The Handbook of
Financial Market
Indexes, Averages,
and Indicators

The Handbook of Financial Market Indexes, Averages, and Indicators

Howard M. Berlin

DOW JONES-IRWIN
Homewood, Illinois 60430

Project editor: Carol Goodfriend Schoen
Production manager: Bette K. Ittersagen
Compositor: Arcata Graphics/Kingsport
Typeface: 11/13 Century Schoolbook
Printer: The Maple-Vail Book Manufacturing Group

Library of Congress Cataloging-in-Publication Data

Berlin, Howard M.
    The handbook for financial market indexes, averages, and indicators /
by Howard M. Berlin.
        p.   cm.
    Includes bibliographical references.
    ISBN 1-55623-125-3
    1. Stock price indexes—Handbooks, manuals, etc.   2. Stock
-exchange—Handbooks, manuals, etc.   I. Title.
HG4636.B49   1990
332.63′222—dc20   89–17197
                                                              CIP

Printed in the United States of America

1 2 3 4 5 6 7 8 9 0   MP   7 6 5 4 3 2 1 0

Trademarks

The following is a list of trademarks used throughout this book. Any omission from this list is unintentional.

AMEX, Major Market Index, Market Value Index, AMEX Oil Index, AMEX Computer Technology Index, Institutional Index, and International Market Index are trademarks of the American Stock Exchange.

BANKXQUOTE is a trademark of Masterfund, Inc.

Dow Jones Averages, Dow Jones Industrials, Dow Jones Transportation, Dow Jones Utilities, Dow Jones Precious Metals Index, and Dow Jones Equity Index are trademarks of Dow Jones & Company.

McDonald's and Big Mac are trademarks of McDonald's Corporation.

NASDAQ, NASDAQ Composite Index, NASDAQ/NMS Composite Index, NASDAQ Bank Index, NASDAQ Insurance Index, NASDAQ Other Finance Index, NASDAQ Finance Index, NASDAQ Transportation Index, NASDAQ Utilities Index, NASDAQ Industrial Index, NASDAQ-100 are trademarks of the National Association of Securities Dealers.

NYSE and NYSE Composite are trademarks of the New York Stock Exchange.

PHLX, Gold/Silver Index, National OTC Index, Utility Index, and Blue Chip CIP Index are trademarks of the Philadelphia Stock Exchange.

Sotheby's Art Index is a registered trademark of Sotheby's, Inc.

Standard & Poor's, S&P, S&P 500, S&P 100, are trademarks of Standard & Poor's Corporation.

Value Line and Value Line Index are trademarks of Value Line, Inc.

Preface

For as long as there has been an organized financial market, someone has tried using some sort of average or index to summarize the price movements or trading activity of that market. The main purpose for such a measure was to forecast market trends to suggest the best time for the purchase or sale of a particular security. Users of these measures hoped that they would prove to be more accurate than following one's horoscope, charting the phases of the moon, or taking the advice of Aunt Sally, whose bunion hurts every time the market is about to go sour.

In many cases, a few carefully selected stocks, bonds, mutual funds, or commodities have been made the basis of inferences about the state of the broader market. Since the October 1987 market crash, investors have been concerned more than ever before with measures of market activity. This is true not only for domestic indicators, such as the ubiquitous Dow Jones Industrial Average, but for many foreign indexes and averages as well.

This book discusses virtually all of the major financial market barometers—market averages, indexes, and indicators—as well as many minor ones. In all, this book discusses over 200 such measures, representing the financial markets of the United States and more than 24 other countries. It is meant to serve as a reference for the investor, naming the issues that are the basis of each average or index and describing how it is calculated. Inasmuch as many averages and indexes are tied to tradable options and futures contracts, it is wise to know the composition of the index and what stocks have the greatest influence. This book was intended to be as complete and accurate as possible, but because financial markets change rapidly, one or more of the components of some of the indexes may have changed during the book's production.

The book is divided into nine chapters. The first chapter discusses the mathematics of how averages and indexes are determined; their characteristics, strengths, and weaknesses; and the differences between them. The next six chapters focus on those measures of U.S. stocks, notes and bonds, commodities, mutual funds, money and the dollar, and foreign stocks. With very few exceptions, no comments are made about the effectiveness (or lack of it) of a particular average or index as a barometer of what it is supposed to measure.

Chapter 8 is concerned primarily with technical indicators that are used by both fundamental and technical analysts to guide their financial decisions. For some, the calculation is easier than the interpretation of the result. The final chapter concerns itself with several financial benchmarks that, while they may not be universally known, accepted, or discussed at trading desks or cocktail parties, poke a little fun at the lengths to which financial analysts will go to relate or predict the price movements of virtually anything carrying a price tag. The appendix gives the names and addresses of virtually every securities market in the world.

As one who was always interested in numbers, I wrote this book as an outgrowth of my research into the various measures used to describe the financial markets. I hope that it will be helpful as a sourcebook of information. While every effort was made to make this book as complete as possible, any comments concerning omissions are welcomed. My address is P.O. Box 9431, Wilmington, DE 19809.

Howard M. Berlin

Acknowledgments

There are always many individuals behind the scenes who have given their assistance in the research and preparation of a book. I would like to thank the following firms and individuals for providing information in the preparation of this book. To those persons employed by the firms that answered my letters and telephone calls and provided helpful information when requested, and whose names I may never know, I also extend my deep-felt thanks.

Affärsvärlden—Viveca Enholm

American Stock Exchange

Asia Securities Trading Co., Ltd.—Sirivat Voravetvuthikhun

Association of Swiss Stock Exchanges

Australian Stock Exchange

The Baltic International Freight Futures Market—Joan Davidson

Banca Commerciale Italiana

Barclays Bank PLC

Alfred Berg Fondkomission AB—Stern Lindquist

The Bond Buyer—Matthew Kreps

Brussels Stock Exchange

Business Times—Mano Sabnani

Chambre de Compensation des Instruments Financiers de Paris—Gilbert Durieux

Chicago Board Options Exchange

Chicago Board of Trade—Patricia J. Mosley

Chicago Mercantile Exchange—Angelo A. Calvello

Commerzbank

The Commodity Exchange

Commodity Research Bureau

Copenhagen Stock Exchange—Jorgen Brisson

Credit Suisse—Rita Cherry

The Delaware Business Review

Dow Jones & Co.—Gilbert Sherman

The Economist—Liz Mann

Federal Home Loan Bank of San Francisco

Federation of the German Stock Exchanges

Futures Magazine

Frankfurt Stock Exchange—Dr. Hamke

Frankfurter Allgemeine Zeitung für Deutschland—Ilse Neuhausen

Hägglöf & Ponsbach Fondkommission AB

Helsinki Stock Exchange—Heli Häivälä

Thomas J. Herzfeld Advisors—Thomas J. Herzfeld

International Federation of Stock Exchanges—Jean Abbey

Johannesburg Stock Exchange—Amelia Soares

Kansas City Board of Trade—Jenell Wallace

Kansallis-Osake-Pankki

Korea Stock Exchange—Chong Yoon Lee

The Kuala Lumpur Stock Exchange—Qua Gek Kim

Lipper Analytical Securities Corporation—Henry Shilling

The London International Financial Futures Exchange—Dilip Bavisha

The Luxembourg Stock Exchange—Paul Marmann, Nadine Jonette-Pomes

McDonald's Corporation—Charles Ebeling

Masterfund, Inc.—Norberto Mehl

Merrill Lynch—Harold Clouser, Jr.

Milan Stock Exchange—Malcom G. Duncan

Morgan Guaranty Trust—Wanda Zoquier

Morgan Stanley Capital International Perspective—Mark H. Sladkus

National Association of Securities Dealers—David Compton

Netherlands Central Bureau of Statistics—H. K. van Tuinen

New York Cotton Exchange/Financial Instruments Exchange

New York Futures Exchange

New York Stock Exchange

New Zealand Stock Exchange—Mrs. H. Mowat

New Zealand Futures Exchange—Susan Pederson

Nihon Keizai Shimbun, Inc.—Akira Higurashi

Nomura Securities International—P. J. Johnson

Osaka Securities Exchange

A/S Oslo Børs Informasjon—Jon Martin Ostby

Oslo Stock Exchange—Heidi Kristensen

Pacific Stock Exchange—Marie Hirsch, Brenda J. Swenson

Philadelphia Stock Exchange—Ken Pietrzak, Steve McEwen, Michelle Wesler-Brown

Prudential-Bache, U.S.A.—Molly Quintana

Prudential-Bache (France) S.A.—M. Raffestin

Reuters—Richard Greb, David Feldheim, Philip J. Wardle

Ryan Financial Strategies Group—Ronald Ryan

Shearson Lehman Hutton—Daniel A. Conners

Singapore International Monetary Exchange—Patrick Chu

Société de Bourses Françaises

Salomon Brothers

Standard & Poor's—Elliot Sheridan

The Stock Exchange of Hong Kong—Cheung Yin Kwan

Stock Exchange of Singapore Ltd.—Patricia Quek

Stockholm Stock Exchange—Cornella Mofors

Stockholm Options Market—Mikael Stenbom

The Straits Times Press (1975) Ltd.

Sweden's Options and Futures Exchange—Ulrika Kjellström

Swiss Bank Corporation—Dr. R. J. Riepl, Dr. R. Loertscher

Swiss Options and Financial Futures Exchange, Ltd.—M. Baur

Sydney Futures Exchange

Taiwan Stock Exchange Corporation—Ju Fu-Chen

Tokyo Stock Exchange—Akira Yoshida, Debbie S. Kesler

Toronto Stock Exchange—Marija Finney

Unitas Ltd.

Value Line—Rudy Carroll

Vienna Stock Exchange—Dr. K. Neuteufel

Wilshire Associates

Zurich Stock Exchange

I would like to offer a special acknowledgment to the following individuals for their generous cooperation:

Anthony P. Arciero, Independent
Market Maker, Chicago Board
Options Exchange

Irwin Axelrod, Independent Market
Maker, Chicago Board Options
Exchange

John A. Bennett, Vice President
(Investments), Janney Montgomery
Scott

H.M.B.

Contents

List of Exhibits

List of Figures

1 The Mathematics of Averages, Indexes, and Technical Indicators

Introduction

This chapter is an introduction to the mathematics of how various types of averages and indicators are defined and calculated. We start here because in order to analyze the performance of a particular stock average or index, we must know how it is constructed, its strengths and weaknesses, and which of its components influence its value more strongly than others.

Averages

An *average* or *mean* is a value typical or representative of a set of values. As barometers of the activity of a group of stocks or of a whole stock market, two major types are often used. These are the unweighted arithmetic average and the geometric average, although the harmonic mean is sometimes used in the construction of indexes.

The Arithmetic Average

1. Definition. The average of a given number of stock prices is determined simply by adding up the individual prices (P_i) and then dividing by the number of prices *(N):*

$$\text{Average} = \frac{\text{Price 1} + \text{Price 2} + \text{Price 3} + \cdots + \text{Price } N}{N} \quad \textbf{(1.1a)}$$

or, in a more compact form

$$\text{Average} = \frac{\Sigma\, P_i}{N} \quad \textbf{(1.1b)}$$

This is often referred to as an *algebraic* or *arithmetic average* or *arithmetic mean* and is intended to be a measure of the central value of a range of values that are closely related in magnitude. In these two equations, the number N is referred to as the *divisor*.

1

Example 1.1

As an example, suppose that the share prices, at the end of today's trading, of four companies that sell hot dogs are:

Company	Price Per Share
A	$25
B	31¼
C	18⅞
D	22½

The average price per share of these four issues is found as follows:

$$\text{Average} = \frac{25 + 31.25 + 18.875 + 22.5}{4}$$

$$= \frac{97.625}{4}$$

$$= \textbf{\$21.41 per share}$$

when rounded to the nearest cent. It should be noted that fractions of a dollar were converted to their decimal equivalents to simplify averaging.

2. Adjusting the Divisor. The Dow Jones Industrial Average (DJIA), like several other indicators of stock prices, is based on the arithmetic average calculation, with provisions made for adding or deleting issues from the list. At first, Dow Jones & Company computed the arithmetic average of 12 stock prices. Over the years, the original list has grown to 30, and many stocks have been added and deleted. To account for such changes in the average and to maintain its historical continuity over the years, the divisor must be changed. Returning to Example 1.1, suppose that at the end of today's trading, Company C is to be replaced with Company E. At the close, suppose that the "Hot Dog Average" of Companies A, B, C, and D is $21.41 with a divisor of 4. Furthermore, Company E's closing price is 36⅜. To provide continuity in the average price from the close of today's trading to the beginning of the next trading day after this change has been made, the average price (i.e., $21.41) must remain the same.

The old divisor must be then *corrected* or *adjusted*. The new divisor is determined by the following formula:

$$\text{New divisor} = \frac{\text{New total of stock prices}}{\text{Old total of stock prices}} \times \text{Old divisor} \qquad \textbf{(1.2a)}$$

In a more compact form,

$$N_i = \frac{\Sigma P_i}{\Sigma P_o} \times N_o \qquad \textbf{(1.2b)}$$

where

N_o = Old divisor
N_i = New divisor
P_o = Total of individual stock prices before the change
P_i = Total of individual stock prices after the change

Example 1.2

The following two lists summarize the components of the four-stock Hot Dog Average before and after the change:

Before		After	
Company	**Price Per Share**	**Company**	**Price Per Share**
A	$25	A	$25
B	31¼	B	31¼
C (deleted)	**18⅞**	D	22½
D	22½	**E (added)**	**36⅜**
Total	$97.625	Total	$115.125

Use of Equation 1.2 gives the new divisor as follows:

$$\text{New divisor} = \frac{115.125}{97.625} \times 4$$

$$= \mathbf{4.717}$$

With the new divisor (4.717), the four-stock average is the same ($21.41) before the change and after the change. The stock average will be $21.41 per share at the beginning of the next day's trading as if nothing had happened. This new divisor is used until the component companies are changed at some future time.

If the average was computed after the change without adjusting the divisor, then its value would always be distorted and would never equal the true average value. As a consequence, the historical continuity would be lost. Without adjusting the divisor, the new four-stock Hot Dog Average at the start of the next day's trading would be 115.125/4, or $28.78 per share, which is in error.

The same method is used if an additional company is added to the list without any deletions. If Company E is added to the original list of hot dog companies, then the new divisor for the resultant five-stock Hot Dog Average will be as follows:

$$\text{New divisor} = \frac{134}{97.625} \times 4$$

$$= \mathbf{5.490}$$

3. Stock Splits. On occasion a company will declare a split in its shares, which will reduce the price per share. The total value of the stock issue remains unchanged, however. Suppose that Company D declares a 3-for-2 stock split. This means that the owner of Company D stock will receive three shares of stock in exchange for every two shares already owned, with the result that the price of each share drops by one-third. If Company D's stock closed at 22½, then it will be priced at ⅔ × 22½ or $15 per share at the start of the next trading day. The total market value of Company D's shares does not change: if you owned 100 shares before the split, the total market value was 100 × $22½, or $2,250; after the split, you own 150 shares, whose total market value is 150 × $15, or $2,250.

Example 1.3

Again using the original four companies, assume that Company D splits 3 for 2 after closing at 22½, as summarized below.

Before 3-for-2 Split		After 3-for-2 Split	
Company	**Price Per Share**	**Company**	**Price Per Share**
A	$25	A	$25
B	31¼	B	31¼
C	18⅞	C	18⅞
D	22½	**D (3/2) split)**	**15**
Total	$97.625	Total	$90.125

The new divisor for the four-stock average after the stock split will be as follows:

$$\text{New divisor} = \frac{90.125}{97.625} \times 4$$

$$= \mathbf{3.693}$$

Depending on the total value of the shares of all the companies in the average, the new divisor—following changes in stocks included in the average or changes in share prices caused by stock splits—may be either larger or smaller than the old divisor.

When a stock split occurs, the divisor must be adjusted. This adjustment is performed in the same way as that made for the deletion of a stock and its subsequent replacement by another. Equation 1.2 is used for both situations.

4. Characteristic Disadvantages. The arithmetic average is often referred to as an *unweighted* arithmetic average, with higher-priced stocks having a greater effect on the resultant average than lower-priced stocks. For example, consider the closing prices of the stocks of four companies that make frozen pizza pies:

Company	Price Per Share
A	$115
B	20
C	70
D	80
Total	$285

If the divisor is 4, then the four-stock Pizza Pie Average is 285/4, or $71.25 per share. Suppose that the price of Company A's stock increases 5 percent to 120¾. The Pizza Pie Average is then $72.69, which represents an increase of 2.4 percent. On the other hand, if Company B's price were to increase 5 percent to 21, then the four-stock average becomes $71.50, which represents an increase of only 0.35 percent.

Another problem with unweighted averages like the Dow Jones

Industrial Average is that the computed average no longer *realistically* reflects the average price of its components. On March 23, 1989, the DJIA closed at 2243.04. This indicated that the "average" price of the 30 stocks, whose share prices ranged from 5⅞ (Navistar) to 114 (Philip Morris), was $2,243.04 per share! Here the average is almost 20 times the largest share price of the 30 stocks. Since the average is a value intended to be typical or representative of a set of values, this clearly cannot be a representative average in the traditional sense.

Because of additions, deletions, and stock splits, the divisor—in order to maintain historical continuity—becomes radically different from its original value, which should always be equal to the number of stock prices used to compute the average. On March 23, 1989, however, the divisor for the 30-stock Dow Jones Industrial Average was 0.700, whereas the divisor would be 30 in a true unweighted average. The effect on the average of a one-point change in the price of one stock would be 1/30, or 0.03, if the divisor were the same as the number of issues. Because the value of the divisor has decreased to 0.700, the effect of a one-point change becomes magnified to 1/0.700, or 1.43. If two stocks each move upward by one point, the average moves upward by 2 × 1/0.700, or 2.86 points.

In a statistical sense, the unweighted arithmetic average best represents the typical value of a set of values only if the difference between the highest and lowest values in this set is relatively small, so that most of the individual prices would be clustered closely about some typical price, some higher, some lower. For the DJIA, however, the stock prices of the 30 companies ranged from 5⅞ to 114, a spread of 108⅛ points. Here the spread is almost as much as the highest-priced component.

The Geometric Average

1. Definition. The geometric mean—or average—is used primarily when there is a large spread between the lowest and highest values of a set. It is determined by taking the Nth root of the product of N prices:

$$\text{Geometric average} = \frac{\sqrt[N]{\text{Price 1} \times \text{Price 2} \times \text{Price 3} \cdots \times \text{Price } N}}{\text{Divisor}} \qquad \textbf{(1.3a)}$$

or, in a more compact form,

$$\text{Geometric average} = \frac{\sqrt[N]{P_1 P_2 P_3 \cdots P_N}}{d} \qquad \textbf{(1.3b)}$$

The divisor shown in Equation 1.3a and symbolized d in Equation 1.3b is not part of the definition of the geometric mean. It is included in these equations as a parameter that allows adjustment of the mean to keep its value unchanged when the list of issues is modified to account for replacements or stock splits.

2. Adjusting the Divisor. Those stock averages computed using the geometric average must be adjusted to preserve their historical continuity—like certain arithmetic stock averages whose divisor must be ad-

Example 1.4

For example, suppose that four companies owning casinos have the following share prices at the end of today's trading:

Company	Price Per Share
A	$95
B	33¾
C	10⅛
D	3⅝

The geometric average price per share of these four stocks (assuming an original divisor of 1) is found as follows:

$$\text{Geometric average} = \sqrt[4]{(95)(33.75)(10.125)(3.625)}$$

$$= \sqrt[4]{117{,}679.39}$$

$$= \textbf{\$18.52 per share}$$

Notice that since there are four values, the fourth root is taken of the product of the four numbers. Two well-known examples of the geometric average are the Value Line Average, which consists of approximately 1,700 stock prices, and the Financial Times (London) 30-Share Index.

Example 1.5

For example, assume that Company B in our Casino Average will split 2 for 1 after closing at 33¾:

Before 2-for-1 Split		After 2-for-1 Split	
Company	**Price Per Share**	**Company**	**Price Per Share**
A	$95	A	$95
B	33¾	**B (2/1 split)**	**16⅞**
C	10⅛	C	10⅛
D	3⅝	D	3⅝

Before the stock split, the fourth root of the product of the four prices is $18.52, and the divisor is 1. After the split, the unadjusted geometric average is as follows:

$$\text{Uncorrected geometric average} = \sqrt[4]{(95)(16.875)(10.125)(3.625)}$$

$$= \sqrt[4]{58{,}839.70}$$

$$= \textbf{\$15.57 per share}$$

The new divisor for the four-stock geometric average, adjusted for the stock split, will be as follows:

$$\text{New divisor} = \frac{18.52}{15.57} \times 1$$

$$= \textbf{1.189}$$

If any of the components is changed again at a later time, the divisor must be readjusted. This adjustment is also carried out if the total number of stock prices increases or decreases, or when substitutions are made in the component companies.

justed for occasional additions/deletions of companies from the list, as well as stock splits.

When required, the new divisor for Equations 1.3a and 1.3b is determined by using the same method as is used for arithmetic stock averages (Equation 1.2).

3. Characteristics.   One property of the geometric average is that price changes of the higher-priced stocks have no greater effect on the average than similar percentage changes in the prices of the lower-priced stocks. Suppose the price of Company A's stock increases 5 percent, to 99¾. The four-stock geometric average is then $18.75, which represents an increase of 1.24 percent. On the other hand, if Company D's price were to increase 5 percent, to $3.81, then the four-stock geometric average would also be $18.75.

Because the change in the geometric average's value is the same for a proportionate change in any of its component values, whether high or low, the geometric average is often referred to as an *equally weighted average.*

Another characteristic of the geometric average is that its value will always be less than the arithmetic average for the same set of numbers. For these four stock prices, the arithmetic average is 142.5/4, or $35.63 per share. Because of the way the geometric average is calculated, low-priced components have the effect of pulling down the average value. This downward bias is the chief criticism of geometric averages, even though its equal weighting characteristic gives the small fry as much power as the big boys. Nobody ever said life was fair!

The Harmonic Mean

The harmonic mean of a given number of stock prices is determined by taking the reciprocal of the arithmetic mean of the reciprocals of the individual prices, so that

$$\text{Harmonic mean} = \cfrac{N}{\cfrac{1}{\text{Price 1}} + \cfrac{1}{\text{Price 2}} + \cfrac{1}{\text{Price 3}} + \cdots + \cfrac{1}{\text{Price } N}} \quad \textbf{(1.4a)}$$

Or, in a more compact form

$$\text{Harmonic mean} = \cfrac{N}{\sum \cfrac{1}{P_i}} \quad \textbf{(1.4b)}$$

Just as the geometric average of a set of values is less than the arithmetic average of the same values, the harmonic mean is less than the geometric average.

Indexes

Introduction

The purpose of an index number, or simply an index, is to relate some current measure of a quantity to some reference or *base value* at a specified previous date, called the *base period*. For most indexes, the base value is set at 100, although any value may be chosen.

The establishment of the base period is very important: it is the time reference to which all comparisons are made. For some financial indexes, this might be an important date relevant to that market. For example, an index for gold prices might have as its base period the date that the United States went off the gold standard or perhaps the date that Americans were once again allowed to own gold coins and bullion. For other indexes, it might be the date that the index was established. For most indexes, the base period is selected as the last business day of a given year.

1. Narrow-Based and Broad-Based Indexes. Regardless of how they are calculated, indexes may be classified as either *narrow-based* or *broad-based*. A narrow-based index has a small number of components and is usually concentrated on a particular market sector or industry. Many of the stock indexes—such as the Philadelphia Stock Exchange's Gold/Silver Index, having 7 companies, or the AMEX Major Market Index, having 20 companies—are considered narrow-based.

By contrast, indexes having a large number of components—such as the NYSE Composite (1,600+ stocks), S&P 500, AMEX Market Value (800+ stocks), and the Wilshire 5000—are considered broad-based indexes; they generally cover either an entire industry or all stocks traded on a particular stock exchange. The terms narrow-based and broad-based are relative designations, and there is no particular dividing line between the two categories.

2. Elementary Indexes. If an index is intended to measure the values of a single variable such as price, it can be directly defined and measured as the ratio of the observed current price (P_t) to a reference price (P_0) of the base period:

$$\text{Index} = \frac{P_t}{P_0} \tag{1.5}$$

To construct a simple gold bullion index, for example, suppose we take the price of gold at the base period of January 1, 1930, which was pegged at the official price of $35 an ounce. If the current price of gold is $395.91 an ounce, our "Gold Bullion Index" is computed as follows:

$$\text{Index} = \frac{\$395.91}{\$35}$$
$$= \mathbf{11.31}$$

Because this index is the ratio of two prices for the same category, it is termed a *price relative index*.

The relative index just discussed generally includes a base index value (I_0) in addition to a base value of the measured variable. The index's current value (I_t) is computed from a base index value as follows:

$$\text{Current index value} = \frac{\text{Current component value}}{\text{Base component value}} \times \text{Base index value} \tag{1.6a}$$

or,

$$I_t = \frac{P_t}{P_0} \times I_0 \qquad \text{(1.6b)}$$

Example 1.6

As an example, let's construct an index representing publicly traded stocks of four companies involved in making left-handed widgets. The base period for this Left-Handed Widget Index was chosen to be December 31, 1984. The following table summarizes the closing market prices of these four stocks.

Company	Price Per Share (12/31/84)
A	$57
B	8½
C	21⅜
D	29¾

The total of the four stock prices is 116.625 (116⅝). Arbitrarily, we can set this equal to a base index value of 100. Suppose that on March 8, 1989, the share prices are as follows:

Company	Price Per Share (3/8/89)
A	$68⅞
B	15¾
C	15
D	31¼

so that the total is 130.875 (130⅞). On March 8, 1989, the value of the Left-Handed Widget Index, according to Equation 1.6, is

$$\text{Current index value} = \frac{130.875}{116.625} \times 100$$

$$= \mathbf{112.22}$$

That is, the index of the stocks of the four companies is 12.22 percent higher on March 8, 1989, when compared to its base period.

On the other hand, suppose that the Left-Handed Widget Index is to be based on the geometric average of the four stock prices instead of the arithmetic average. For the base period, the geometric average of the four stocks is $23.56 per share. This time, instead of setting the index base value at 100, let's arbitrarily set it at 250, so that a geometric average of 23.56 for the four stock prices corresponds to an index value of 250. On March 8, 1989, the geometric average of the four component stocks is $26.70 per share. The current value of our Left-Handed Widget Index is calculated as follows:

$$\text{Current index value} = \frac{26.70}{23.56} \times 250$$

$$= \mathbf{283.32}$$

3. Composite Indexes. A low-priced stock has a small effect on the value of an average. Because of the low price, however, the issuing company may have many more shares outstanding (i.e., publicly owned) than does a company whose shares are relatively high-priced. A price-weighted index is frequently used to take into account both the share price and the number of shares outstanding.

The product of a company's stock price and the number of its shares outstanding is termed the company's *market value* or its *capitalization*. An index based on the market value of a given group of stocks is said to be *price-weighted* or *capitalization-weighted*. In general, the index value of a capitalization-based index is determined as follows:

$$\text{Current index value} = \frac{\text{Current total market value}}{\text{Base-period total market value}} \times \text{Base index value}$$

$$\text{(1.7)}$$

An index of a set of combined variables such as price and number of shares outstanding is called a *composite index*. The fundamental problem in devising a composite index is to find the appropriate formula to express the combined effect of the relevant variables. The most widely used formulas for constructing composite indexes were developed by the German economists E. Laspeyres in 1864 and H. Paäsche in 1874 and the U.S. economist Irving Fisher in 1927.

The *Laspeyres Index formula,* the basis of the *base-year method,* is defined as follows:

$$I_L = \frac{\Sigma\, P_{ni} Q_{0i}}{\Sigma\, P_{0i} Q_{0i}} \times I_0 \qquad\qquad \text{(1.8)}$$

where

P_{0i} = Share price for the ith stock in the base period
P_{ni} = Share price for the ith stock in the current period
Q_{0i} = Number of shares of the ith stock outstanding in the base period
I_0 = Index level of the base period.

The product $P_{ni} Q_{0i}$ is the market value or capitalization of the ith stock in the index, calculated on the basis of its *current* price and the base-period number of shares outstanding. The product $P_{0i} Q_{0i}$ is the market value of the same stock, calculated on the basis of its *base-period* price and number of shares.

The *Paäsche Index formula,* the basis of the *current-year method,* is defined as follows:

$$I_P = \frac{\Sigma\, P_{ni} Q_{ni}}{\Sigma\, P_{0i} Q_{ni}} \times I_0 \qquad\qquad \text{(1.9)}$$

where Q_{ni} is the number of shares of the ith stock outstanding in the current period. Unlike the Laspreyes formula of Equation 1.8, the Paäsche formula is based on the number of outstanding shares in the current period for each stock.

The *Fisher Index,* also called the *ideal index,* is the geometric mean of the Laspeyres and Paäsche indexes. From Equations 1.8 and 1.9, we have

$$I_F = \sqrt{I_L I_P}$$
$$= I_0\, \sqrt{\left(\frac{\Sigma\, P_{ni} Q_{0i}}{\Sigma\, P_{0i} Q_{0i}}\right)\left(\frac{\Sigma\, P_{ni} Q_{ni}}{\Sigma\, P_{0i} Q_{ni}}\right)} \qquad\qquad \text{(1.10)}$$

Example 1.7

An index is to be constructed for the hot dog stock prices given in Example 1.1. Suppose that on the base date, the companies have the following stock prices, numbers of outstanding shares, and capitalizations:

Company	Price Per Share (P_{0i})	Outstanding Shares (Q_{0i})	Capitalization $(P_{0i}Q_{0i})$
A	$25	1,500	$ 37,500
B	31¼	2,000	62,500
C	18⅞	800	15,100
D	22½	3,400	76,500

Total value = $191,600

Suppose that two years later, the corresponding figures are as follows:

Company	Price Per Share (P_{ni})	Outstanding Shares (Q_{0i})	Capitalization $(P_{ni}Q_{0i})$
A	$30½	1,500	$ 45,750
B	28⅞	2,000	57,750
C	18	800	14,400
D	25⅜	3,400	86,275

Total value = $204,175

If the base index level is arbitrarily chosen to be 250, then the current index level, as defined by the Laspeyres formula (Equation 1.8), is:

$$I_L = \frac{\$204,175}{\$191,600} \times 250$$

$$= \mathbf{266.41}$$

4. Total-Return Indexes. Most stock indexes using the Laspeyres, Paäsche, or Fisher formulas are *capital* indexes, with no provision for correcting the price of a stock when it pays a dividend (ex-dividend). In the case of note and bond indexes, usually no provision is made for reinvestment of the interest received from the semiannual coupon. A *total-return index* (for stocks) makes adjustments for dividends paid (cum-dividend), or in the case of notes and bonds, the payment of semiannual interest to obtain the overall increase (or decrease) of the value of a basket of stocks compared with a given base-period value.

A simple total-return index, with the Laspeyres formula as a basis, could then be written as:

$$I_L = \frac{\Sigma \, (P_{ni}Q_{0i} + D_i)}{\Sigma \, P_{0i}Q_{0i}} \times I_0 \qquad\qquad \textbf{(1.11)}$$

where D_i is the total dividend paid for the ith stock since the base period.

Example 1.8

As an example, suppose that we are constructing a total-return index for three bonds whose base values are as follows:

Bond	Coupon (%)	Face Value	Price	Market Value
A	10¼	$10,000	$105	$10,500
B	6.70	10,000	98	9,800
C	9½	10,000	103	10,300

Total value = $30,600
Index value = 100

Suppose that three months later the bond prices are as follows:

Bond	Coupon (%)	Face Value	Price	Market Value
A	10¼	$10,000	$106	$10,600
B	6.70	10,000	98	9,800
C	9½	10,000	104	10,400

Total value = $30,800

and that bond B had paid its semiannual interest of $335 during this three-month period. The total-return index for these three bonds is then

$$\text{Index value} = \frac{\$30,800 + \$335}{\$30,600} \times 100$$

$$= \mathbf{101.75}$$

Without the inclusion of the interest, the value of the corresponding capital index would equal 100.65.

5. Adjusting the Base Level. As with arithmetic stock averages, whose divisor must be adjusted for occasional additions/deletions of companies from the list and for stock splits, the base level of stock indexes must be similarly adjusted to preserve their historical continuity. When required, the following formula is used:

$$\text{New base value} = \frac{\text{Total capitalization before adjustment}}{\text{Total capitalization after adjustment}} \times \text{Old base value} \qquad \textbf{(1.12a)}$$

Or in a more compact form,

$$B_i = \frac{C_0}{C_i} \times B_0 \qquad \textbf{(1.12b)}$$

where

B_0 = Old base value
B_i = New base value
C_0 = Total capitalization value before adjustment
C_i = Total capitalization value after adjustment.

Example 1.9

Suppose that Company B, whose shares are a component of the Hot Dog Index of example 1.7, issues a preemptive right of one new share for every old share at the subscription price of $5 per share plus the price on that day. Let's also assume that, as a result, the price of Company B stock drops from 27⅞ to 25. After the change, the four companies have the following stock prices, numbers of outstanding shares, and capitalizations:

Company	Price per Share (P_{ni})	Outstanding Shares (Q_{oi})	Capitalization $(P_{ni}Q_{oi})$
A	$30½	1,500	$ 45,750
B	25	2,000	50,000
C	18	800	14,400
D	25⅜	3,400	86,275

Total value = $196,425

From Example 1.7, the total market value before the adjustment was $204,175 with a base level of 250.00. From Equation 1.12,

$$B_i = \frac{\$205,175}{\$196,425} \times 250.00$$

$$= \mathbf{259.86}$$

Technical Indicators

For the purposes of this book, a technical indicator is a value used by analysts as a gauge of financial or economic activity. It may be the result of the simplest of calculations, requiring only finding the difference between two specific numbers, such as the International Money Market's Treasury Bill Futures Index. It may be computed by taking the ratio of the highest value to lowest value of the same group, such as the advance-decline ratio. On the other hand, the value may be the result of a very complicated series of calculations, some of which are proprietary, and some of whose derivations may be of questionable validity.

Some indicators, although called "averages" or "indexes," are really not. For example, the Misery Index (Chapter 9) does not compare its current value to a base period. Some indexes are really averages, while some averages are in reality indexes. On the other hand, some indicators are based on subjective assessments, such as the Wall Street Week Technical Index, which is based on the number of subjective negative (bearish) and positive (bullish) ratings given for each of its 10 categories.

2 The Domestic Stock Market

People interested in the stock market will often ask the proverbial question, "How is the market?" For the domestic market, this could be answered in a number of ways. Most of the time, the Dow Jones Industrial Average is given as *the* measure of market activity. On the other hand, those who manage stock portfolios tend to use the S&P 500 as their yardstick. Defining the "market" is often a source of heated debate. This chapter discusses over 45 indexes and averages that serve as either narrow- or broad-based barometers of stock prices.

The Dow Jones Stock Averages and Indexes

The Dow Jones averages and indexes are perhaps the best-known and most often quoted of the world's market indicators. The editors of *The Wall Street Journal* currently maintain and publish the following averages and indexes:

> 30-Stock Industrial Average
> 20-Stock Transportation Average
> 15-Stock Utilities Average
> 65-Stock Composite Average
> The Dow Jones Equity Index
> Dow Jones Precious Metals Index

The Dow Jones Stock Averages

In 1882, Charles Henry Dow attempted to identify underlying trends in each day's stock price changes by computing the arithmetic average of the prices of 11 stocks he regarded as representative of the market as a whole: the shares of nine railroad companies and only two industrial firms. In the following years, more industrial issues were added to the average, and the list expanded, first to 20 stocks, then to 30. A

EXHIBIT 2.1 Chronology of the Dow Jones Averages

November 1882	Charles H. Dow, Edward D. Jones, and Charles M. Bergstrasser found Dow Jones & Company as a news agency at 15 Wall Street.
July 3, 1884	Dow writes the *Customer Afternoon Letter,* in which he presents his initial average of 11 stocks, 9 of which are railroad issues.
February 16, 1885	14-stock average (9 railroad issues).
January 2, 1886	12-stock average (2 railroad issues).
July 8, 1889	First issue of *The Wall Street Journal,* 12-stock average appears.
September 3, 1889	20-stock average (18 railroad issues).
May 26, 1896	The first Dow Jones Industrial Average of 12 stocks appears in *The Wall Street Journal* with a value of 40.94.
October 7, 1896	12-stock Dow Jones Industrial Average is published daily in *The Wall Street Journal.*
October 26, 1896	Dow Jones Railroad Average (20 stocks) first calculated.
September 30, 1916	Dow Jones Industrial Average consists only of common stocks.
October 4, 1916	20-stock Dow Jones Industrial Average published in *The Wall Street Journal.*
October 1, 1928	Dow Jones Industrial Average increases to 30 stocks.
January 2, 1929	15-stock Dow Jones Utility Average published in *The Wall Street Journal.*
January 1, 1970	20-stock Dow Jones Railroad Average renamed the Dow Jones Transportation Average.

brief chronology[1] of the evolution of the Dow Jones Averages is given in Exhibit 2.1.

The present standard of the Dow Jones Industrial Average having 30 stocks was first published in *The Wall Street Journal* on October 1, 1928; that average is one of four compiled by the editors of the *Journal:*

Dow Jones Industrial Average

Dow Jones Transportation Average

Dow Jones Utilities Average

Dow Jones Composite Average

Dow Jones Industrial Average

The Dow Jones Industrial Average (DJIA), in addition to being the best-known and most often quoted barometer of the stock market (U.S. or worldwide), is the oldest continuous price measure in the United States. It is currently based on 30 blue-chip issues whose value alone accounts for over one-fourth the value of the stocks listed on the New York Stock Exchange (Exhibit 2.2). It is a price-weighted average of the 30 issues; changes in the DJIA's composition result in adjustments of the divisor, which is currently 0.700, so that a 1-point change in any one of the 30 components results in a 1.429-point change in the DJIA.

---

[1] A comprehensive history of the Dow Jones Industrial Average can be found in Richard J. Stillman, *Dow Jones Industrial Average* (Homewood, Ill.: Dow Jones-Irwin, 1986).

EXHIBIT 2.2   The Dow Jones Stock Averages

Average/Divisor/Companies	Ticker Symbol	Percent Weight (3/16/89)
1. 30-Stock Industrial Average (0.700)		
Allied-Signal	ALD	2.09%
Alcoa	AA	3.76
American Express	AXP	1.88
American Telephone & Telegraph	T	2.00
Bethlehem Steel	BS	1.53
Boeing	BA	4.23
Chevron	CHV	3.36
Coca-Cola	KO	3.16
E.I. Du Pont de Nemours	DD	6.38
Eastman Kodak	EK	2.87
Exxon	XON	2.82
General Electric	GE	2.84
General Motors	GM	5.16
Goodyear Tire & Rubber	GT	2.91
International Business Machines	IBM	7.21
International Paper	IP	2.84
McDonald's Corporation	MCD	3.11
Merck & Company	MRK	4.04
Minnesota Mining & Manufacturing	MMM	4.24
Navistar International	NAV	0.38
Philip Morris	MO	7.30
Primerica	PA	1.37
Procter & Gamble	PG	5.56
Sears, Roebuck	S	2.65
Texaco	TX	3.27
USX	X	2.01
Union Carbide	UK	1.88
United Technologies	UTX	2.76
Westinghouse Electric	WX	3.33
F.W. Woolworth	Z	3.06
2. 20-Stock Transportation Average (0.733)		
AMR Corporation	AMR	7.32
Alaska Air Group	ALK	3.02
American President	APS	4.49
Burlington Northern	BNI	2.86
CSX	CSX	3.94
Carolina Freight	CAO	3.00
Consolidated Freightways	CNF	3.73
Consolidated Rail	CRR	4.23
Delta Air Lines	DAL	7.12
Federal Express	FDX	5.94
NWA Inc.	NWA	7.96
Norfolk Southern	NSC	4.29
Pan American	PN	0.52
Ryder System	RDR	3.12
Santa Fe Southern Pacific	SFX	2.65
Southwest Airlines	LUV	3.02
UAL	UAL	14.83
Union Pacific	UNP	8.34
US Air Group	U	5.03
XTRA	XTR	4.59
3. Stock Public Utilities Average (2.109)		
American Electric Power	AEP	6.82
Centerior Energy	CX	4.10
Columbia Gas System	CG	9.10
Commonwealth Edison	CWE	8.69
Consolidated Edison of New York	ED	11.73

EXHIBIT 2.2 *(concluded)*

Average/Divisor/Companies	Ticker Symbol	Percent Weight (3/16/89)
Consolidated Natural Gas	CNG	10.00%
Detroit Edison	DTE	4.55
Houston Industries	HOU	7.05
Niagara Mohawk Power	NMK	3.14
Pacific Gas & Electric	PCG	4.42
Panhandle Eastern	PEL	5.58
Peoples Energy	PGL	5.29
Philadelphia Electric	PE	5.13
Public Service Enterprises	PEG	6.15
Southern California Edison	SCE	8.20
4. 65-Stock Composite Average (3.221)		

Source: *The Wall Street Journal.*

DJIA fluctuations are shown in Figure 2.1 for a time period chosen specifically to include the dramatic, record-setting 508-point plunge (−22.6%) on October 19, 1987—the "black Monday" stock market crash. Exhibit 2.3 summarizes the largest one-day gains and losses in the value of the DJIA. From the original DJIA list of 12 stocks which appeared on a daily basis in *The Wall Street Journal,* not including changes in company name, General Electric is the only company that still remains.

Dow Jones Transportation Average.   Formerly known as the Dow Jones Railroad Average—which was published in the *The Wall Street Journal* from October 26, 1986, until January 2, 1970—the Dow Jones Transportation Average is a price-weighted average based on 20 NYSE-listed transportation stocks.

Dow Jones Utilities Average.   The Dow Jones Utilities Average, published in the *The Wall Street Journal* since January 2, 1929, is a price-weighted average based on 15 NYSE-listed public utility stock issues. Since the prices of the stocks of companies involved in the generation of electric power are more sensitive to interest rates than are stock prices in most other sectors of the economy, this average is considered a leading indicator of interest rate changes.

Dow Jones Composite Average.   The Dow Jones Composite Average is a price-weighted average of the 65 stocks included in the Dow Jones Industrial, Transportation, and Utilities Averages.

Dow Jones Equity Index.   The Dow Jones Equity Index is a broad-based index of the share prices of approximately 700 companies chosen to reflect the movements of over 80 percent of the broad stock market, including NYSE, American Stock Exchange, and over-the-counter (OTC) issues. The index is subdivided into 82 industry groups clustered into nine sectors that represent larger segments of the U.S. economy

FIGURE 2.1 Dow Jones Industrial Average, July 1987–January 1988

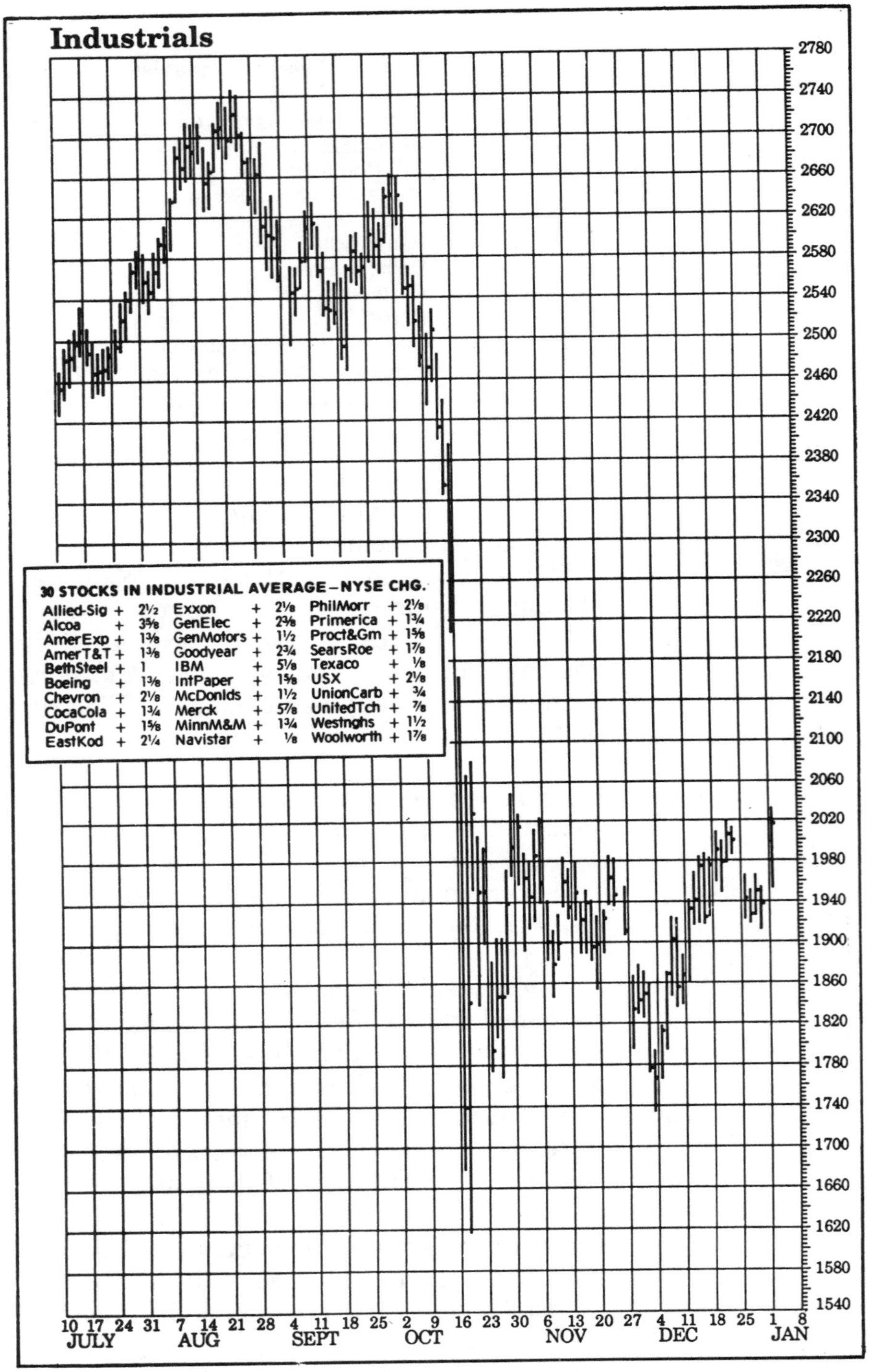
Industrials
2780
2740
2700
2660
2620
2580
2540
2500
2460
2420
2380
2340
2300
2260
2220
2180
2140
2100
2060
2020
1980
1940
1900
1860
1820
1780
1740
1700
1660
1620
1580
1540
30 STOCKS IN INDUSTRIAL AVERAGE—NYSE CHG.
Allied-Sig + 2 1/2 Exxon + 2 1/8 PhilMorr + 2 1/8
Alcoa + 3 5/8 GenElec + 2 3/8 Primerica + 1 3/4
AmerExp + 1 3/8 GenMotors + 1 1/2 Proct&Gm + 1 5/8
AmerT&T + 1 3/8 Goodyear + 2 3/4 SearsRoe + 1 7/8
BethSteel + 1 IBM + 5 1/8 Texaco + 1/8
Boeing + 1 3/8 IntPaper + 1 5/8 USX + 2 1/8
Chevron + 2 1/8 McDonlds + 1 1/2 UnionCarb + 3/4
CocaCola + 1 3/4 Merck + 5 7/8 UnitedTch + 7/8
DuPont + 1 5/8 MinnM&M + 1 3/4 Westnghs + 1 1/2
EastKod + 2 1/4 Navistar + 1/8 Woolworth + 1 7/8
10 17 24 31 7 14 21 28 4 11 18 25 2 9 16 23 30 6 13 20 27 4 11 18 25 1 8
JULY AUG SEPT OCT NOV DEC JAN

EXHIBIT 2.3 Biggest One-Day Gains and Losses of the Dow Jones Industrial Average

Date	Close	Gain	Percent Change
October 21, 1987	2027.85	186.84	10.15%
October 20, 1987	1841.01	102.27	5.88
October 29, 1987	1938.33	91.51	4.96
October 16, 1989	2657.38	88.12	3.43
January 4, 1988	2015.25	76.42	3.94

Date	Close	Loss	Percent Change
October 19, 1987	1738.74	508.00	−22.61%
October 13,1989	2569.26	190.58	−6.91
October 26, 1987	1793.93	156.83	−8.04
January 8, 1988	1911.31	140.58	−6.85
October 16, 1987	2246.74	108.35	−4.60

Source: *The Wall Street Journal.*

FIGURE 2.2 Dow Jones Transportation Average, July 1987–January 1988

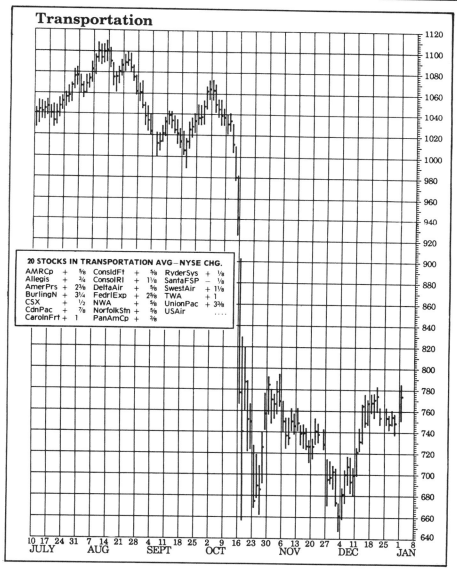

FIGURE 2.3 Dow Jones Utilities Average, July 1987–January 1988

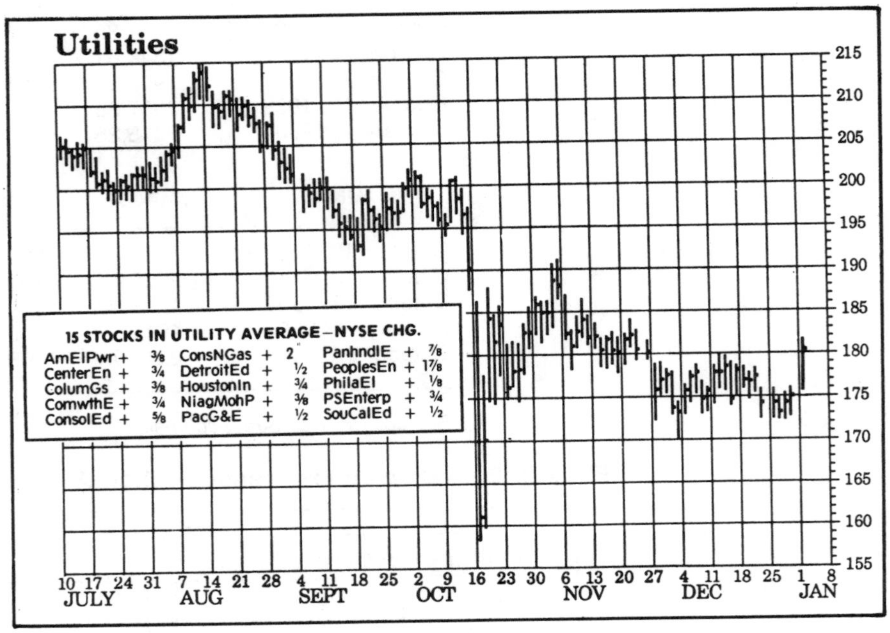
Utilities
215
210
205
200
195
190
185
180
175
170
165
160
155
15 STOCKS IN UTILITY AVERAGE–NYSE CHG.
AmElPwr + 3/8 ConsNGas + 2 PanhndlE + 7/8
CenterEn + 3/4 DetroitEd + 1/2 PeoplesEn + 1 7/8
ColumGs + 3/8 HoustonIn + 3/4 PhilaEl + 1/8
ComwthE + 3/4 NiagMohP + 3/8 PSEnterp + 3/4
ConsolEd + 5/8 PacG&E + 1/2 SouCalEd + 1/2
10 17 24 31 7 14 21 28 4 11 18 25 2 9 16 23 30 6 13 20 27 4 11 18 25 1 8
JULY AUG SEPT OCT NOV DEC JAN

(Exhibit 2.4). Unlike the Dow Jones averages, the index is capitalization-weighted, and its present base level of 100 was assigned on June 30, 1982.

Dow Jones Precious Metals Index Components. The Dow Jones Precious Metals Index is one of the narrow-based indexes within the Dow Jones Equity Index. It is based on the prices of the shares of

EXHIBIT 2.4 The Dow Jones Equity Index Component Sectors (as of 10/7/88)

Sectors/Number of Companies
1. Basic materials (66)
2. Energy (45)
3. Industrial (97)
4. Consumer, cyclical (116)
5. Consumer, noncyclical (85)
6. Technology (94)
7. Financial services (112)
8. Utilities (90)
9. Conglomerates (7)
Total: 712 companies

Source: *The Wall Street Journal.*

FIGURE 2.4 The Dow Jones Equity Index, 1982–1988

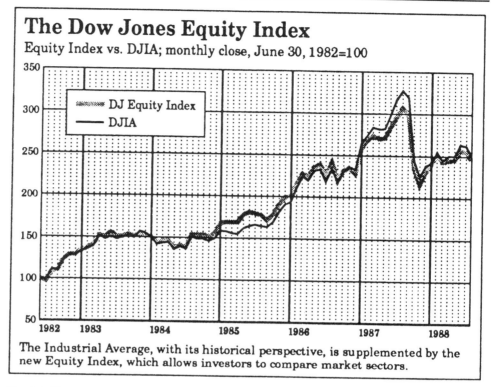

The Dow Jones Equity Index

Equity Index vs. DJIA; monthly close, June 30, 1982=100

The Industrial Average, with its historical perspective, is supplemented by the new Equity Index, which allows investors to compare market sectors.

four NYSE-listed companies involved in the mining of precious metals, such as platinum, silver, and gold (Exhibit 2.5). The four stocks are also components of the Philadelphia Stock Exchange's Gold/Silver Index, while ASA and Homestake Mining are two of the four stocks in Barron's Gold Mining Index.

The index is capitalization-weighted, and its base level of 100 was determined on June 30, 1982. Currently, Homestake Mining and Battle Mountain Gold together account for approximately 75 percent of the index's value.

EXHIBIT 2.5 Dow Jones Precious Metals Index Components

	Company	Ticker Symbol	Capitalization Weight (%) (2/24/89)
1.	Homestake Mining	HM	43.10%
2.	Battle Mountain Gold	BMG	32.06
3.	ASA Ltd.	ASA	12.49
4.	Hecla Mining	HL	12.35

Source: *The Wall Street Journal.*

FIGURE 2.5   Dow Jones Precious Metals Index, 1987–1989

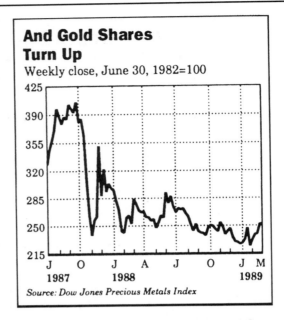

American Stock Exchange Indexes

The American Stock Exchange (AMEX) is the NYSE's little brother.
Stocks listed on the AMEX are issues of those corporations that are
generally smaller and financially less strong than those on the NYSE.
To be listed, the firm must have:

- A corporate net worth of $4 million.
- Annual earnings of $400,000 after all charges and taxes, not including
  nonrecurring items.
- 500,000 shares of common stock, not including those held by corporate
  officers and directors, but including 150,000 shares held in lots of
  100 or more.
- 1,000 public shareholders, of whom 500 each owns 100 or more shares.
- A market value of $3 million.

Besides trading stocks, American Depository Receipts (ADRs),[2] and
warrants, the AMEX also maintains an active market in options on
many stocks as well as several specialized stock indexes.

---

[2] An American Depository Receipt (ADR) is a U.S. security representing ownership of a specified number of
ordinary shares of a foreign company traded on either the NYSE, AMEX, or OTC. The physical shares are
held by an agent or foreign branch of an American bank (ADR bank). The custodian bank is usually an office
of the American bank in the country of the company whose ADR is issued. If not, the custodian bank is then
a bank closest to the foreign country.

Currently, the AMEX maintains one broad-based and four narrow-based indexes of domestic stocks issues:

AMEX Market Value Index
AMEX Computer Technology Index
AMEX Institutional Index
Major Market Index
AMEX Oil Index

A sixth index, the International Market Index, was developed jointly by the AMEX and the Coffee, Sugar & Cocoa Exchange. As it is based entirely on foreign shares, it is discussed in Chapter 7.

AMEX Market Value Index

The Market Value Index is the broad-based composite index of the prices of all the (800+) common stocks, ADRs of foreign stocks, and warrants listed on the AMEX; it covers nine industrial sectors (Exhibit 2.6). To be included in the index, new listings must first be traded for a full business day. Although the index is capitalization-weighted, it is unique among stock indexes in that it includes the reinvestment of stock dividends. As a consequence, it is really a total return index.

On September 4, 1973, the Market Value Index replaced a price change index that had been maintained since April 1966. The original base date was August 31, 1973, and the base value for the Market Value Index was set at 100; in July 1983, the base level was adjusted to 50. The Market Value Index was the basis for cash-settled index option contracts that formerly were traded on the AMEX but are now delisted. As it still remains the primary measure of the trading activity on the AMEX, the index's value is still maintained and reported on most quotation machines under ticker symbol XAM.

EXHIBIT 2.6   AMEX Market Value Index Components

Industry Sector	Approximate Weight (%)
1. Natural resources	36%
2. High technology	15
3. Service	12
4. Consumer goods	10
5. Capital goods	7
6. Financial	5
7. Housing, construction, land	5
8. Retail	3
9. Unclassified	7

Source: American Stock Exchange.

FIGURE 2.6   AMEX Market Value Index

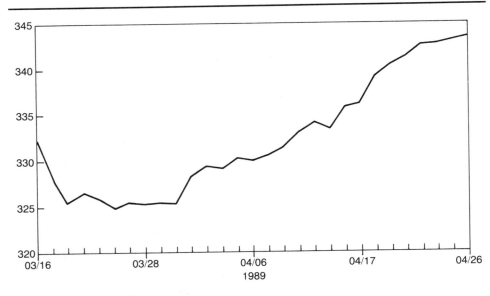

Source: American Stock Exchange.

AMEX Computer Technology Index

The Computer Technology Index is a narrow-based index of the share prices of 30 leading companies involved in the production of computers, related equipment, and semiconductor devices (Exhibit 2.7). The index is capitalization-weighted and has a base level of 100 as of July 29, 1983. On the basis of market capitalization, IBM currently accounts for approximately 44 percent of the index's value; the addition of Hewlett-Packard and Digital Equipment increases the share to approximately 60 percent. Since August 26, 1983, the index is the basis for cash-settled index option contracts that are traded on the AMEX under the ticker symbol XCI.

AMEX Institutional Index

The Institutional Index is a broad-based index based on the share prices of 75 companies most widely held as equity investments by the nation's largest institutions; it is designed to reflect the performance of their core stock holdings (Exhibit 2.8). Of these 75 companies, 20 are components of the 30-stock Dow Jones Industrial Average and 3 are components of the 15-stock Dow Jones Transportation Average.

The underlying companies are selected on the basis of stock positions in 13(f) reports filed periodically with the Securities and Exchange Commission by institutions with portfolios valued at more than $100 million. To be included in the index, component stocks must (1) be held by a minimum of 200 of the reporting institutions, and (2) have had at least 7 million shares traded in each of the two preceding calendar quarters. The list is reviewed quarterly and updated when needed.

EXHIBIT 2.7   AMEX Computer Technology Index Components

Company	Ticker Symbol	Capitalization Weight (%) (3/23/89)
1. IBM Corporation	IBM	44.20%
2. Hewlett-Packard Company	HWP	8.26
3. Digital Equipment	DEC	8.04
4. Xerox Corporation	XRX	4.12
5. Motorola, Inc.	MOT	3.52
6. NCR Corporation	NCR	2.94
7. Apple Computer, Inc.	AAPL	2.89
8. Intel Corporation	INTC	2.84
9. Unisys Corporation	UIS	2.72
10. Tandy Corporation	TAN	2.58
11. Texas Instruments	TXN	2.05
12. Honeywell, Inc.	HON	1.93
13. Automatic Data Processing	AUD	1.88
14. Microsoft Corporation	MSFT	1.87
15. COMPAQ Computer Corporation	CPQ	1.79
16. Cray Research, Inc.	CYR	1.41
17. Amdahl Corporation	AMH	1.21
18. Tandem Computers	TDM	1.15
19. Wang Laboratories "B"	WAN.B	0.95
20. Control Data Corporation	CDA	0.58
21. Prime Computer	PRM	0.56
22. National Semiconductor	NSM	0.52
23. Computer Sciences	CSC	0.51
24. Advanced Micro Devices	AMD	0.45
25. Commodore International	CBU	0.37
26. Storage Technology	STK	0.31
27. Data General Corporation	DGN	0.30
28. Datapoint Corporation	DPT	0.03
29. NBI, Inc.	NBI	0.01
30. Quantel Corporation	BQC	0.01

Source: American Stock Exchange.

FIGURE 2.7   AMEX Computer Technology Index

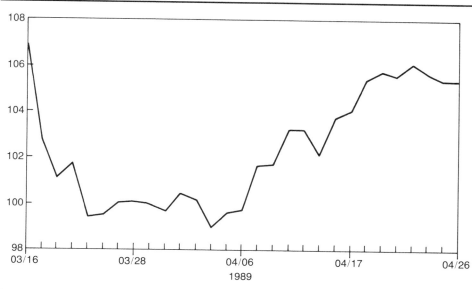

Source: American Stock Exchange.

EXHIBIT 2.8 AMEX Institutional Index Components

Company	Ticker Symbol	Capitalization Weight (%) (3/23/89)
1. International Business Machines	IBM	6.24%
2. Exxon Corporation	XON	5.52
3. General Electric Company	GE	3.82
4. American Telephone & Telegraph	T	3.24
5. Royal Dutch Petroleum	RD	3.19
6. Philip Morris Companies, Inc.	MO	2.56
7. General Motors Corporation	GM	2.44
8. Merck & Company	MRK	2.42
9. E.I. Du Pont de Nemours	DD	2.31
10. Ford Motor	F	2.30
11. Amoco Corporation	AN	1.99
12. Mobil Corporation	MOB	1.95
13. BellSouth Corporation	BEL	1.88
14. Wal-Mart Stores	WMT	1.74
15. Coca-Cola	KO	1.73
16. Chevron	CHV	1.70
17. Dow Chemical Company	DOW	1.61
18. Sears, Roebuck & Company	S	1.55
19. Atlantic Richfield Company	ARC	1.49
20. Procter & Gamble Company	PG	1.48
21. Minnesota Mining & Manufacturing	MMM	1.46
22. Bell Atlantic Corporation	BEL	1.43
23. GTE Corporation	GTE	1.43
24. Johnson & Johnson	JNJ	1.42
25. Eastman Kodak	EK	1.40
26. Pacific Telsis Group	PAC	1.39
27. American International Group	AIG	1.36
28. Ameritech	AIT	1.36
29. Eli Lilly & Company	LLY	1.34
30. NYNEX	NYN	1.32
31. Bristol Meyers	BMY	1.29
32. Southwestern Bell Corporation	SBC	1.28
33. Abbott Laboratories	ABT	1.27
34. Texaco, Inc.	TX	1.24
35. American Express	AXP	1.20
36. American Home Products	AHP	1.19
37. Hewlett-Packard	HWP	1.16
38. Digital Equipment	DEC	1.13
39. Pepsico, Inc.	PEP	1.10
40. US West, Inc.	USW	1.08
41. Walt Disney Company	DIS	0.97
42. Boeing	BA	0.96
43. Waste Management	WMX	0.94
44. Anheuser Busch Companies, Inc.	BUD	0.93
45. Dun & Bradstreet Corporation	DNB	0.92
46. Pfizer, Inc.	PFE	0.89
47. McDonald's	MCD	0.88
48. Citicorp	CCI	0.85
49. USX Corporation	X	0.77
50. Westinghouse Electric	WX	0.73
51. K-Mart Corporation	KM	0.72
52. Kellogg Company	K	0.70
53. Union Pacific Corporation	UNP	0.70
54. Schering Plough Corporation	SGP	0.67
55. ITT Corporation	ITT	0.66
56. Emerson Electric Company	EMR	0.65
57. Time, Inc.	TL	0.65
58. SmithKline Beckman Corporation	SKB	0.64
59. MCI Communications Corporation	MCIC	0.62

EXHIBIT 2.8   *(concluded)*

Company	Ticker Symbol	Capitalization Weight (%) (3/23/89)
60. Monsanto	MTC	0.62%
61. J.C. Penney Co.	JCP	0.62
62. Squibb Corporation	SQB	0.61
63. General Re Corporation	GRN	0.60
64. Xerox	XRX	0.58
65. Gannett Company, Inc.	GCI	0.57
66. Norfolk Southern Corporation	NSC	0.57
67. Caterpillar	CAT	0.56
68. Chrysler Corporation	C	0.55
69. Aetna Life & Casualty	AET	0.54
70. Warner Lambert Company	WLA	0.52
71. Motorola, Inc.	MOT	0.50
72. Aluminum Company of America	AA	0.49
73. J.P. Morgan & Company	JPM	0.45
74. AMP, Inc.	AMP	0.43
75. Burlington Northern, Inc.	BNI	0.16

Source: American Stock Exchange.

The Institutional Index is capitalization-weighted and has a base level of 25 as of June 24, 1986. Five of the 75 companies (IBM, Exxon, General Electric, AT&T, and Royal Dutch Petroleum) currently account for approximately 25 percent of the index's value. The index is the basis for European-style[3] cash-settled index option contracts that are traded on the AMEX under the ticker symbol XII, as well as cash-

FIGURE 2.8   AMEX Institutional Index

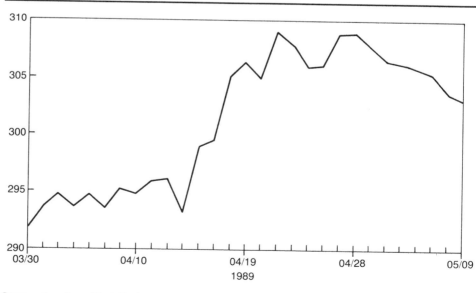

Source: American Stock Exchange.

---

[3] Unlike American-style options, European-style index option contracts can be exercised only on the last day of the contract.

settled futures contracts on the Chicago Board of Trade (CBOT), under the symbol XI.

Major Market Index—MMI

The Major Market Index (MMI) is a narrow-based index of the share prices of 20 blue-chip NYSE-listed companies (Exhibit 2.9). It is designed to follow the Dow Jones Industrial Average closely without actually duplicating it. The MMI is highly correlated to the DJIA as 17 of the 20 MMI companies are components of the DJIA. Dow Jones & Company does not license the use of either the "Dow Jones" name or its market averages as the basis for exchange-traded index contracts.

Although called an index, with a base level of 200 set in 1983, the MMI is actually calculated as a price-weighted arithmetic average. IBM and Exxon currently account for approximately 27 percent of the index's value on the basis of capitalization, but for only 13 percent of the index on the basis of market price. Since April 29, 1983, the MMI is the basis for cash-settled index option contracts that are traded on both the AMEX and European Options Exchange (Amsterdam) under the ticker symbol XMI; similar cash-settled stock index futures contracts began trading July 23, 1984, on the Chicago Board of Trade under the ticker symbol BC (for "blue chip").

EXHIBIT 2.9   Major Market Index Components

	Company	Ticker Symbol	Capitalization Weight (%) (2/15/89)	Price as a Percent of Index (2/15/89)
1.	IBM*	IBM	15.03%	9.80%
2.	Exxon*	XON	12.07	3.47
3.	General Electric*	GE	8.69	3.57
4.	American Telephone & Telegraph*	T	6.99	2.41
5.	General Motors*	GM	5.69	6.90
6.	Merck & Company*	MRK	5.23	4.92
7.	Philip Morris*	MO	5.22	8.38
8.	E.I. Du Pont de Nemours*	DD	4.87	7.55
9.	Mobil Oil	MOB	4.00	3.60
10.	Dow Chemical	DOW	3.73	7.43
11.	Coca-Cola*	KO	3.55	3.68
12.	Chevron*	CHV	3.41	3.70
13.	Sears, Roebuck*	S	3.31	3.24
14.	Eastman Kodak*	EK	3.20	3.68
15.	Procter & Gamble*	PG	3.20	7.00
16.	Minnesota Mining & Mfg.*	MMM	3.17	5.20
17.	Johnson & Johnson	JNJ	3.13	6.93
18.	American Express*	AXP	2.68	2.38
19.	USX*	X	1.72	2.44
20.	International Paper*	IP	1.12	3.74

* Components of the Dow Jones Industrial Average (17).

Source: Chicago Board of Trade; American Stock Exchange.

FIGURE 2.9 AMEX Major Market Index

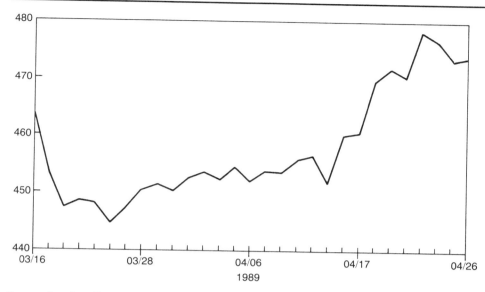

Source: American Stock Exchange.

AMEX Oil Index

The Oil Index, formerly known as the Oil & Gas Index, is a narrow-based index of the share prices of 15 leading NYSE-listed companies involved in the exploration, production, and development of petroleum (Exhibit 2.10). The index is capitalization-weighted and has a base

EXHIBIT 2.10 AMEX Oil Index Components (Formerly, Oil & Gas Index)

	Company	Ticker Symbol	Capitalization Weight (%) (3/23/89)
1.	British Petroleum	BP	61.11%
2.	Exxon	XON	9.82
3.	Royal Dutch Petroleum	RD	5.67
4.	E.I. Du Pont de Nemours	DD	4.14
5.	Amoco	AN	3.54
6.	Mobil	MOB	3.46
7.	Chevron	CHV	2.97
8.	Atlantic Richfield	ARC	2.65
9.	Texaco	TX	2.21
10.	Occidental Petroleum	OXY	1.21
11.	Phillips Petroleum	P	0.94
12.	Unocal	UCL	0.81
13.	Sun Company	SUN	0.63
14.	Amerada Hess	AHC	0.50
15.	Kerr-McGee	KMG	0.34

Source: American Stock Exchange.

FIGURE 2.10   AMEX Oil Index

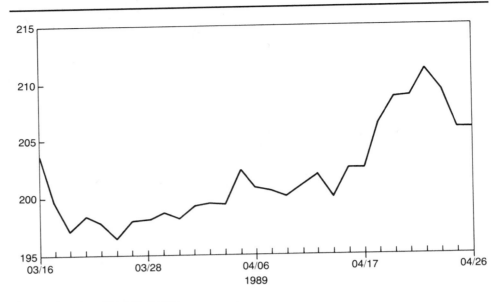

Source: American Stock Exchange.

level of 125 as of August 27, 1984. On the basis of market capitalization, British Petroleum currently accounts for approximately 61 percent of the index's value; the addition of Exxon and Royal Dutch Petroleum increases the share to approximately 75 percent. The index is the basis for cash-settled index option contracts that are traded on the AMEX under the ticker symbol XOI.

Barron's Averages

Barron's is a weekly financial newspaper published by Dow Jones & Company. It currently maintains the following stock price measures:

> Barron's 50-Stock Average
> Barron's Low-Price Stock Average
> Barron's Gold Mining Index

Barron's 50-Stock Average

Barron's 50-Stock Average represents 50 leading NYSE-listed issues, 20 of which are components of the Dow Jones 65-Stock Composite Average (Exhibit 2.11). The 50 are currently divided as follows:

> 42 industrial stocks
> 5 transportation
> 3 public utility stocks

EXHIBIT 2.11 Barron's 50-Stock Average Components as of 1/16/89

Sector/Companies	Ticker Symbol
Industrials (42)	
Allied-Signal*	ALD
American Telephone & Telegraph*	T
Amoco	AN
Baxter Travenol Laboratories	BAX
Boeing*	BA
CPC International	CPC
Caterpillar Tractor	CAT
Citicorp	CCI
Coca-Cola*	KO
Control Data	CDA
R.R. Donnelley & Sons	DNY
E.I. Du Pont de Nemours*	DD
General Electric*	GE
General Mills	GIS
General Motors*	GM
Goodyear Tire & Rubber*	GT
International Business Machines*	IBM
Inco Ltd.	N
Inland Steel	IAD
James River	JR
Kellogg	K
Lone Star Industries	LCE
Minnesota Mining & Manufacturing*	MMM
Mobil Corporation	MOB
Monsanto	MTC
NCR Corporation	NCR
National Intergroup	NII
Pittsburgh Plate Glass	PPG
Pfizer	PFE
Procter & Gamble*	PG
Raytheon	RTN
RJR Nabisco	RJR
Schlumberger Ltd.	SLB
Squibb	SQB
TRW	TRW
Timken	TKR
Union Carbide*	UK
United Technologies*	UTX
USG	USG
Westinghouse Electric*	WX
Weyerhaeuser	WY
Wrigley	WWY
Transportation (5)	
CSX*	CSX
Delta Air Lines*	DAL
GATX	GMT
Norfolk Southern*	NSC
Union Pacific*	UNP
Utilities (3)	
Detroit Edison*	DTE
Southern California Edison*	SCE
Wisconsin Energy	WEC

* Components of the Dow Jones 65-stock composite average (20).

Source: *Barron's.*

FIGURE 2.11   Barron's 50-Stock Average

Barron's 50- Stock Average

This 50-stock index is an unweighted average of 50 leading issues with each stock given equal weight in determining the average. It offers comparisons to the projected quarterly and annual earnings which appear in the table. The earnings yield, which is the reciprocal of the Price/Earnings Ratio (1 divided by the P/E), can be compared to bond yields in the table. The dividend yield equals the dividend divided by the price of the average.

	June 1 1989	May 25 1989	June 1988
Average price index	1382	1375	1211
Projected quarterly earn	32.50	32.50	29.14
Annualized projected earn	130.00	130.00	116.56
Annualized projected P/E	10.6	10.6	10.4
Five-year average earn	85.29	85.29	75.48
Five-year average P/E	16.2	16.1	16.1
Year-end earn	125.46	125.46	104.35
Year-end P/E	11.0	10.9	11.6
Year-end earns yield, %	9.1	9.2	8.61
Best grade bond yields, %	9.41	9.46	9.44
Bond yields/stock ylds, %	1.03	1.03	1.09
Actual year-end divs	53.70	53.70	40.43
Actual yr-end divs yld, %	3.88	3.90	3.34

The average and the associated statistics of the component companies (Figure 2.11) are intended to be used as yardsticks in deciding whether the market at any given time is reasonably priced, overvalued, or undervalued in view of what the investor believes to be the most probable course of the business cycle.

Unlike other stock price averages and indexes, it is an unweighted price average—calculated from the closing prices each Thursday—which (1) includes both earnings and dividends of the 50 issues, and (2) assumes that the same dollar investment is made in each component company instead of one share of each company.

Barron's Low-Price Stock Average

The Low-Price Stock Index is based on 20 speculative, lower-quality, low-priced issues that tend to be more volatile than the blue-chip stocks that make up the Dow Averages (Exhibit 2.12). Currently, 12 of the issues are listed on the NYSE and 8 on the AMEX.

Barron's Gold Mining Index

Barron's Gold Mining Index is a weighted average of the prices of four gold mining stocks, all of which except LAC Minerals also are

EXHIBIT 2.12   Barron's Low-Price Stock Index Components as of 1/16/89

Company	Ticker Symbol
NYSE-Listed (12)	
Core Industries	CRI
DiGiorgio Corporation	DIG
Flow General	FGN
Limited Inc.	LTD
Navistar International	NAV
Nortek Inc.	NTK
Ohio Mattress	OMT
Parker Drilling	PKD
SL Industries	SL
Skyline	SKY
Suave Shoe	SWV
Trans Technology	TT
AMEX-Listed (8)	
American Precision Industries	APR
Cubic Corporation	CUB
Genisco Technologies	GES
Met-Pro Corporation	MPR
Penril Corporation	PNL
Superior Surgical Manufacturing	SGC
United Foods "A"	UFD.A
Vicon Industries	VII

Source: *Barron's.*

FIGURE 2.12   Barron's Low-Price Stock Index

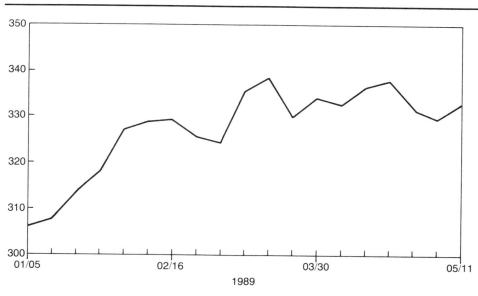

Source: *Barron's.*

EXHIBIT 2.13 Barron's Gold Mining Index Components

Company	Multiplier (1/16/89)	Ticker Symbol
ASA Ltd.*	39.9120	ASA
Homestake Mining*	20.0000	HM
LAC Minerals	9.3957	LAC
Placer Dome*	36.0000	PDG

* Components of PHLX Gold/Silver Index (3).
Source: *Barron's*.

Example 2.1

The prices of the four stocks of the Gold Mining Index at the close on Thursday, May 4, 1989, were:

> ASA Ltd. 41
> Homestake Mining 13¼
> LAC Mineral 10½
> Placer Dome 12⅜

The Gold Mining Index was then computed as follows:

Stock	Closing Price	Multiplier	Weighted Price
ASA	41	39.9120	1636.3920
Homestake	13.25	20.0000	265.0000
LAC	10.5	9.3957	98.6549
Placer Dome	12.375	36.0000	445.5000
		Total =	2445.5469
		Group divisor	4.0
		Gold Mining Index =	611.39

---

components of the larger Philadelphia Stock Exchange's Gold/Silver Index (Exhibit 2.13). Although called an index, it is actually a weighted arithmetic average based on the stocks' weekly Thursday closing prices.

The computation of the Gold Mining Index is illustrated in Example 2.1.

CBOE 250 Stock Index

The CBOE 250 Stock Index is the result of a joint venture of the Chicago Board of Trade (CBOT), the world's oldest and largest futures exchange, and the Chicago Board Options Exchange (CBOE), which is the world's oldest and largest options exchange. It is a broad-based stock price index of the 250 largest-capitalized NYSE stock issues (Exhibit 2.14), representing about 70 percent of the total market value of all NYSE issues. The components are revised on a quarterly cycle, except for

EXHIBIT 2.14   CBOE 250 Futures Index Components (Top 10 Ranked by Capitalization)

Company	Ticker Symbol	Index Weight (%) (1/5/89)
1. IBM	IBM	4.33%
2. Exxon Corporation	XON	3.44
3. General Electric	GE	2.42
4. American Telephone & Telegraph	T	1.85
5. Royal Dutch Petroleum	RD	1.84
6. General Motors	GM	1.53
7. Ford Motor	F	1.52
8. Philip Morris	MO	1.41
9. Merck & Company	MRK	1.35
10. E.I. Du Pont de Nemours	DD	1.27
Total		20.94%

Source: Chicago Board Options Exchange.

revisions as a result of mergers, acquisitions, etc. The CBOE 250 Index was originally designed in part to attract hedging trades from traders located at the S&P 100 stock index options pit at the CBOE.

The index is capitalization-weighted and has a base level of 100 as of July 29, 1983. On the basis of market capitalization, the top 10 ranked companies represent almost 21 percent of the index's weight. The CBOE 250 Index is the basis for cash-settled futures contracts

FIGURE 2.13   CBOE 250 Index (January 4, 1982, to December 31, 1988)

Source: Chicago Board Options Exchange.

that have been traded on the CBOT under the ticker symbol JV since November 11, 1988.

Financial News Composite Index—FNCI

The Financial News Composite Index (FNCI, pronounced "fancy"), based on 30 blue-chip stocks, was designed to track the modern stock market and was developed by the Financial News Network. Its components (Exhibit 2.15), all highly capitalized NYSE firms, are very liquid, have listed options, and represent industries chosen to model the contemporary American economy.

The FNCI is a price-weighted arithmetic average, and its correlation with the DJIA is very high, as 17 of the FNCI component companies are also components of the DJIA. In addition, 15 of the 20 Major Market Index stocks are included in the FNCI. Since November 13, 1986, the index has been the basis for cash-settled, European-style index option

EXHIBIT 2.15   Financial News Composite Index Components

	Company	Ticker Symbol	(%) Index Weight (12/30/88)
1.	International Business Machines*†	IBM	13.17%
2.	Exxon Corporation*†	XON	11.59
3.	General Electric Company*†	GE	8.03
4.	American Telephone & Telegraph*†	T	6.81
5.	Philip Morris Companies*†	MO	5.40
6.	General Motors Company *†	GM	5.14
7.	Merck & Company*†	MRK	5.12
8.	BellSouth Corporation	BLS	3.98
9.	Coca-Cola Co.*†	KO	3.66
10.	Dow Chemical Company†	DOW	3.35
11.	Sears, Roebuck & Company*†	S	3.25
12.	Minnesota Mining & Manufacturing*†	MMM	3.07
13.	Eastman Kodak Company*†	EK	2.95
14.	American Express Company*†	AXP	2.61
15.	American Home Products	AHP	2.50
16.	Digital Equipment Corporation	DEC	2.49
17.	Walt Disney Company	DIS	2.05
18.	Boeing Company*	BA	2.01
19.	Schlumberger Ltd.	SLB	1.81
20.	Citicorp	CCI	1.80
21.	SCECorp	SCE	1.41
22.	H. J. Heinz Company	HNZ	1.27
23.	Aetna Life & Casualty Company	AE	1.15
24.	Aluminum Company of America*	AA	1.05
25.	International Paper Company*†	IP	1.02
26.	Allied-Signal, Inc.*†	ALD	0.98
27.	CSX Corporation	CSX	0.71
28.	Delta Air Lines, Inc.	DAL	0.57
29.	Merrill Lynch & Company	MER	0.55
30.	Goodyear Tire & Rubber Company*	GT	0.52

* Component of Dow Jones Industrial Average (17).

† Component of Major Market Index (15).

Sources: Financial News Network; Pacific Stock Exchange.

FIGURE 2.14   Financial News Composite Index

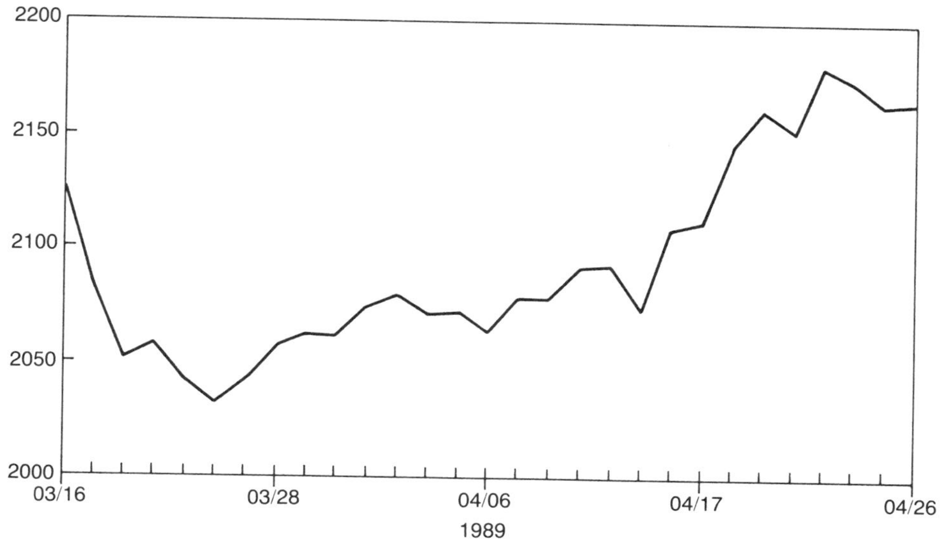

Source: Pacific Stock Exchange.

contracts that are traded on the Pacific Stock Exchange under the ticker symbol FNC.

NASDAQ Indexes

Public stock issues not traded on any domestic stock exchange are traded in the OTC market. Unlike stock exchanges, which are *auction* markets, the OTC market is a *negotiated* market. The National Association of Securities Dealers (NASD) represents thousands of brokers and dealers who trade OTC stocks. Since 1970, the prices of over 5,000 of the more than 40,000,000 OTC issues have been reported through the National Association of Securities Dealers Automatic Quotation System, called NASDAQ (pronounced *naz-dak*). The NASDAQ system is divided into two broad classifications: the National Market System and the OTC market. The National Market System (NMS) comprises so-called Tier 1 OTC stocks, a select subset of the OTC market whose issues meet higher volume and price requirements than the remainder of the OTC market.

The NASD maintains and publishes two composite indexes and six subindexes daily:

NASDAQ Composite Index

NASDAQ/NMS Composite Index

NASDAQ Bank Index

NASDAQ Insurance Index

NASDAQ Other Finance Index

NASDAQ Transportation Index

NASDAQ Utilities Index

NASDAQ Industrial Index

All eight stock price indexes are capitalization-weighted; each was assigned a base level of 100 as of February 5, 1971. Adjustments for the addition or deletion of securities or for capitalization changes are made after the market closes on the day of the change. Adjustments for stock splits and stock dividends are made in the same manner, but no adjustments are made for cash dividends. The prices used in the computation of each index are the *median bid prices* at the time the index is computed. Because of the bid-asked price spreads associated with the OTC market, index levels may be affected by dealer judgments (bid prices). In addition, there may be as few as one or two market makers for some stock issues, so that a dealer's change in bid price can substantially affect the median price that is used in the calculation of the index.

In the case of the NASDAQ indexes, most of which include larger numbers of issues than other stock groups, the weighting by capitalization may tend to skew the performance of OTC stocks more than do other measures such as the S&P 500, DJIA, or the NYSE Composite. Only about 15 (or 0.9 percent) of the issues traded on the NYSE have market capitalizations of less than $10 million. However, more than 1,500 (or 35 percent) NASDAQ issues represent less than $10 million each in capitalization. Furthermore, these 1,500 issues collectively have a capitalization that is smaller than the combined capitalization of NASDAQ's six largest issues.

NASDAQ Composite Index

As its name implies, the NASDAQ Composite Index is a measure of all of NASDAQ's 2,900+ National Marketing System (NASDAQ/NMS)

FIGURE 2.15   NASDAQ Composite Index

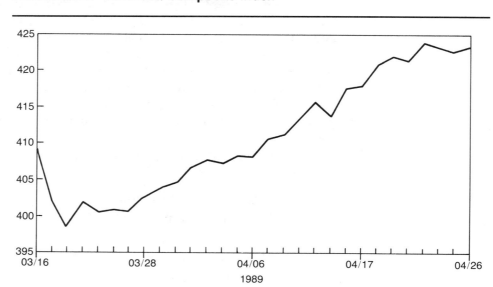

Source: National Association of Securities Dealers.

FIGURE 2.16   NASDAQ/NMS Composite Index

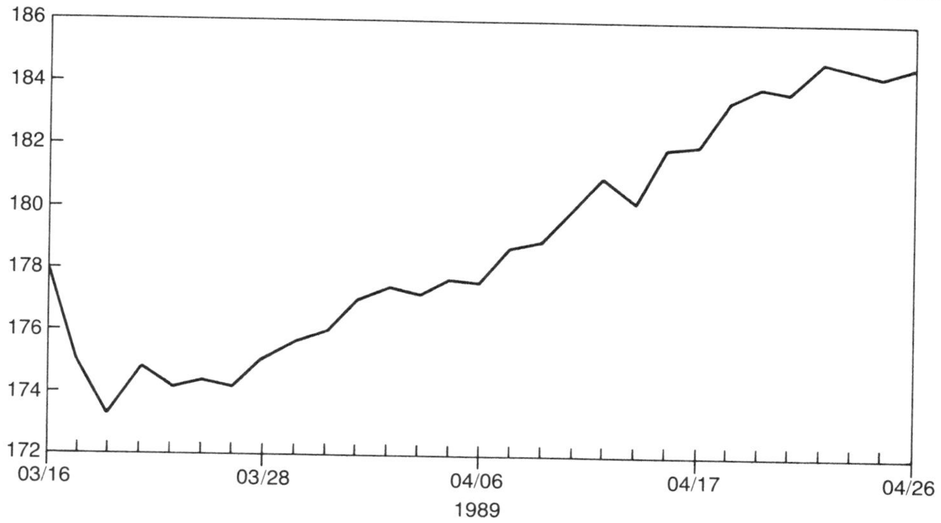

Source: National Association of Securities Dealers.

issues, exclusive of warrants, as well as all domestic common stocks traded in the regular NASDAQ market that are not part of NASDAQ/ NMS. Every one of the 4,300+ securities making up the Composite Index is also assigned to one of the six subindexes. The placement within a particular subindex is based upon the federally sponsored Standard Industrial Classification (SIC) codes applicable to a company's major source of revenues.

NASDAQ/NMS Composite Index

The NASDAQ/NMS Composite Index is a subindex of the NASDAQ Composite Index; it includes only the 2,900+ National Market System (NASDAQ/NMS) issues, exclusive of warrants.

NASDAQ Bank Index

The NASDAQ Bank Index is a broad-based index that includes the securities of all types of banks, including trust companies not engaged in deposit banking, as well as those establishments performing functions closely related to banking, such as check-cashing agencies, currency exchanges, safe deposit companies, and corporations for banking abroad (Exhibit 2.16).

This may be misleading, as the index (which contains approximately 240 issues) does not include most of the approximately 800 NASDAQ banking stocks but does include all of the approximately 220 savings bank issues. When the index was formed in 1971, all commercial and savings banks had the same SIC code number. The NASD, faced with the huge and constantly changing OTC market, opted to use the SIC codes as the basis for its subindexes. Since 1971, however, most commer-

**EXHIBIT 2.16 NASDAQ Bank Index Components
(Top 10 Ranked by Capitalization; as of 6/30/88)**

	Company	Ticker Symbol
1.	National Community Bank of New Jersey	NCBR
2.	Wilmington Trust Company	WILM
3.	California First Bank	CFBK
4.	Merchants Bank of New York	MBNY
5.	Banco Popular de Puerto Rico	BPOP
6.	Washington Mutual Savings Bank	WAMU
7.	Home Savings Bank	HMSB
8.	Bank of Delaware	BDEL
9.	Rochester Community Savings Bank	RCSB
10.	Sumitomo Bank of California	SUMI
	Total 241	

Source: National Association Securities Dealers.

FIGURE 2.17 NASDAQ Bank Index

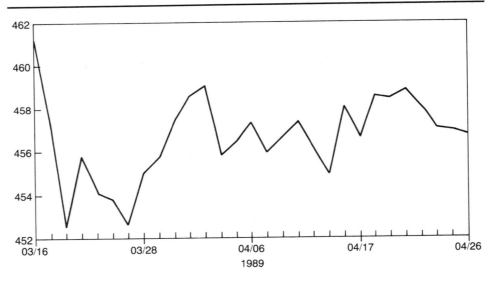

Source: National Association of Securities Dealers.

cial banks have restructured themselves as holding companies with new SIC codes that have moved them out of the Bank Index.

NASDAQ Insurance Index

The NASDAQ Insurance Index is a broad-based index that includes 130+ issues representing all types of insurance companies, including brokers, agents, and related services (Exhibit 2.17).

EXHIBIT 2.17   NASDAQ Insurance Index Components (Top 10 Ranked by Capitalization; as of 12/30/88)

Company	Ticker Symbol
1. St. Paul Companies (The)	STPL
2. SAFECO Corporation	SAFC
3. First Executive Corporation	FEXC
4. Roadway Services	ROAD
5. Ohio Casualty Corporation	OCAS
6. Provident Life & Accident Insurance of America "B"	PACCB
7. Hannover Insurance Company	HINS
8. Argonaut Group	AGII
9. 20th Century Industries	TWEN
10. Old Republic International	OLDR
Total 133	

Source: National Association of Securities Dealers.

FIGURE 2.18   NASDAQ Insurance Index

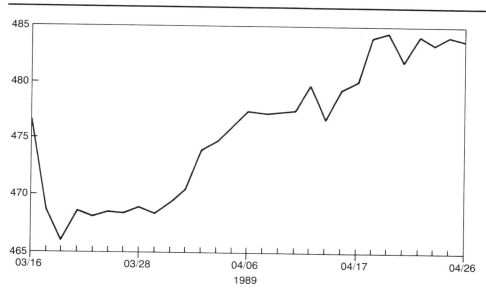

Source: National Association of Securities Dealers.

NASDAQ Other Finance Index

The NASDAQ Other Finance Index is a broad-based index representing the securities of approximately 760 credit agencies other than banks (Exhibit 2.18). These include savings and loan associations, security and commodity brokers, Exchanges, and investment companies other than those subject to regulation under the Investment Company Act of 1940. Since 1971, most commercial banks have restructured them-

EXHIBIT 2.18   NASDAQ Other Finance Index Components (Top 10 Ranked by Capitalization; as of 6/30/88)

	Company	Ticker Symbol
1.	First Union Corporation	FUNC
2.	Sovran Financial Corporation	SOVN
3.	Shawmut National Corporation	SHNA
4.	Citizens & Southern Corporation	CSOU
5.	Midlantic Corporation	MIDL
6.	Corestates Financial Corporation	CSTN
7.	Kemper Corporation	KEMC
8.	National City Corporation	NCTY
9.	M N C Financial	MNCF
10.	Rouse Company	ROUS
	Total 769	

Source: National Association of Securities Dealers.

FIGURE 2.19   NASDAQ Other Finance Index

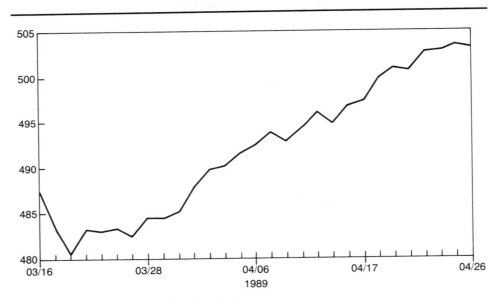

Source: National Association of Securities Dealers.

selves as regional holding companies with new SIC codes that have moved them out of the Bank Index into the Other Finance Index.

NASDAQ Finance Index

The NASDAQ Finance Index tracks the 100 largest banks and insurance companies whose stocks are traded in the OTC market. It is a hybrid measure made up of some of the companies included in NASDAQ's Bank, Insurance, and Other Finance indexes.

FIGURE 2.20   NASDAQ Finance Index

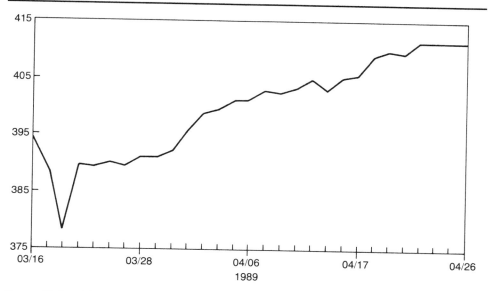

Source: National Association of Securities Dealers.

NASDAQ Transportation Index

The NASDAQ Transportation Index is a narrow-based index representing all types of approximately 75 transportation companies (Exhibit 2.19). These include pipelines (except natural gas) and services incidental to transportation, such as warehousing, travel arrangements, and packing.

EXHIBIT 2.19   NASDAQ Transportation Index Components (Top 10 Ranked by Capitalization; as of 12/30/88)

	Company	Ticker Symbol
1.	Laidlaw Transportation "B"	LDMFB
2.	Interhome Energy	IHEIF
3.	Alexander & Baldwin	ALEX
4.	Roadway Services	ROAD
5.	Yellow Freight Delivery	YELL
6.	Laidlaw Transportation "A"	LDMFA
7.	J. B. Hunt Transport Services	JBHT
8.	Gotaas-Larsen Shipping	GOTLF
9.	Stolt Tankers & Terminals (Holdings) S. A.	STLTF
10.	Trans World Airlines, preferred	TWAXP
	Total 79	

Source: National Association of Securities Dealers.

FIGURE 2.21 NASDAQ Transportation Index

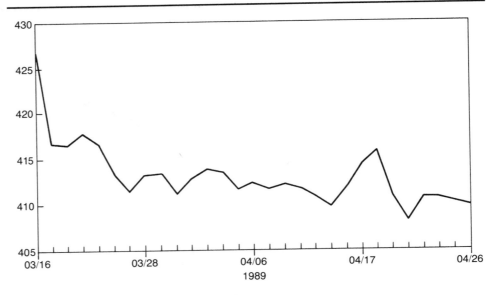

Source: National Association of Securities Dealers.

NASDAQ Utilities Index

The NASDAQ Utilities Index is a broad-based index representing all types of approximately 170 utility companies and natural gas pipelines, but it excludes railroads and buses (Exhibit 2.20). Contrary to what its name implies, the Utility Index is dominated largely by broadcasting, communications, and cable-television companies, rather than by companies involved in generation of electrical power.

EXHIBIT 2.20 NASDAQ Utilities Index Components (Top 10 Ranked by Capitalization; as of 7/14/88)

	Company	Ticker Symbol
1.	MCI Communications	MCIC
2.	Tele-Communications "A"	TCOMA
3.	LIN Broadcasting	LINB
4.	American Television & Communications Corporation "A"	STCMA
5.	Citizens Utilities "A"	CITUA
6.	Wheelabrator Technologies	WHTI
7.	Scripps Howard Broadcasting	SCRP
8.	Metro Mobile CTS "B"	MMCTB
9.	Cellular Communications	COMM
10.	Tele-Communications "B"	TCOMB
	Total 173	

Source: National Association of Securities Dealers.

FIGURE 2.22   NASDAQ Utilities Index

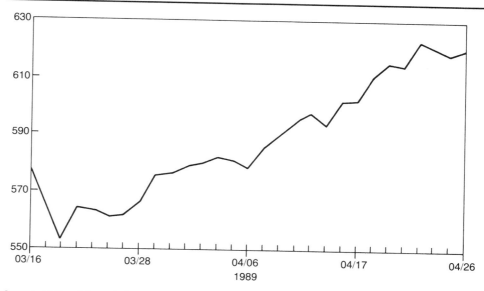

Source: National Association of Securities Dealers.

NASDAQ Industrial Index

The NASDAQ Industrial Index represents those 2,900+ issues that are not included in NASDAQ's Bank, Insurance, Other Finance, Transportation, or Utilities indexes (Exhibit 2.21).

EXHIBIT 2.21   NASDAQ Industrial Index Components (Top 20 Ranked by Capitalization; as of 6/30/88)

	Company	Ticker Symbol
1.	Intel Corporation	INTC
2.	Apple Computer Corporation	AAPL
3.	Microsoft Corporation	MSFT
4.	Nordstrom	NOBE
5.	The Henley Group	HNCO
6.	The Price Company	PCLB
7.	Food Lion "A"	FDLNA
8.	Consolidated Papers	CPER
9.	MacMillan Bloedel Ltd.	MMBLF
10.	Food Lion "B"	FDLNB
11.	Liz Claiborne	LIZC
12.	Sonoco Products	SONO
13.	Paccar Corporation	PCAR
14.	Sun Microsystems	SUNW
15.	Reuters Holdings PLC, ADR	RTRSY
16.	Willamette Industries	WMTT
17.	Massachusetts Computer Corp.	MSCP
18.	Pioneer Hi-Bred International	PHYB
19.	United Artists Communications	UACI
20.	Oracle Systems Corporation	ORCL
	Total 2,986	

Source: National Association of Securities Dealers.

FIGURE 2.23   NASDAQ Industrials Index

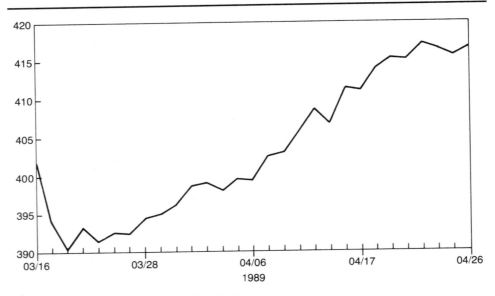

Source: National Association of Securities Dealers.

New York Stock Exchange Averages and Indexes

The New York Stock Exchange (NYSE), known as the "Big Board," is the second oldest and the largest of the 16 principal U.S. financial markets; it accounts for over 80 percent of all domestic stock exchange activity. Once the largest world market in total market capitalization, it now ranks second to the Tokyo Stock Exchange.

As the story goes, the forerunner of the New York Stock Exchange was a group of 24 stock traders who met under a buttonwood tree in the financial district of lower Manhattan, somewhere on Wall Street, on May 17, 1792, to arrange for a permanent place for organized stock trading.[4] On March 8, 1817, the association of traders became known as the New York Stock & Exchange Board, which was renamed the New York Stock Exchange in 1869.

Currently, the NYSE computes the following indexes:

NYSE Composite Index

NYSE Industrial Index

NYSE Utilities Index

NYSE Transportation Index

NYSE Financial Index

NYSE Composite Index

The NYSE Composite Index is a broad-based index of the share prices of all the 1,600+ companies listed on the NYSE, representative of 46 industrial sectors. In addition to the all-share Composite Index, there

[4] The address of this original meeting has been reported to be 62 Wall Street. The current address of the NYSE is 11 Wall Street (the corner of Wall and Broad streets).

are four major subindexes: Industrial, Transportation, Utility, and Finance (Exhibit 2.22). Like the NASDAQ indexes, the placement of a company within a particular subindex is based upon SIC codes relative to the company's major source of revenues.

The NYSE began daily computation of the Composite Index on

EXHIBIT 2.22 New York Stock Exchange Index Components

Index/Sectors	Companies (3/3/89)
1. NYSE Industrial Index	**1,012**
Aerospace	17
Business Supplies & Services	38
Chemicals	47
Computers, Data Processing	47
Construction	65
Electrical Equipment	13
Electronics	51
Environmental Control	8
Foods, Beverages	47
Health & Beauty Products	11
Health Care Services	28
Household Goods	34
Industrial Machinery & Equipment	56
Lodging, Restaurants	25
Mining, Refining, Fabricating	70
Motor Vehicles	22
Oil & Gas	80
Packaging	12
Paper Production	14
Pharmaceuticals	18
Publishing	15
Recreation Services & Products	45
Retail Trade	81
Textiles, Apparel	38
Tires, Rubber	6
Tobacco	7
Wholesalers, Distributors	19
Multi-Industry	83
Other	15
2. NYSE Transportation Index	**41**
Air	16
Rail	10
Trucking	4
Other Transportation Services	11
3. NYSE Utility Index	**178**
Electric Services	69
Gas Services	51
Telecommunications	25
Water Supply Companies	4
Multi-Service Companies	29
4. NYSE Financial Index	**409**
Banks	87
Brokerage Services	18
Closed-End Investment Companies	148
Finance Companies	7
Insurance	46
Trusts	55
Real Estate	21
Diversified Financial Services	27
5. NYSE Composite Index	**1,640**

Source: New York Stock Exchange.

FIGURE 2.24   NYSE Composite Index

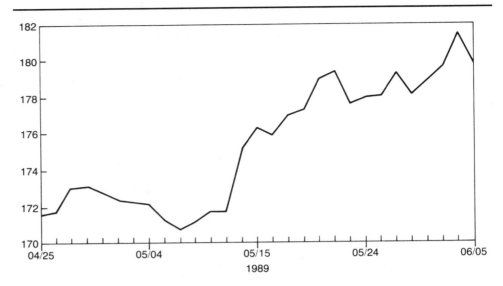

Source: New York Stock Exchange.

May 28, 1964. The Composite and the four subindexes are all capitalization-weighted, and each was assigned a base level of 50 on December
31, 1965. The market capitalization of the top ranked companies is
similar to that of the companies covered by the S&P 100/500 Indexes
and other indexes of blue-chip companies, such as the Major Market
Index. Adjustments are made for new listings and delistings, for the
change in capitalization that occurs when a listed company acquires
an unlisted company, and for the offering of rights to compensate for
the value of new shares being added to the value of the issue. Since
December 23, 1983, the index is the basis for cash-settled index option
contracts that are traded on the New York Futures Exchange under
the ticker symbol YX.

FIGURE 2.25   NYSE Industrial Index

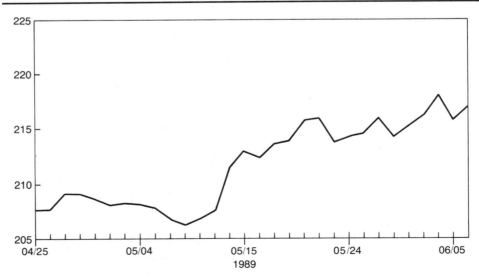

Source: New York Stock Exchange.

FIGURE 2.26   NYSE Utility Index

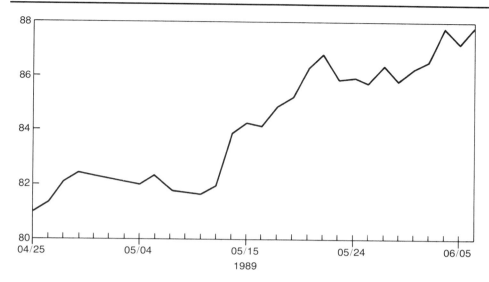

Source: New York Stock Exchange.

1. Industrial. The NYSE Industrial Index is a broad-based index representing over 1,000 NYSE-listed industrial companies distributed over 29 industrial groups.

2. Utilities. The NYSE Utilities Index is a narrow-based index representing approximately 40 NYSE-listed public utility companies involved in electric power, natural gas, telecommunications, and water supply.

3. Transportation. The NYSE Transportation Index is a broad-based index representing over 175 NYSE-listed companies involved in transportation services in air, rail, trucking, and miscellaneous.

FIGURE 2.27   NYSE Transportation Index

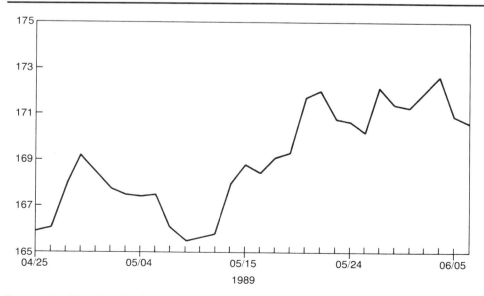

Source: New York Stock Exchange.

FIGURE 2.28   NYSE Financial Index

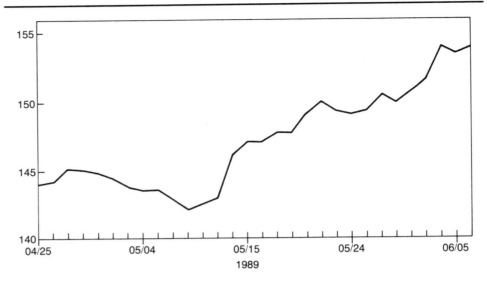

Source: New York Stock Exchange.

4. Financial.   The NYSE Financial Index is a broad-based index representing approximately 400 NYSE-listed credit agencies, banks, savings and loan associations, security and commodity brokers, exchanges, insurance, and investment companies.

Philadelphia Stock Exchange Indexes

The Philadelphia Stock Exchange (PHLX), the nation's first securities exchange, has been in operation since 1790. Currently, the PHLX maintains the following indexes:

>   PHLX Gold/Silver Index
>   PHLX National OTC Index
>   PHLX Utility Index
>   PHLX Blue Chip CIP Index

PHLX Gold/Silver Index

The PHLX Gold/Silver Index is a narrow-based index of the share prices of seven NYSE-listed companies involved in the mining of silver and gold (Exhibit 2.23). The index is capitalization-weighted and has a base level of 100 as of 1983. On the basis of market capitalization, Placer Dome and Newmont Mining currently account for approximately 57 percent of the index's value. Since December 19, 1983, the index is the basis for cash-settled index option contracts that are traded on the PHLX under the ticker symbol XAU.

EXHIBIT 2.23   Philadelphia Stock Exchange Gold/Silver Index Components

	Company	Ticker Symbol	Capitalization Weight (%) (2/24/89)
1.	Placer Dome	PDG	30.54%
2.	Newmont Mining	NEM	26.99
3.	Echo Bay Mines	ECO	14.22
4.	Homestake Mining	HM	12.18
5.	Battle Mountain Gold	BMG	9.06
6.	ASA Ltd.	ASA	3.53
7.	Hecla Mining	HL	3.49

Source: Philadelphia Stock Exchange.

FIGURE 2.29   PHLX Gold/Silver Index

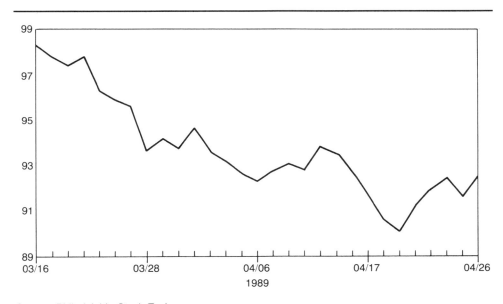

Source: Philadelphia Stock Exchange.

PHLX National OTC Index

The PHLX National OTC Index is a broad-based index of the share prices of the 100 largest U.S. companies whose common stocks are (1) traded over-the-counter by at least four market makers, (2) Tier 1 National Market System issues, and (3) not listed on any of the regional or national stock exchanges (Exhibit 2.24). It was developed to compete with other tradable OTC stock indexes, such as S&P 250 OTC.

The index, which is capitalization-weighted, has a base level of 150 as of September 28, 1984. The list of component stocks is reviewed at least semiannually. The market capitalization of Apple Computer and MCI Communications currently accounts for approximately 13 percent of the index's value. The index is the basis for cash-settled index option contracts that are traded on the PHLX under the ticker symbol XOC.

EXHIBIT 2.24 Philadelphia Stock Exchange National OTC Index Components

	Company	Ticker Symbol	Capitalization Weight (%) (2/24/89
1.	Apple Computer	AAPL	8.64%
2.	MCI Communications	MCIC	4.37
3.	McCaw Cellular Communications "A"	MCAWA	3.74
4.	LIN Broadcasting "B"	LINB	3.55
5.	Tele-Communications "A"	TCOMA	3.40
6.	Intel Corporation	INTC	3.13
7.	American Television & Communication "A"	ATCMA	2.73
8.	Food Lion "B"	FDLNB	2.63
9.	Microsoft	MSFT	2.46
10.	Laidlaw Transportation "B"	LDMFB	2.14
11.	Nordstrom	NOBE	1.94
12.	St. Paul Companies	STPL	1.61
13.	The Price Company	PCLB	1.33
14.	Contel Cellular "A"	CCXLA	1.31
15.	Kemper	KEMC	1.28
16.	SAFECO	SAFC	1.28
17.	Alexander & Baldwin	ALEX	1.27
18.	Corestates Financial	CSFN	1.22
19.	Liz Claiborne	LIZC	1.17
20.	Sonoco Products	SONO	1.17
21.	Citizens & Southern	CSOU	1.15
22.	Consolidated Papers	CPER	1.14
23.	Oracle Systems	ORCL	1.14
24.	Midlantic	MIDL	1.12
25.	Sun Microsystems	SUNW	1.12
26.	PACCAR, Inc.	PCAR	1.09
27.	U.S. West New Vector Grp "A"	USWNA	1.09
28.	E. W. Scripps "A"	EWSCA	1.04
29.	Citizens Utilities "B"	CITUB	0.96
30.	Rouse	ROUS	0.96
31.	Roadway Services	ROAD	0.95
32.	United Artists Communications	UACI	0.95
33.	Comcast "A"	CMCSA	0.93
34.	First Executive Corporation	FEXC	0.93
35.	Jefferson Smurfit Corporation	JJSC	0.92
36.	Wheelabrator Technologies	WHTI	0.88
37.	Willamette Industries	WHTG	0.86
38.	Sigma-Aldrich Corporation	SIAL	0.85
39.	Cellular Communications	COMM	0.84
40.	Intergraph	INGR	0.84
41.	Centel Cable Television "A"	CNCAA	0.83
42.	Nike, Inc.	NIKE	0.81
43.	Pioneer Hi-Bred International	PHYB	0.80
44.	U.S. Bancorp of Oregon	USBC	0.80
45.	Fifth Third Bancorp	FITB	0.78
46.	Multimedia Incorporated	MMEDC	0.76
47.	American National Insurance	ANAT	0.74
48.	State Street Boston	STBK	0.74
49.	Tyson Foods "A"	TYSNA	0.74
50.	Cincinnati Financial	CINF	0.73
51.	Novell, Inc.	NOVL	0.73
52.	Commerce Clearing House	CCLR	0.69
53.	Ameritrust	AMTR	0.68
54.	Lotus Development Corporation	LOTS	0.68
55.	Bruno's, Inc.	BRNO	0.66
56.	Molex, Inc.	MOLX	0.66
57.	Kelly Services "A"	KELYA	0.65

EXHIBIT 2.24 *(concluded)*

	Company	Ticker Symbol	Capitalization Weight (%) (2/24/89)
58.	MASCO Industries	MASX	0.65%
59.	Worthington Industries	WTHG	0.64
60.	Ohio Casualty Corporation	OCAS	0.63
61.	Noxell "B"	NOXLB	0.62
62.	Charming Shoppes	CHRS	0.61
63.	Yellow Freight System	YELL	0.61
64.	Hartford Steam Boiler Inspection & Insurance	HBOL	0.60
65.	Provident Life & Accident Insurance of America "B"	PACCB	0.59
66.	Mobile Communications "B"	MCCAB	0.58
67.	Society Corporation	SOCI	0.58
68.	Tecumseh Products	TECU	0.58
69.	3Com Corporation	COMS	0.57
70.	Betz Laboratories	BETZ	0.56
71.	Hechinger "A"	HECHA	0.56
72.	National Health Laboratories	NHLI	0.56
73.	Comerica Corporation	CMCA	0.55
74.	Crestar Financial	CRFC	0.52
75.	Micron Technology	MCRN	0.52
76.	Meridian Bancorp	MRDN	0.52
77.	Northern Trust	NTRS	0.52
78.	Autodesk	ACAD	0.51
79.	American Greetings "A"	AGREA	0.51
80.	Baybanks, Inc.	BBNK	0.51
81.	Dominion Bankshares	DMBK	0.51
82.	First Maryland Bancorporation	FMDB	0.51
83.	Manufacturers National	MNTL	0.51
84.	Huntington Bancshares	HBAN	0.50
85.	Michigan National	MNCO	0.50
86.	Adolph Coors "B"	ACCOB	0.49
87.	Hamilton Oil	HAML	0.49
88.	Amgen, Inc.	AMGN	0.48
89.	Fisher Scientific Group	FSHG	0.48
90.	Figgie International	FIGI	0.47
91.	MEDCO Containment Services	MCCS	0.47
92.	Scripps Howard Broadcasting	SCRP	0.46
93.	Marshall & Ilsley Corporation	MRIS	0.46
94.	Neutrogena Corporation	NGNA	0.46
95.	Boatmens Bancshares	BOAT	0.45
96.	City National Corporation	CTYN	0.45
97.	Lance, Inc.	LNCE	0.45
98.	McCormick & Company	MCCRK	0.45
99.	Block Drug "A"	BLOCA	0.43
100.	Wheelabrator Group	WHGP	0.43

Source: Philadelphia Stock Exchange.

FIGURE 2.30   PHLX National OTC Index

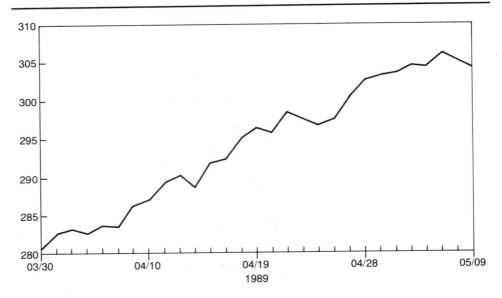

Source: Philadelphia Stock Exchange.

EXHIBIT 2.25   Philadelphia Stock Exchange Utility Index Components

	Company	Ticker Symbol	Capitalization Weight (%) (2/24/89)
1.	Southern Company	SO	8.64%
2.	Pacific Gas & Electric*	PCG	8.61
3.	Southern California Edison*	SCE	8.28
4.	Commonwealth Edison*	CWE	8.25
5.	American Electric Power*	AEP	6.05
6.	Consolidated Edison of New York*	CE	5.99
7.	Public Service Enterprises*	PEG	5.75
8.	Texas Utilities	TXU	5.67
9.	Duke Power	DUK	5.20
10.	Philadelphia Electric*	PE	4.84
11.	Dominion Resources	D	4.71
12.	FPL Group	FPL	4.64
13.	Houston Industries*	HOU	3.87
14.	Ohio Edison	OEC	3.75
15.	Detroit Edison*	DTE	3.11
16.	Union Electric	UEP	2.87
17.	Pacificorp	PPW	2.78
18.	Centerior Energy	CX	2.65
19.	Northeast Utilities	NU	2.46
20.	Niagara Mohawk Power*	NMK	1.88

* Components of the Dow Jones Utilities Average (10).

Source: Philadelphia Stock Exchange.

FIGURE 2.31   PHLX Utility Index

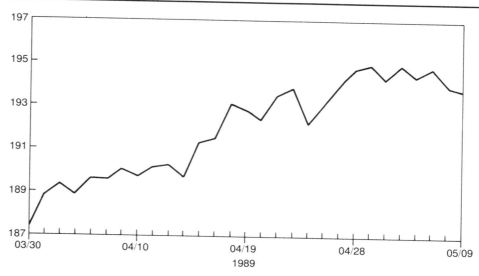

Source: Philadelphia Stock Exchange.

PHLX Utility Index

The PHLX Utility Index is a narrow-based index of the share prices of 20 NYSE-listed utility companies involved in the production of electrical energy (Exhibit 2.25). (Of these 20, 10 companies are components of the Dow Jones Utility Average.) It is a capitalization-weighted index, with a base level of 200 as of May 1, 1987. Based on market capitalization, four companies (Southern Company, Pacific Gas & Electric, Southern California Edison, and Commonwealth Edison) currently account for approximately 33 percent of the index's value. Since September 22, 1987, the index has been the basis for cash-settled index option contracts that are traded on the PHLX under the ticker symbol UTY.

PHLX Blue Chip CIP Index

The PHLX Blue Chip Cash Index Participation (CIP) index is a narrow-based index—derived from the share prices of 25 NYSE-listed blue-chip companies—that correlates with the Dow Jones Industrial Average (Exhibit 2.26).[5] Currently, 17 of the Index's 25 components are also part of the DJIA.

The index is price-weighted; it equals the total of the prices of one share of each of the 25 underlying companies. Since May 13, 1989, the index has been the basis for cash-settled index instruments that are traded on the PHLX under the ticker symbol MKX.

---

[5] A Cash Index Participation (CIP) is perhaps the newest investment instrument to date. It allows investors to purchase the equivalent of a portfolio of specific stocks, including dividends.

EXHIBIT 2.26   Philadelphia Stock Exchange Blue Chip CIP Index Components

	Company	Ticker Symbol	Share Price Weight (%) (8/12/88)
1.	IBM*	IBM	8.73%
2.	Philip Morris*	MO	6.60
3.	Dow Chemical	DOW	6.19
4.	E. I. Du Pont de Nemours*	DD	6.10
5.	Johnson & Johnson	JNJ	5.91
6.	General Motors*	GM	5.60
7.	Procter & Gamble*	PG	5.34
8.	Caterpillar	CAT	4.36
9.	Goodyear Tire & Rubber	GT	4.28
10.	Merck & Company*	MRK	4.02
11.	Reynolds Metal Company	RLM	3.58
12.	J. C. Penney	JCP	3.53
13.	Exxon*	XON	3.43
14.	Mobil Oil	MOB	3.26
15.	McDonald's Corporation	MCD	3.25
16.	Eastman Kodak*	EK	3.20
17.	TRW	TRW	3.16
18.	General Electric*	GE	2.98
19.	Mead Corporation	MEA	2.89
20.	Pepsico	PEP	2.58
21.	Allied-Signal*	ALD	2.50
22.	K-Mart	KM	2.40
23.	USX*	X	2.15
24.	American Express*	AXP	2.06
25.	American Telephone & Telegraph*	T	1.87

* Components of the Dow Jones Industrial Average (17).
Source: Philadelphia Stock Exchange.

The Russell Indexes

A series of indexes was developed jointly by the Frank Russell Company and the New York Futures Exchange (NYFE) to represent investment-grade equities. Whereas the S&P 500 represents approximately 75 percent of the investment-grade stocks held by most institutional investors, the Russell 1000, 2000, and 3000 indexes track almost 99 percent of the stocks included in portfolios of institutional investors.

Although there are more than 6,000 publicly traded U.S. stocks, the Russell 3000 Index confines itself to the 3,000 most actively traded shares and is divided into the Russell 1000 and Russell 2000 subindexes. The Russell 1000 Index represents the prices of the top tier of the domestic equity market—companies with market values greater than $300 million, which typically comprise approximately 90 percent of the market. The Russell 2000 Index represents the second tier of U.S. equities—companies with market values between $20 million and $300 million, which account for approximately 8 to 9 percent of the total market.

All three indexes are capitalization-weighted, and adjustments are made for cross-ownership. For example, if IBM owns 20 percent of

FIGURE 2.32   Russell 1000, 2000, and 3000 Indexes

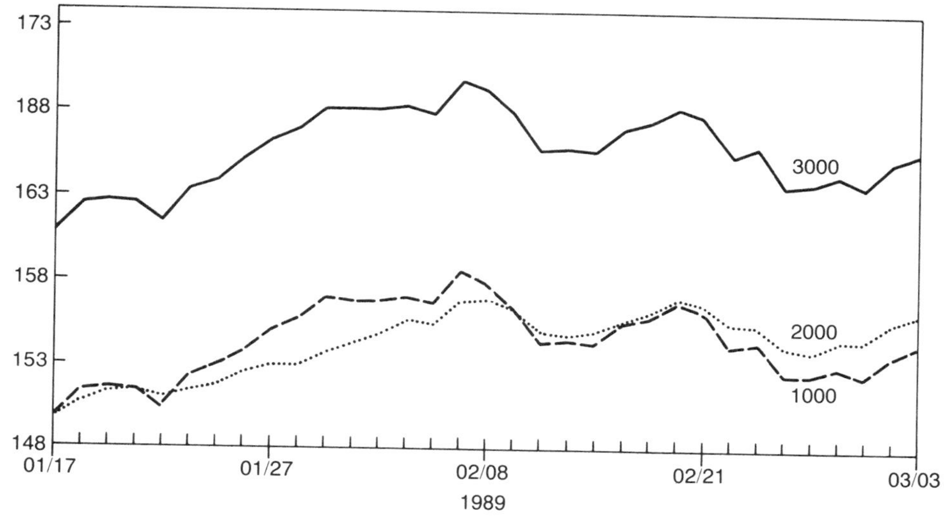

Source: New York Futures Exchange.

Intel, the index includes only 80 percent of Intel's outstanding shares. Furthermore, all three indexes exclude non-U.S. stocks—both ADRs and the ordinary shares that are traded on U.S. stock exchanges. The base level for all three indexes was set at 100 in 1979.

Standard & Poor's Indexes

Standard & Poor's stock price index, first published in 1923, was based on 233 stocks broken down into 26 subindexes. In 1957, this list was expanded to a composite index of 500 companies, known as the S&P 500, which represents 95 industrial sectors. Currently, Standard and Poor's maintains the S&P 500 Index and S&P 100 Index, as well as several bond indexes (see Chapter 3).

S&P 500 Index

The original S&P 500 was divided into three main groups similar to those of the early Dow Jones averages. The 500 stocks consisted of 425 industrial, 60 public utility, and 15 railroad stocks, all of which were listed on the NYSE and were selected to approximate the same proportion of the NYSE's major industrial sectors. On July 1, 1976, the composition of the S&P 500 was changed to the following four groups, which included stocks traded on the NYSE, the AMEX, and in the OTC market.

Group	Stocks
Industrial	400
Financial	40
Utility	40
Transportation	20

**EXHIBIT 2.27   Standard & Poor's 500 Index Components
(Top 20 Companies Ranked by Capitalization)**

	Company	Ticker Symbol	Percent of Index* (12/31/88)
1.	International Business Machines	IBM	3.80%
2.	Exxon	XON	3.02
3.	General Electric	GE	2.12
4.	American Telephone & Telegraph	T	1.63
5.	Royal Dutch Petroleum	RD	1.61
6.	General Motors	GM	1.35
7.	Ford Motor	F	1.33
8.	Philip Morris	MO	1.24
9.	Merck & Company	MRK	1.19
10.	E. I. Du Pont de Nemours	DD	1.11
11.	RJR Nabisco	RJR	1.08
12.	Amoco	AN	1.02
13.	Mobil Corporation	MOB	0.99
14.	BellSouth	BLS	0.99
15.	Wal-Mart Stores	WMT	0.93
16.	Dow Chemical	DOW	0.88
17.	Coca-Cola	KO	0.84
18.	Chevron Corporation	CHV	0.83
19.	Sears, Roebuck	S	0.82
20.	Procter & Gamble	PG	0.78
	Total		27.56%

Source: Standard & Poor's.

The composite index of 500 stocks, as are the four main subindexes, is capitalization-weighted with the average base level equal to 10 for the 1941–43 base period. IBM alone accounts for nearly 4 percent of the total capitalization, while the top-ranked 20 companies account for approximately 28 percent of the total (Exhibit 2.27).

FIGURE 2.33   S&P 500 Index

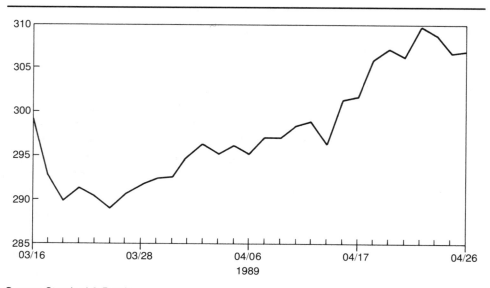

Source: Standard & Poor's.

Because of its breadth, the S&P 500, not the highly visible DJIA, is used as the benchmark against which all money managers compare the performance of their portfolios. In addition, it is one of the 12 components that make up the U.S. Commerce Department's Index of Leading Economic Indicators. There are many reasons for this favored treatment.

- First, the Dow Jones Industrial Average is, as its name states, an *average* of only 30, albeit blue-chip, stocks. Consequently, higher-priced shares carry more weight than lower-priced ones. With the divisor currently below 1.000, a dramatic price change in a single stock can result in a disproportionate move in the DJIA.
- Second, many of the Dow stocks have industrial or cyclical characteristics and may not accurately reflect the broader market.

In order to promote flexibility in the makeup of the S&P 500, Standard & Poor's Corporation, on April 6, 1988, stopped requiring that there be precisely 400 industrial, 40 financial, 40 utility, and 20 transportation stocks in the index. Instead, the four categories were allowed to vary in size when an issue was to be replaced. Candidate issues to fill the proposed vacancy were to be selected according to the following standards:

- *Industry classification.* Profitability within an industry.
- *Size.* Measured by market value of common shares.
- *Capitalization.* Number of common shares outstanding, controlling interests, float, and institutional holdings.
- *Trading volume/turnover.* Measured by average daily volume divided by shares outstanding over a reasonable period of time.
- *Emerging companies/industries.*
- *Stock price.* Movements must be responsive to changes in industry affairs.

The S&P 500 Index is the basis for cash-settled stock index options contracts. Since July 3, 1983, European-style options contracts have been traded on the Chicago Board Options Exchange (CBOE) under the ticker symbol SPX. On the Index and Options Market Division of the Chicago Mercantile Exchange (CME), cash-settled futures contracts have been traded since April 21, 1982, under the ticker symbol SP. Futures options contracts are also traded on the CME under the ticker symbols CS and PS, respectively, for calls and puts.

1. S&P Industrial Subindex. The S&P Industrial Subindex consists of 390 companies not categorized as financial, public utilities, or transportation-based. It accounts for approximately 84 percent of the S&P 500 index's total capitalized value.

2. S&P Financial Subindex. The S&P Financial Subindex consists of 50 companies involved in banking, insurance, and other aspects of the financial sector. It accounts for approximately 8 percent of the S&P 500 Index's total capitalized value (Exhibit 2.28).

EXHIBIT 2.28   Standard & Poor's Financial Index Components

Company	Ticker Symbol	Capitalization Weight (%) (11/30/88)	Percent of S&P 500 (11/30/88)
1. American Express	AXP	7.59%	0.59%
2. American International Group	AIG	7.19	0.56
3. Citicorp	CCI	5.58	0.44
4. Morgan (J. P.) & Company	JPM	4.28	0.34
5. Aetna Life & Casualty	AET	3.68	0.29
6. General Re Corporation	GRN	3.63	0.28
7. Security Pacific Corporation	SPC	2.80	0.22
8. American General	AGC	2.64	0.21
9. Federal National Mortgage	FNM	2.60	0.20
10. CNA Financial	CNA	2.58	0.20
11. CIGNA	CI	2.54	0.20
12. Wells Fargo & Company	WFC	2.39	0.19
13. Travelers Corporation	TIC	2.38	0.19
14. PNC Financial Corporation	PNC	2.37	0.19
15. Salomon, Inc.	SB	2.22	0.17
16. BankAmerica Corporation	BAC	2.20	0.17
17. Banc One Corporation	ONE	2.07	0.16
18. Bankers Trust N.Y.	BT	2.03	0.16
19. Chemical Banking Corporation	CHL	1.99	0.16
20. Merrill Lynch	MER	1.86	0.15
21. SunTrust Banks	STI	1.81	0.14
22. Fleet/Norstar Financial	FNG	1.76	0.14
23. USF&G Corporation	FG	1.66	0.13
24. Transamerica	TA	1.64	0.13
25. Chase Manhattan	CMB	1.63	0.13
26. Chubb Corporation	CB	1.55	0.12
27. NCNB Corporation	NCB	1.54	0.12
28. Fidelity Bancorp	FFB	1.46	0.11
29. First Interstate Bancorp	I	1.40	0.11
30. Household International	HI	1.38	0.11
31. Barnett Banks	BBI	1.30	0.10
32. Lincoln National	LNC	1.30	0.10
33. St. Paul Companies	STPL	1.30	0.10
34. Continental Corporation	CIC	1.28	0.10
35. Great Western Financial	GWF	1.26	0.10
36. First Chicago Corporation	FNB	1.18	0.09
37. NBD Bancorp	NBD	1.16	0.09
38. Ahmanson (H. F.) & Company	AHM	1.06	0.08
39. SAFECO	SAFC	1.06	0.08
40. Bank of Boston	BKB	1.04	0.08
41. Primerica Corporation	PA	1.01	0.08
42. Capital Holding	CPH	0.98	0.08
43. Manufacturers Hanover	MHC	0.98	0.08
44. Norwest Corporation	NOB	0.96	0.08
45. Jefferson-Pilot	JP	0.84	0.07
46. Beneficial Corporation	BNL	0.69	0.05
47. Commercial Credit Group	CCC	0.64	0.05
48. Golden West Financial	GDW	0.63	0.05
49. Mellon Bank Corporation	MEL	0.47	0.04
50. USLIFE Corporation	USH	0.40	0.03
Totals		100%	7.84%

Source: Standard & Poor's.

3. S&P Utility Subindex.   The S&P Utility Subindex consists of 40 public utility companies and accounts for approximately 11 percent of the S&P 500 Index's total capitalized value (Exhibit 2.29). Fourteen

EXHIBIT 2.29 Standard & Poor's Utilities Index Components

Company	Ticker Symbol	Capitalization Weight (%) (11/30/88)	Percent of S&P 500 (11/30/88)
1. Bell South	BLS	8.98%	1.02%
2. GTE	GTE	6.88	0.78
3. Bell Atlantic	BEL	6.56	0.74
4. Pacific Telesis	PAC	6.17	0.70
5. Nynex	NYN	6.07	0.69
6. Ameritech	ATI	5.98	0.68
7. Southwestern Bell	SBC	5.84	0.66
8. US West	USW	4.97	0.56
9. Pacific Gas & Electric*	PCG	3.43	0.39
10. Southern California Edison*	SCE	3.37	0.38
11. Southern Company	SO	3.13	0.35
12. Commonwealth Edison*	CWE	3.12	0.35
13. American Electric Power*	AEP	2.45	0.28
14. Consolidated Edison of New York*	ED	2.40	0.27
15. Public Service Enterprises*	PEG	2.40	0.27
16. Duke Power	DUK	2.17	0.25
17. Texas Utilities	TXU	2.12	0.24
18. Dominion Resources	D	1.93	0.22
19. FPL Group	FPL	1.89	0.21
20. Philadelphia Electric*	PE	1.83	0.21
21. Houston Industries*	HOU	1.54	0.17
22. Consolidated Natural Gas*	CNG	1.53	0.17
23. Middle South Utilities	MSU	1.52	0.17
24. Central & Southwest	CSR	1.38	0.16
25. Ohio Edison	OEC	1.35	0.15
26. Baltimore Gas & Electric	BGE	1.17	0.13
27. Detroit Edison*	DTE	1.13	0.13
28. Pacific Enterprises	PET	1.13	0.13
29. Coastal Corporation	CGP	1.01	0.11
30. Northern States Power	NSP	0.96	0.11
31. Enron Corporation	ENE	0.84	0.09
32. Niagara Mohawk Power	NMK	0.80	0.09
33. Columbia Gas System*	CG	0.76	0.09
34. Texas Eastern Corporation	TET	0.73	0.08
35. Panhandle Eastern*	PEL	0.65	0.07
36. Sonat	SNT	0.54	0.06
37. ENSERCH	ENE	0.50	0.06
38. PSI Holding	PIN	0.35	0.04
39. Peoples Energy*	PGL	0.31	0.04
40. ONEOK	OKE	0.12	0.01
Totals		100%	11.31%

* Components of the Dow Jones Utilities Average (14)
Source: Standard & Poor's.

of the subindex's underlying stocks are also components of the 15-stock Dow Jones Utility Average.

4. S&P Transportation Subindex. The S&P Transportation Subindex consists of 40 transportation-based companies and accounts for approximately 2.5 percent of the S&P 500 index's total capitalized value (Exhibit 2.30). Fifteen of the subindex's underlying stocks are also components of the 20-stock Dow Jones Transportation Average.

EXHIBIT 2.30   Standard & Poor's Transportation Index Components

	Company	Ticker Symbol	Capitalization Weight (%) (11/30/88)	Percent of S&P 500 (11/30/88)
1.	Burlington Northern*	BNI	12.11%	0.30%
2.	Norfolk Southern Corporation*	NSC	12.02	0.30
3.	CSX Corporation*	CSX	7.57	0.19
4.	AMR Corporation*	AMR	6.61	0.16
5.	Sante Fe Southern Pacific*	SFX	5.80	0.14
6.	Federal Express*	FDX	5.35	0.13
7.	Delta Air Lines*	DAL	5.10	0.13
8.	Consolidated Rail*	CRR	4.98	0.12
9.	UAL Corporation*	UAL	4.92	0.12
10.	Union Pacific Corporation*	UNP	4.91	0.37
11.	Ryder System*	R	4.06	0.10
12.	NWA, Inc.*	NWA	3.42	0.08
13.	USAir Group*	U	3.25	0.08
14.	Roadway Service	ROAD	2.59	0.06
15.	Consolidated Freightways*	CNF	2.51	0.06
16.	Yellow Freight System	YELL	2.03	0.05
17.	Tiger International	TGR	0.94	0.02
18.	CNW Corporation	CNW	0.88	0.02
19.	Pan American World Airways*	PN	0.72	0.02
20.	Emery Air Freight	EAF	0.23	0.01
	Totals		100%	2.47%

* Components of the Dow Jones Transportation Average (15).

Source: Standard & Poor's.

S&P 100 Index

The S&P 100 Index is based on 100 highly capitalized stocks for which index option contracts are currently traded on the CBOE (Exhibit 2.31). Like the larger S&P 500 Index, it is capitalization-weighted; its base level of 100 was set in 1983. IBM makes up approximately 8 percent of the index's total capitalization; the three top-ranked companies—IBM, Exxon, and GE—account for about 20 percent of the total.

EXHIBIT 2.31   Standard & Poor's 100 Index Components

	Company	Ticker Symbol	Capitalization Weight (%) (12/31/88)
1.	International Business Machines	IBM	8.47%
2.	Exxon	XON	6.73
3.	General Electric	GE	4.74
4.	American Telephone & Telegraph	T	3.63
5.	General Motors	GM	3.01
6.	Ford Motor	F	2.96
7.	Merck & Company	MRK	2.66
8.	E. I. Du Pont de Nemours	DD	2.48
9.	RJR Nabisco	RJR	2.41
10.	Amoco	AN	2.28
11.	Mobil Corporation	MOB	2.20
12.	Wal-Mart Stores	WMT	2.07
13.	Dow Chemical	DOW	1.96

EXHIBIT 2.31 *(continued)*

	Company	Ticker Symbol	Capitalization Weight (%) (12/31/88)
14.	Coca-Cola	KO	1.88%
15.	Sears, Roebuck	S	1.82
16.	Eastman Kodak	EK	1.72
17.	Johnson & Johnson	JNJ	1.71
18.	Atlantic Richfield	ARC	1.68
19.	Bell Atlantic	BEL	1.65
20.	Minnesota Mining & Manufacturing	MMM	1.65
21.	Ameritech	AIT	1.55
22.	Bristol Meyers	BMY	1.53
23.	Hewlett-Packard	HWP	1.50
24.	Digital Equipment	DEC	1.46
25.	American Express	AXP	1.30
26.	American International Group	AIG	1.30
27.	Pepsico	PEP	1.22
28.	Boeing	BA	1.09
29.	McDonald's Corporation	MCD	1.06
30.	Walt Disney Company	DIS	1.02
31.	Citicorp	CCI	0.97
32.	Schlumberger	SLB	0.91
33.	Southern Corporation	SO	0.83
34.	Commonwealth Edison	CWE	0.82
35.	K-Mart	KM	0.82
36.	Occidental Petroleum	OXY	0.80
37.	ITT	ITT	0.79
38.	Squibb	SQB	0.76
39.	Xerox	XRX	0.70
40.	H. J. Heinz	HNZ	0.70
41.	Capital Cities/ABC	CCB	0.69
42.	Norfolk Southern Corporation	NSC	0.68
43.	Rockwell International	ROK	0.67
44.	Monsanto	MTC	0.67
45.	Ralston Purina	RAL	0.66
46.	United Technologies	UTX	0.64
47.	Upjohn	UPJ	0.63
48.	American Electric Power	AEP	0.62
49.	International Paper	IP	0.61
50.	Weyerhaeuser	WY	0.60
51.	Aluminum Company of America	AA	0.58
52.	Limited, Inc.	LTD	0.57
53.	Toys "R" Us	TOY	0.56
54.	Gulf & Western	GW	0.56
55.	AMP	AMP	0.56
56.	Warner Communications	WCI	0.54
57.	Unisys	UIS	0.52
58.	Raytheon Company	RTN	0.52
59.	NCR Corporation	NCR	0.51
60.	Baxter International	BAX	0.51
61.	Northern Telecom	NT	0.46
62.	Teledyne, Inc.	TDY	0.45
63.	CIGNA Corporation	CI	0.44
64.	Tandy Corporation	TAN	0.43
65.	Texas Instruments	TXN	0.39
66.	Colgate-Palmolive	CL	0.38
67.	BankAmerica	BAC	0.38
68.	Champion International	CHA	0.36
69.	Halliburton Company	HAL	0.35
70.	Polaroid Company	PRD	0.31
71.	Federal Express	FDX	0.31
72.	Honeywell	HON	0.30

EXHIBIT 2.31   *(concluded)*

	Company	Ticker Symbol	Capitalization Weight (%) (12/31/88)
73.	Humana, Inc.	HUM	0.29%
74.	Delta Air Lines	DAL	0.29
75.	Merrill Lynch	MER	0.28
76.	UAL, Inc.	UAL	0.28
77.	General Dynamics	GD	0.25
78.	International Flavors	IFF	0.22
79.	Great Western Financial	GWF	0.22
80.	Boise Cascade	BCC	0.22
81.	Fluor Corporation	FLR	0.22
82.	Litton Industries	LIT	0.21
83.	Bethlehem Steel	BS	0.20
84.	Burlington Northern	BNI	0.20
85.	Baker Hughes	BHI	0.19
86.	NWA, Inc.	NWA	0.18
87.	Brunswick Corporation	BC	0.17
88.	Black & Decker	BDK	0.16
89.	Homestake Mining	HM	0.14
90.	Williams Companies	WMB	0.14
91.	Harris Corporation	HRS	0.12
92.	Avon Products	AVP	0.12
93.	National Semiconductor		
94.	International Minerals	IGL	0.11
95.	Control Data	CDA	0.10
96.	Computer Sciences Corporation	CSC	0.09
97.	Holiday Corporation	HIA	0.08
98.	Tektronix	TEK	0.07
99.	Skyline Corporation	SKY	0.02
100.	Datapoint	DPT	0.01

Source: Standard & Poor's.

FIGURE 2.34   S&P 100 Index

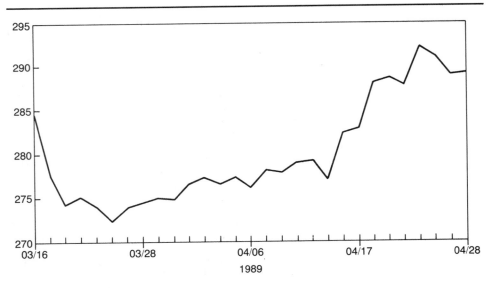

Source: Standard & Poor's.

When introduced on March 11, 1983, the S&P 100 Index was called the CBOE-100 Index, and it was the basis for the first "home-grown" tradable stock index that was not based on an already-existing index like the Value Line, Market Value Index, and NYSE Composite Index, to name a few. However, its name was shortly changed to S&P 100. The CBOE-100/S&P 100 Index was the basis for the first cash-settled tradable stock index options contracts, which are still traded on the CBOE under the ticker symbol OEX. On the Index and Options Market Division of the CME, cash-settled futures contracts are traded under the ticker symbol SX.

Value Line Averages

The Value Line Composite Index is a broad-based measure of the prices of approximately 1,700 NYSE, AMEX, and OTC blue-chip and second-tier stocks; it represents approximately 95 percent of the market value of all U.S. securities. It was developed and has been maintained, and published since 1961 by Arnold Bernhard and Co., which was renamed Value Line, Inc., upon its reorganization in October 1982.

To be included, a stock must (1) have a reasonable market value, or capitalization, (2) have a strong trading volume, which is a measure of investor interest, and (3) have a high degree of investor interest, as represented by the number of requests for information on a specific stock by the subscribers of the *Value Line Investment Survey*. Component stocks are rarely dropped from the index; if one is, it is because the company has either (1) gone bankrupt with little hope of revitalization and continued investor interest, (2) merged with another company, or (3) gone private.

From 1961 until 1988, the "Value Line Index," as it is commonly known, was computed only as a price-weighted geometric average of the approximately 1,700 prices, with a base level of 100 as of June 30, 1961. Each stock price therefore has the same weight. Many analysts feel that the use of a geometric average imparts a downward bias to the index, so that it climbs slower and declines faster than a measure based on an arithmetic average. Because of the inclusion of many second-tier issues, the index is also much more volatile than most broad-based indexes.

In March 1988, Value Line began publishing a second price index, called the Value Line Arithmetic Index. The only difference between the Value Line Composite and Arithmetic indexes is the method used in calculating them. As shown in the graph of Figure 2.35, the Value Line Composite Index is lower than the Value Line Arithmetic Index.

Besides the geometric and arithmetic averages, Value Line maintains three lesser-known price averages representing industrial, railroad, and utility issues:

Measure	Stocks
Value Line Industrial Average	1,500
Value Line Utility Average	177
Value Line Railroad Average	14

FIGURE 2.35 Value Line Indexes

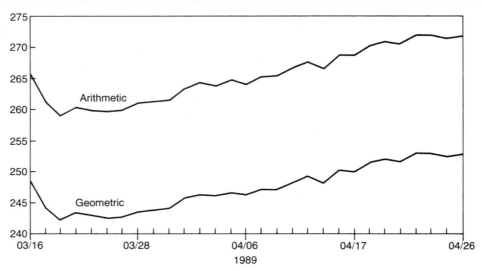

Source: Value Line.

The Value Line Composite Index was the basis for the first cash-settled tradable stock index contract, initially traded on February 24, 1982, on the Kansas City Board of Trade (KCBT). Here, "maxi" and "mini" index futures contracts are still traded on the KCBT under the ticker symbols KV and MV, respectively. In addition, similar stock index option contracts began trading January 11, 1985, on the PHLX under the ticker symbol XVL.

Wilshire 5000 Equity Index

Developed in 1974 by Wilshire Associates of Santa Monica, California, the Wilshire 5000 Equity Index currently includes over 6,000 common

FIGURE 2.36 Wilshire 5000 Equity Index

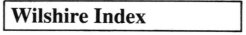
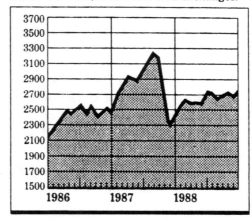

stocks that are traded on the NYSE (86%), the AMEX (3%), and OTC (11%). It is capitalization-weighted and has a base of 1,404.596, set on December 31, 1980. The unusual base level represents the total capitalization of $1,404.596 billion on that date.

Delisted Indexes

Like television programs, the staying power of a given average or index primarily depends on its relevance and investor interest. Most of those that have fallen by the wayside were specifically created to be tradable indexes. The following is a selection of those indexes that have been delisted from further index trading.

AMEX Transportation Index

The AMEX Transportation Index was a narrow-based index of 20 transportation industry stocks; it closely resembled the Dow Jones Transportation Average (Exhibit 2.32). With the exception of Chicago & Northwestern Transportation, RLC Corporation, and Western Air Lines, the companies were also components of the Dow Jones Transportation Average at that time. Capitalization-weighted, with a base index level of 150 as of December 30, 1983, the index was the basis for cash-settled options contracts traded on the AMEX.

EXHIBIT 2.32   AMEX Transportation Index Components

Company	Ticker Symbol
AMR	AMR
Allegis	AEG
Burlington Northern	BNI
CSX Corporation	CSX
Canadian Pacific	CP
Carolina Freight	CAO
Chicago & Northwestern Transportation	CNW
Consolidated Freightways	CNF
Delta Air Lines	DAL
Federal Express	FDX
Norfolk Southern	NSC
Northwest Airlines	NWA
Overnite Transportation Corp.	OVT
RLC	RLC
Sante Fe Southern Pacific	SFX
Transway International Corporation	TNW
Trans World Airlines	TWA
US Air Group	U
Union Pacific	UNP
Western Air Lines	WAL

Source: American Stock Exchange.

NASDAQ-100 Index

The NASDAQ-100 Index represented the 100 largest industrial, nonfinancial issues drawn from the NASDAQ/NMS issues (Exhibit 2.33). It was constructed in 1985 as a broad-based OTC index options contract

EXHIBIT 2.33   NASDAQ-100 Components

	Company	Ticker Symbol		Company	Ticker Symbol
1.	ASK Computer Systems	ASKI	51.	Masco Industries	MASX
2.	Adolph Coors Company "B"	ACCOB	52.	Maxicare Health Plans, Inc.	MAXI
3.	Alexander & Baldwin, Inc.	ALEX	53.	McCormick & Co., Inc.	MCCRK
4.	American Greetings	AGREA	54.	Mentor Graphics Corporation	MENT
5.	Andrew Corporation	ANDW	55.	Metro Mobile CTS, Inc.	MMCT
6.	Apollo Computer, Inc.	APCI	56.	Micom Systems, Inc.	MICS
7.	Apple Computer, Inc.	AAPL	57.	Micron Technology, Inc.	DRAM
8.	Avantek, Inc.	AVAK	58.	Microsoft Corporation	MSFT
9.	Bassett Furniture Industries	BSET	59.	Miller, Inc.	MLHR
10.	Betz Laboratories, Inc.	BETZ	60.	Molex Incorporated	MOLX
11.	Bob Evans Farms, Inc.	BOBE	61.	Multimedia, Inc.	MMEDC
12.	Bruno's, Inc.	BRNO	62.	Network Systems Corporation	NSCO
13.	Cetus Corporation	CTUS	63.	Nordstrom, Inc.	NOBE
14.	Charming Shoppes, Inc.	CHRS	64.	Noxell Corporation "B"	NOXLB
15.	Cipher Data Products, Inc.	CIFR	65.	Ogilvy Group, Inc.	OGIL
16.	Citizens Utilities "A"	CITUA	66.	Optical Radiation	ORCO
17.	Comcast Corporation "A"	CMCSA	67.	Oracle Systems Corporation	ORCL
18.	Commerce Clearing House, Inc.	CCLR	68.	PACCAR, Inc.	PCAR
19.	Comprehensive Care Corporation	CMPH	69.	Petrolite Corporation	PLIT
20.	Consolidated Papers, Inc.	CPER	70.	Pic 'n Save Corporation	PICN
21.	Convergent, Inc.	CVGT	71.	Pioneer Hi-Bred Intn'l	PHYB
22.	Cross & Trecker Corporation	CTCO	72.	Policy Management Systems	PMSC
23.	Cyprus Minerals Company	CYPM	73.	The Price Company	PCLB
24.	DSC Communications Corporation	DIGI	74.	Quantum Corporation	QNTM
25.	Daisy Systems Corporation	DAZY	75.	Roadway Services, Inc.	ROAD
26.	Dollar General Corporation	DOLR	76.	SafeCard Services, Inc.	SFCD
27.	El Paso Electric Company	ELPA	77.	Seagate Technology	SGAT
28.	Fisher Scientific Group, Inc.	FSHG	78.	Service Merchandise Company	SMCH
29.	Food Lion, Inc. "B"	FDLNB	79.	Shared Medical Systems	SMED
30.	Gibson Greetings, Inc.	GIBG	80.	Shoney's, Inc.	SHON
31.	Goulds Pumps, Inc.	GULD	81.	Sigma-Aldrich Corporation	SIAL
32.	HBO & Company	HBOC	82.	Sonoco Products Company	SONO
33.	Hamilton Oil Corporation	HAML	83.	Standard Register Company	SREG
34.	Henley Group, Inc.	HENG	84.	Stratus Computer, Inc.	STRA
35.	Highland Superstores	HIGH	85.	Subaru of America, Inc.	SBRU
36.	I.M.S. International, Inc.	IMSI	86.	Sun Microsystems, Inc.	SUNW
37.	Intel Corporation	INTC	87.	Tandon Corporation	TCOR
38.	Intergraph Corporation	INGR	88.	Tecumseh Products Company	TECU
39.	Jerrico, Inc.	JERR	89.	Tele-Communications "A"	TCOMA
40.	KLA Instruments Corporation	KLAC	90.	Tyson Foods "A"	TYSNA
41.	Kelly Services "A"	KELYA	91.	Ungermann-Bass, Inc.	UNGR
42.	Kinder-Care Learning Centers	KNDR	92.	United Artists	UACI
43.	Lance, Inc.	LNCE	93.	United States Healthcare	USHC
44.	LIN Broadcasting Corporation	LINB	94.	United Stationers, Inc.	USTR
45.	LSI Logic Corporation	LLSI	95.	Wetterau Incorporated	WETT
46.	Liz Claiborne, Inc.	LIZC	96.	Willamette Industries, Inc.	WMTT
47.	Lotus Development Corporation	LOTS	97.	Worthington Industries, Inc.	WTHG
48.	Lyphomed, Inc.	LMED	98.	Wyman-Gordon Company	WYMN
49.	MCI Communications Corporation	MCIC	99.	Xidex Corporation	XIDX
50.	Mack Trucks, Inc.	MACK	100.	Yellow Freight System, Inc.	YELL

Source: National Association of Securities Dealers.

FIGURE 2.37   NASDAQ-100 Index

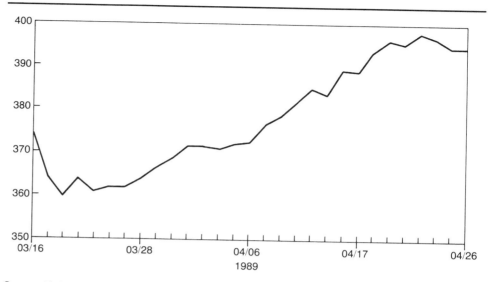

Source: National Association of Securities Dealers.

to compete with tradable indexes like the Philadelphia Stock Exchange's National OTC Index (options) and the now-delisted S&P 250 OTC Industrial Index (SPOC),[6] whose cash-settled futures contracts were once traded on the Chicago Mercantile Exchange. Like the SPOC, the NASDAQ-100 was the basis for cash-settled futures contracts that were traded on the Chicago Board of Trade. It was delisted as a tradable index in mid-1988, so that none of the NASDAQ indexes is currently the basis for stock index options or futures contracts, but the NASDAQ-100 Index is still computed for historical continuity. Although the index is capitalization-weighted, it differs from the NASDAQ Composite Index and its six subindexes in that the base value was set at 250 on February 1, 1985.

NYSE Beta Index

The NYSE Beta Index was a narrow-based index of 100 NYSE-listed stocks that had the highest *beta,* which is a measure of the sensitivity of a stock's price to fluctuations in the S&P 500 Index. Besides the beta, each stock issue had more than 7 million shares outstanding and sold for more than $10 per share. It was once the basis for cash-settled index option contracts that were traded on the NYSE.

New York Stock Exchange Telephone Index

The NYSE Telephone Index was a narrow-based index of the stocks of AT&T and the seven "baby Bell" companies that were formed upon the divestiture of AT&T in 1983 (Exhibit 2.34). The index was capitalization-weighted and its base level was set at 100 on December 30, 1983,

---

[6] The SPOC Index had a base level set at 150 on December 31, 1884.

FIGURE 2.38   NYSE Beta Index

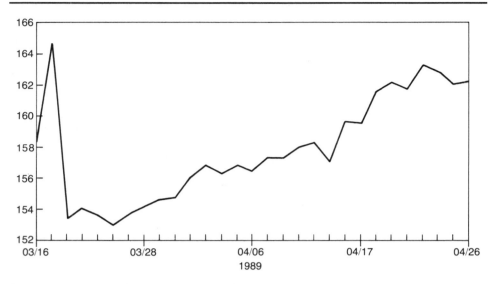

Source: New York Stock Exchange.

EXHIBIT 2.34   New York Stock Exchange Telephone Index Components

	Company	Ticker Symbol
1.	American Telephone & Telegraph	T
2.	BellSouth	BLS
3.	Bell Atlantic	BEL
4.	Pacific Telesis	PAC
5.	Nynex	NYN
6.	Ameritech	AIT
7.	Southwestern Bell	SBC
8.	US West	USW

Source: New York Stock Exchange.

which was the last trading day before the AT&T breakup. In addition, it was once the basis for cash-settled index option contracts that were traded on the NYSE using the ticker symbol NTI.

PSE Technology Index

The Pacific Stock Exchange's Technology Index is composed of 100 stocks representing 49 NYSE, 5 AMEX, and 46 OTC-listed companies involved in a broad spectrum of high-technology industries (Exhibit 2.35). The index is a price-weighted average based on the last sale price of each stock. It was once the basis for cash-settled index option contracts that were traded on the PSE starting January 13, 1984, but was delisted as a tradable index on September 18, 1987. The index is still maintained, however, and can be obtained on many quotation machines by using the ticker symbol PSE.

EXHIBIT 2.35   Pacific Stock Exchange Technology Index

Company	Ticker Symbol	Company	Ticker Symbol
1. Advanced Micro Devices	AMD	51. Harris Corporation	HRS
2. Altos Computer Systems	ALTO	52. Healthydyne, Inc.	HDYN
3. Amdahl Corporation	AMH	53. Hewlett-Packard Company	HWP
4. Analog Devices, Inc.	ADI	54. Honeywell, Inc.	HON
5. Apollo Computer, Inc.	APCI	55. Intel Corporation	INTC
6. Apple Computer, Inc.	AAPL	56. Intergraph Corporation	INGR
7. Applied Magnetics Corporation	APM	57. Intermedics, Inc.	ITM
8. Applied Materials, Inc.	AMAT	58. Int'l Business Machines	IBM
9. Ashton-Tate	TATE	59. KLA Instruments Corporation	KLAC
10. ASK Computer Systems, Inc.	ASKI	60. Kulicke and Soffa Industries	KLIC
11. Avantek, Inc.	AVAK	61. Lotus Development Corp.	LOTS
12. AVX Corporation	AVX	62. Medtronic, Inc.	MDT
13. Biogen, N.V.	BGENF	63. Micom Systems, Inc.	MICS
14. BMC Industries, Inc.	BMC	64. Microsoft Corporation	MSFT
15. Centronics Data Computer Corp.	CEN	65. Millipore Corporation	MILI
16. Cetus Corporation	CTUS	66. Monolithic Memories, Inc.	MMIC
17. Cipher Data Products, Inc.	CIFR	67. Motorola, Inc.	MOT
18. Cobe Laboratories, Inc.	COBE	68. National Micronetics, Inc.	NMIC
19. Coherent, Inc.	COHR	69. National Semiconductor Corp.	NSM
20. Commodore International, Ltd.	CBU	70. NBI, Inc.	NBI
21. Communications Satellite Corp.	CQ	71. NCR Corporation	NCR
22. Computervision Corporation	CVN	72. Network Systems Corporation	NSCO
23. Conrac Corporation	CAX	73. Nicolet Instrument Corp.	NIC
24. Control Data Corporation	CDA	74. Novo Industri A/S	NVO
25. Control Laser Corporation	CLSR	75. Optical Radiation Corp.	ORCO
26. Convergent Technologies, Inc.	CVGT	76. Pansophic Systems	PNS
27. Corvus Systems, Inc.	CRVS	77. Paradyne Corporation	PDN
28. CPT Corporation	CPTC	78. Perkin-Elmer Corporation	PKN
29. Cray Research, Inc.	CYR	79. Prime Computer, Inc.	PRM
30. Cullinet	CUL	80. Quantum Corporation	QNTM
31. Daisy Systems Corporation	DAZY	81. Rogers Corporation	ROG
32. Data I/O Corporation	DAIO	82. Scientific-Atlanta, Inc.	SFA
33. Data General Corporation	DGN	83. Seagate Technology	SGAT
34. Datapoint Corporation	DPT	84. Silicon Systems, Inc.	SLCN
35. Datum	DATM	85. Spectra Physics, Inc.	SPY
36. Digital Equipment Corporation	DEC	86. Standard Microsystems Corp.	SMSC
37. Digital Switch	DIGI	87. Tandem Computers, Inc.	TNDM
38. Electro-Biology, Inc.	EBII	88. Tandon Corporation	TCOR
39. Electronic Associates, Inc.	EA	89. Tektronix, Inc.	TEK
40. Enzo Biochem	ENZO	90. TeleVideo Systems, Inc.	TELV
41. Evans & Sutherland Computer	ESCC	91. Telex Corporation	TC
42. Finnigan Corporation	FNNG	92. Teradyne, Inc.	TER
43. Floating Point Systems, Inc.	FLP	93. Texas Instruments, Inc.	TXN
44. Flow General, Inc.	FGN	94. Timplex Communications, Inc.	TIX
45. John Fluke Manufacturing Company	FKM	95. Titan Corporation	TTN
46. GCA Corporation	GCA	96. Ultimate Corporation	ULT
47. Genentech, Inc.	GENE	97. Unisys Corporation	UIS
48. General DataComm Industries, Inc.	GDC	98. Varian Associates, Inc.	VAR
49. GenRad, Inc.	GEN	99. Wang Laboratories, Inc. "B"	WAN.B
50. Gould, Inc.	GLD	100. Xidex Corporation	XIDX

Source: Pacific Stock Exchange.

FIGURE 2.39   Pacific Stock Exchange Technology Index

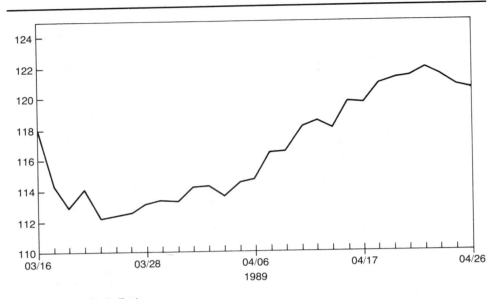

Source: Pacific Stock Exchange.

PHLX Gaming/Hotel Index

The PHLX Gaming/Hotel Index was a narrow-based index of stocks of nine companies involved in various aspects of the hotel and gaming industry (Exhibit 2.36). Its establishment was prompted by the proximity of Philadelphia to the casinos of Atlantic City. Capitalization-weighted and set at a base level of 100 on December 19, 1983, the index was once the basis for cash-settled index option contracts that were traded on the PHLX under the ticker symbol XGH.

EXHIBIT 2.36   Philadelphia Stock Exchange Gaming/Hotel Index Components

	Company	Ticker Symbol
1.	Bally Manufacturing	BLY
2.	Caesar's World	CAW
3.	Golden Nugget	GNG
4.	Holiday Inns	HIA
5.	Hilton Hotel Corp.	HLT
6.	MGM Grand Hotels	GRH
7.	Ramada Inns	RAM
8.	Resorts International	RTA
9.	Showboat	SBO

Source: Philadelphia Stock Exchange.

3

Notes and Bonds

The stock and bond markets are forever linked. Bonds respond to changes in interest rates, and in turn often affect the stock market. On the other hand, changes in stock market prices can affect bond prices. After a while, however, it sometimes is difficult to determine which is the dog and which is the tail. Like the stock market, the bond market has no single indicator, although the price of the most recently issued 30-year Treasury bond is frequently used as the bellwether standard.

Unlike stocks, which are classified as equity investments, notes and bonds are *debt issues,* an IOU paying a stated rate of periodic interest and, at maturity, the principal amount. Bonds are issued by corporations, as well as federal, state, and local governments and agencies.

Bond Ratings

The system of rating debt securities was originated in 1909 by John Moody. Its purpose is to assess the issuer's ability to (1) pay the interest and (2) repay the principal of a specific debt issue when due. Although there are many different types of debt that may be serviced, the types that receive the primary focus of commercial rating companies such as Moody's, Standard & Poor's, Duff & Phelps, and Fitch, are corporate and municipal bond issues. Of these four rating companies, the first two are the best-known and their ratings are the most widely used.

A bond's rating is related to its investment risk: the higher the rating, the lower the risk, although nothing is absolutely guaranteed. As a consequence, those bond issues that have higher ratings generally have lower interest rates. A rating assigned by a given firm is simply that firm's best assessment of the creditworthiness of the issue, based on the facts at hand. If the underlying considerations change, then the bond rating may change. Furthermore, bonds of different issues that carry the same rating are not necessarily of equal quality.

The rating scale used by the four major bond rating firms is summarized in Exhibit 3.1. Of all debt issues, the direct obligations of the

EXHIBIT 3.1 Bond Rating Scales

Category	Moody's	Standard & Poor's	Duff & Phelps	Fitch	Criteria
High Grade	Aaa	AAA	1	AAA	Issues judged to be of the best quality; they carry the lowest degree of investment risk and are frequently referred to as "gilt edged." The capacity to pay principal and interest is extremely strong.
	Aa	AA	2–4	AA	Issues judged to be of high quality by all standards, whose issuers have strong capacity to pay interest and principal. These are rated lower because the margins of protection are not as strong as those of higher ratings.
Medium Grade	A	A	5–7	A	Issues judged to have many favorable investment attributes, issued by firms with a strong capacity to pay interest and principal. They are somewhat more susceptible to changes in economic conditions than those of higher ratings.
	Baa	BBB	8–10	BBB	Bonds whose issuers are judged to have an adequate capacity to pay interest and principal. Although these issues exhibit adequate protection, changes in economic or changing circumstances are more likely to weaken the capacity of the firm to pay interest and repay principal for debt in this category than in higher rated categories.
Speculative Grade	Ba	BB	11–13	BB	Issues judged as having speculative elements; their future cannot be considered as well assured. Bonds in this category are frequently referred to as "junk bonds."
	B	B	14	B	Issues that generally lack the characteristics of a desirable investment, also referred to as "junk bonds." Assurance of interest and principal payments over any long period of time may be small.
Default	Caa	CCC	15	CCC	Issues of poor quality that may be in default or in danger of default with respect to payments of interest or principal.
	Ca	CC	16	CC	Issues judged to be highly speculative, which are either in default or have other market shortcomings.

EXHIBIT 3.1 *(concluded)*

Category	Moody's	Standard & Poor's	Duff & Phelps	Fitch	Criteria
Default	C		17		The lowest class of rated bonds, regarded as having extremely poor prospects of ever attaining any real investment standing.
		C		C	Issues on which no interest is being paid.
		D		DDD, DD, D	Issues in default, with principal and interest payments in arrears.

Sources: *Moody's Bond Record*, Standard & Poor's *Bond Guide*, and Fitch Investor Service's *Rating Register*.

U.S. government, such as Treasury bills, notes, and bonds, enjoy the highest credit rating. The rating scales used by the rating companies can be divided into investment-grade (high and medium grade), and noninvestment-grade (speculative and default) categories. Since the mid-1980s, speculative, high-yield bonds have received the name "junk bonds," because of the high probability that the periodic interest payments and repayment of principal at maturity will not occur as promised.

Standard & Poor's Corporation sometimes uses plus (+) and minus (−) modifiers to those ratings from AA to CCC (e.g., A+ or BB−) to show relative standing with a given major rating category. Moody's Investor Service applies the numerical modifiers 1, 2, or 3 to each major rating category from Aa to B for corporate bonds. The modifier 1 (e.g., Aa1) indicates that the issue ranks at the higher end of its rating category; the modifier 2 indicates a midrange ranking; and the modifier 3 indicates that the issue ranks at the lower end of the rating category. For municipal bonds, Moody's uses the modifier 1 only for bonds in the Aa, A, Baa, Ba, and B groups to indicate the strongest investment attributes.

On the other hand, when no rating is assigned, or when a rating has been suspended or withdrawn, the reasons may be unrelated to the quality of the issue. Such might be the case if (1) a bond issue was not submitted to be rated, (2) the issue belongs to a group of securities that are not rated as a matter of policy, (3) there is insufficient data on which to base a rating, or (4) the bonds are privately placed and their issue is not published.

Barron's Confidence Index

Since July 1976, *Barron's* Confidence Index has been based on 20 bonds (Exhibit 3.2). It is calculated as the ratio of the yield to maturity of 10 "best" or high-grade bonds, rated AAA (Aaa) or AA (Aa), relative

EXHIBIT 3.2 Barron's Confidence Index—Component Bonds as of April 10, 1989

Issuer	Rate	Maturity
Best Grade Bonds (10)		
AT&T	8¾%	2000
Anheuser Busch	8⅝	2016
Baltimore Gas & Electric	8⅜	2006
Du Pont	8½	2006
Exxon Pipeline	8¼	2001
GMAC	8¼	2006
General Electric	8½	2004
IBM	9⅜	2004
Illinois Bell Telephone	7⅝	2006
Procter & Gamble	8¼	2005
Intermediate Grade Bonds (10)		
Alabama Power	9¾%	2004
Beneficial	9	2005
Caterpillar Tractor	8	2001
Commonwealth Edison	9⅛	2008
Firestone Tire & Rubber	9¼	2004
GTE	9⅜	1999
Honeywell	9⅜	2009
USX Corporation	7¾	2001
Union Carbide	8½	2005
F.W. Woolworth	9	1999

Source: *Barron's.*

FIGURE 3.1 Barron's Confidence Index

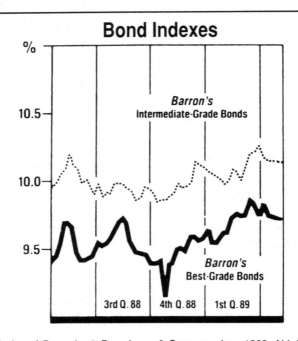

to 10 intermediate, or medium grade bonds, which are rated either A or BBB (Baa). When the ratio decreases, bond buyers are willing to accept a lower relative yield on the better quality bonds, which implies that they are losing confidence in lesser quality issues.

The Bond Buyer Indexes

The Bond Buyer is a daily newspaper that has covered the municipal bond market since 1891. It currently maintains and publishes the following four municipal bond indexes:

> 40-Municipal Bond Index
>
> 11-Bond Index
>
> 20-Bond Index
>
> 25-Revenue Bond Index

The Bond Buyer 40-Municipal Bond Index

The Bond Buyer 40-Municipal Bond Index, as its name implies, consists of 40 actively traded, tax-exempt revenue and general-obligation municipal bonds (Exhibit 3.3). The components have the following characteristics:

- Issue exceeds $50 million ($75 million for housing issues).
- Rated A or higher by Moody's or A− or higher by Standard & Poor's.
- Maturity of at least 19 years when included in the index.
- Bonds must be callable at par (100) prior to maturity. The first call data must be between 7 and 16 years when included in the index.
- Coupon must be fixed and paid semiannually.
- No more than two issues of a single entity can be included in the index at any one time.

The 40 bonds are changed frequently in order to keep the index a current picture of the market.

The index is calculated from the market prices for each bond[1] obtained daily at about 3 p.m. from five principal municipal bond dealers. Currently, they are:

> Cantor, Fitzgerald Municipal Brokers, Inc.
>
> Chapdelaine & Co., Inc.
>
> Clifford Drake & Company, Inc.
>
> J. F. Hartfield & Company, Inc.
>
> Titus & Donelly, Inc.

The highest and lowest prices for each bond are dropped, and the average price is computed from the remaining three prices. This average is

---

[1] This is the broker's assessment of the price at which $100,000 face value of each bond will trade.

EXHIBIT 3.3 The Bond Buyer 40-Municipal Bond Index Components

Type/Issue	Maturity	Rating*
Education (3)		
Clark County (NV) School District 8s	3/1/08	A1/A+
Maryland Health & Education 7½	7/1/20	Aa/AA
New York State Dorms (CUNNY) 8⅛	7/1/17	A/A
G.O. et al (8)		
Baltimore County (MD) 7¾	7/1/16	Aaa/AA+
New York City 7¾	8/15/28	A/A−
New York MAC series 62 6¾	7/1/06	Aa/A+
New York MAC series 62 6.90	7/1/07	Aa/A+
Philadelphia Municipal Authority 7.80	4/1/18	Aaa/AAA
Puerto Rico 7¾	7/1/13	Baa1/A
Tampa Florida 8⅛	10/1/15	Aaa/AAA
Tampa Florida 8⅜	10/1/18	NR/AA
Hospital (4)		
Jackson (TN) Health/Ed Board 8½	7/15/08	A/NR
Missouri Health & Education 7¾	6/1/16	Aaa/AAA
New York State Med Care Facility 8.10	2/15/22	NR/AA
New York State Med Care Facility 8s	2/15/28	NR/AA
Pollution Control (2)		
Brazos River (TX) Authority 8¼	5/1/19	A2/A−
Brazos River (TX) Authority 8.10	5/1/19	Aaa/AAA
Power (13)		
Georgia Municipal Electrical 7.80	1/1/20	Aaa/AAA
Georgia Municipal Electrical 8⅛	1/1/17	A/AA−
Grand River Dam (OK) 7s	6/1/06	A/A−
Grand River Dam (OK) 7s	6/1/10	A/A−
Intermountain Power (UT) FGIC 7s	7/1/15	Aaa/AAA
North Carolina Eastern MPA 7¼	1/1/21	A/A−
North Carolina Eastern MPA 8s	1/1/21	A/A−
North Carolina Catawba 7⅝	1/1/14	Aaa/AAA
North Carolina Catawba 7⅞	1/1/19	A/A
New York State Energy Research 7⅛	3/15/22	Aa2/AA−
New York State Power Authority 7⅞	1/1/13	Aaa/AAA
New York State Power Authority 8s	1/1/17	Aa/AA
Salt River Power (AZ) 7⅞	1/1/28	Aa/AA
Transportation (7)		
Allegheny (PA) airport 8.20	1/1/08	Aaa/AAA
Allegheny (PA) airport 8¼	1/1/16	Aaa/AAA
Chicago airport 8.20	1/1/18	A1/A
Greater Orlando (FL) aviation 8¾	10/1/16	A/A−
Greater Orlando (FL) aviation 8⅛	10/1/13	Aaa/AAA
Harris County (TX) tollroad 8.30	8/15/17	Baa1/A
Triborough Bridge (NY) 8s	1/1/18	A/A
Water (3)		
California Dept Water 7.70	12/1/24	Aa/AA
Lancaster Solid Waste 8½	12/15/10	A/A
NYC Municipal Water Finance 7.80	6/15/18	Aaa/AAA

* Moody's/S&P as of 8/29/88

Sources: *The Bond Buyer;* Chicago Board of Trade.

then divided by a conversion factor equal to the price at which the given bond would yield 8 percent. The conversion factor is determined from the following formula:

$$CV = \frac{1}{(1 + Y/2)^{X/6}} \left[\frac{i}{2} + \left\{ \frac{i}{Y} \left(1 - \frac{1}{(1 + Y/2^{2N})} \right) + \frac{1}{(1 + Y/2)^{2N}} \right\} \right] - \frac{i(6 - X)}{12} \quad (3.1)$$

FIGURE 3.2   The Bond Buyer Municipal Bond Index

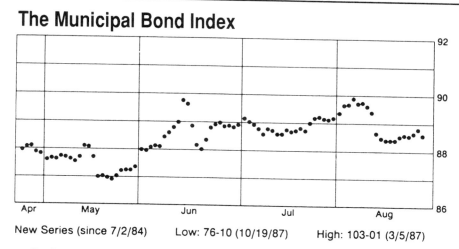

Source: *Credit Markets,* August 29, 1988. Reprinted with permission of American Banker/Bond Buyer.

where

i = Coupon interest rate (as a decimal)

Y = 0.08

N = Whole number of years to call if callable, or number of years to maturity if not callable, or number of years to first call at par for municipal bonds.

X = Number of months that maturity exceeds N, rounded down to the nearest quarter (e.g., X = 0, 3, 6, 9).

The 40 converted prices are then averaged and multiplied by a coefficient to maintain the continuity of the index when its composition changes.

The Bond Buyer 40-Municipal Bond Index was once the basis for cash-settled index futures contracts that were traded on the Chicago Board of Trade using the ticker symbol MB.

The Bond Buyer 20-Bond and 11-Bond Indexes

The Bond Buyer 20-Bond Index consists of 20 general-obligation municipal bonds having a minimum rating of approximately A1 (Moody's) or A+ (S&P) and maturities of 20 years (Exhibit 3.4). The Bond Buyer 11-Bond Index is a component of the 20-bond index; it consists of high-grade general-obligation municipal bonds with AA or Aa ratings and maturities of 20 years. It is compiled weekly and published in *The Bond Buyer.*

The Bond Buyer 25-Revenue Bond Index

The Bond Buyer 25-Revenue Bond Index consists of 25 revenue municipal bonds having a maturity of 30 years (Exhibit 3.5). It is compiled weekly and published in *The Bond Buyer.*

EXHIBIT 3.4 The Bond Buyer 20-Bond (GO, 20 year) Index Components

Issue	Rating†
Alaska*	Aa/AA−
Baltimore, Maryland	A1/A
California*	Aa/AAA
Chicago, Illinois	A/A−
Dade Co., Florida	A1/A+
Denver, Colorado*	Aa/AA
Florida*	Aa/AA
Georgia*	Aaa/AA+
Hawaii*	Aa/AA
Illinois*	Aaa/AA+
Massachusetts	AA/AA+
Memphis, Tennessee*	Aa/AA
Milwaukee, Wisconsin	Aa/AA+
Nassau Co., New York	A1/NR
New York City	A/A−
New York State*	A1/AA−
North Carolina*	Aaa/AAA
Pennsylvania	A1/AA−
Puerto Rico	Baa1/A
Seattle, Washington*	Aa/AA

* Components of the 11-Bond Index.
† Moody's/S&P as of 8/29/88.
Source: *MuniWeek/Credit Markets.*

EXHIBIT 3.5 The Bond Buyer 25-Revenue (30 year) Bond Index Components

Issue	Rating*
Atlanta (GA) airport	Baa1/A
California Housing Finance Agency, multi-unit rental	A1/A+
Connecticut Housing Finance Authority	Aa/AA
Dallas-Fort Worth (TX) Regional Airport Board	A/A
Illinois Health Facilities Authority (Northwestern Memorial Hospital)	Aa/AA
Illinois Housing Development Authority, multi-family	A1/AA
Intermountain Power Agency (UT)	Aa/AA
Jacksonville Electric Authority (FL), electric revenue	A1/AA
Kentucky Turnpike Authority	A/A
Los Angeles Dept Water & Power, electric revenue	Aa/AA
Maricopa Co. (AZ) Ind Devel Auth (Samaritan Health Service)	A1/A+
Massachusetts Port Authority	A/A
New York City MAC, 2nd general bond resolution	Aa/A+
Municipal Electric Authority of Georgia	A/AA−
Nebraska Public Power District, power supply	A1/A+
New Jersey Turnpike Authority, turnpike revenue	A/A
New York State Power Authority, general purpose	Aa/A+
N. Carolina Muni Pwr No. 1, Catawba electric revenue	A/A
Philadelphia (PA), water and sewer	A/A
Port Authority of New York & New Jersey, consolidated	A1/AA−
Puerto Rico Telephone Authority	A1/AA−
Salt River Project (AZ) Agri Impr & Pwr Dist, electric revenue	Aa/AA
South Carolina Public Service Authority, electric system	A1/A+
Texas Municipal Power Agency	A/A+
Virginia Housing Development Authority	A1/AA

* Moody's/S&P as of 8/29/88.
Source: *MuniWeek/Credit Markets.*

EXHIBIT 3.6   Dow Jones 20-Bond Average Components as of February 20, 1989

Issuer	Coupon Rate	S&P Rating	Maturity
Public Utilities (10)			
AT&T	8.8%	AA	2005
Alabama Power	9¾	A	2004
Commonwealth Edison	8¾	BBB+	2005
Consolidated Edison of NY	7.9	AA	2001
Consumers Power Company	9¾	BBB−	2006
Detroit Edison	9	BBB	1999
Michigan Bell Telephone	7	AAA	2012
Pacific Gas & Electric	7¾	A	2005
Philadelphia Electric	7⅜	BBB−	2001
Public Service Industries	9.6	BBB+	2005
Industrials (10)			
BankAmerica	7⅞%	BBB−	2003
Bethlehem Steel	6⅞	B	1999
Eastman Kodak	8⅝	A−	2016
Exxon	6	AAA	1997
Ford Motor	8⅛	AA	1990
GMAC	12	AA−	2005
General Electric	8½	AAA	2004
IBM	9⅜	AAA	2004
Socony Mobil Oil	4¼	AA	1993
Weyerhaeuser	5.20	A+	1991

Source: *Barron's.*

Dow Jones Bond Averages

The first Dow Jones Bond Average was published in April 1915. Currently, the Dow Jones 20-Bond Average is based on 10 utility and 10 industrial bonds (Exhibit 3.6). The utility and industrial bond groups by themselves make up the Dow Jones 10-Utility and 10-Industrial Bond Averages. Before July 1976, the composite bond average included 20 railroad stocks, and was known as the Dow Jones 40-Bond Average. The three averages are calculated as simple arithmetic averages of the closing prices of the component bonds, and are reported weekly in *Barron's,* as illustrated in Figure 3.3.

Moody's Bond Indexes

Since 1918, Moody's Investors Service has maintained and published on a monthly basis a number of averages and indexes covering corporate, municipal, and government bonds. Separate bond averages are calculated for all categories of high-grade bonds for each of the following sectors:

Moody's Industrial Bond Averages (Aaa, Aa, A, and Baa)
Moody's Public Utility Bond Averages (Aaa, Aa, A, and Baa)

FIGURE 3.3 Weekly Summary of Dow Jones Bond Averages

Dow Jones Bond Averages					
Daily	Apr. 3	4	5	6	7
20 Bonds	87.65	87.73	87.93	87.92	87.72
10 Util	87.45	87.54	87.73	87.65	87.45
10 Ind	87.85	87.93	88.14	88.20	88.99

Dow Jones Weekly Bond Averages				
	First	High	Low	Last	Chg.
20 Bonds	87.65	87.93	87.65	87.72 +	0.13
10 Util	87.45	87.73	87.45	87.45 +	0.07
10 Ind	87.85	88.99	87.85	88.99 +	1.18

Dow Jones Bond Averages For 1989					
	First	High	Low	Last	Chg	%
20 Bds	88.47	89.62	87.35	87.72 −	0.87 −	0.98
10 Util	88.16	89.74	86.95	87.45 −	0.83 −	0.94
10 Ind	88.78	89.76	87.60	88.99 +	0.08 +	0.09

Moody's Railroad Bond Averages (Aa, A, and Baa)

Moody's Corporate Composite Bond Averages (Aaa, Aa, A, and Baa)

Separate composite averages cover all the categories for public utility, railroad, and corporate issues.

Of these, Moody's Corporate Bond Index is the best-known. It is a price-weighted total-return index of approximately 80 investment-grade (Aaa to Baa) corporate bonds. All underlying bonds are nonconvertible and taxable, have maturities of less than five years, and have fixed coupons. The index was initialized at 100 on December 31, 1979. Its current level is determined by incrementing total return based on the average of the price valuations (on a $1 million transaction) obtained from a survey of bond dealers and brokers at approximately 3 p.m. daily. At one time, the Moody's Corporate Bond Index served as the basis for cash-settled index futures contracts that were traded on the Commodity Exchange (COMEX) under the ticker symbol MI.

The Ryan Index

Introduced in March 1983, the Ryan Index is a total-return index based on the prices of the most recently auctioned Treasury notes and bonds. It was developed by the Ryan Financial Strategies Group and is made up of the current 2-, 3-, 4-, 5-, 7-, 10-, and 30-year Treasury issues that are auctioned by the Treasury on a periodic schedule, as is summa-

EXHIBIT 3.7 Auction Schedule of U.S. Treasury Notes and Bonds

Security	Auction Date	Maturity Date
2-yr T-note	Every 4 weeks	2 years from issue
3-yr T-note	February, May, August, November	3 years from February 15, May 15, August 15, and November 15
4-yr T-note	March, June, September, December	4 years from issue on business day of March, June, September, and December
5-yr T-note	February, May, August, November	5 years, 2 months from issue on February 15, May 15, August 15, and November 15
7-yr T-note	March, June, September, December	7 years from issue on January 15, April 15, July 15, and October 15
10-yr T-note	February, May, August, November	10 years from February 15, May 15, August 15, and November 15
30-yr T-bond	February, May, August, November	30 years from February 15, May 15, August 15, and November 15

Adapted from Howard M. Berlin, *The Dow Jones-Irwin Guide to Buying and Selling Treasury Securities,* 2nd ed. (Homewood, Ill.: Dow Jones-Irwin, 1988), p. 9.

rized in Exhibit 3.7.[2] Newly auctioned Treasury notes have maturities that range from 2 to 10 years; Treasury bonds have 30-year maturities.

Price and income return are calculated for each maturity on the basis of market price changes and actual accrued interest. Each of the seven active maturities comprises a subindex; these are averaged to obtain the composite Ryan Index level, whose base level was set at 100 on December 31, 1979. The Ryan Index is published weekly in *Barron's.*

Shearson Lehman Hutton Treasury Bond Index

The Shearson Lehman Hutton Treasury Bond Index evaluates the performance of all outstanding U.S. Treasury notes and bonds, exclusive of "flower bonds."[3] Unlike most bond indexes, the index is market-

---

[2] The 15- and 20-year Treasury bonds are no longer issued but are still available for purchase on the secondary market. The 15-year bond was last issued in 1980, while the 20-year bond was last issued in 1986. Only 30-year noncallable bonds are now being auctioned.

[3] Flower bonds are deeply discounted Treasury bonds that are acceptable at par value in payment of federal estate taxes when owned by the decedent at the time of death. The currently available flower bonds are:

Maturity	Coupon
8/15/1992	4¼%
2/15/1993	4
5/15/1994	4⅛
2/15/1995	3
11/15/1998	3½

FIGURE 3.4   Shearson Lehman Hutton T-Bond Index

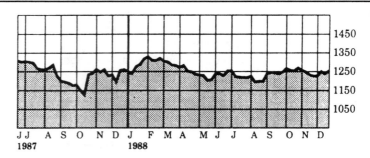

weighted; the weighting factor is the principal amount of the issue
that is publicly held times its current market price. The index is the
combination of two major subindexes. The Long Treasury Index charac-
terizes the performance of issues having maturities from 10 to 30 years.
The Intermediate Treasury Index represents those issues having maturities from 1 to 9.99 years. The index uses a base level of 1000 as of
December 31, 1980. Index levels are published daily in *The Wall Street
Journal* (Figure 3.4) and weekly in *Barron's.*

Salomon Brothers Broad Investment-Grade Bond Index

Salomon Brothers, like Moody's and Standard & Poor's, maintains a
large number of bond indexes, both domestic and foreign. Of these,
the Salomon Brothers Broad Investment-Grade Bond Index is the most
comprehensive; it measures the total rate-of-return performance of all
Treasury/agency, corporate, and mortgage securities with a stated maturity of at least one year and with at least $25 million outstanding.
Issues of less value are not considered large enough to be reasonably
available for institutional transactions nor to be reasonably priced.
The 3,700+ issues are subdivided into the following sectors:

- Treasury/agency—400+ issues (145+ Treasuries, 255+ agencies)
  All issues except flower bonds
- Corporate—3,200+ issues
  Utilities, financials, industrials, world banks, U.S. pay Canadians
- Mortgage—130+ issues
  GNMA, FHLMC, FNMA, FHA projects, conventional pass-throughs

Every issue is priced by traders at the end of each month. Total
returns are made up of price changes, principal payments, interest
payments, accrued interest, and reinvestment income. The index is
reweighted each month to reflect new issues, rating changes, etc. The

three sector subindexes and the overall index all are based on a base level of 100 as of December 31, 1979.

Standard & Poor's Averages & Indexes

Standard & Poor's Corporation, well known for its stock indexes and bond ratings, also maintains and publishes a number of averages and indexes covering corporate, municipal, and government bonds.

Standard & Poor's Corporate Bond Yield Averages

Since January 1937, Standard & Poor's has maintained a series of bond yield averages to gauge the average yield to maturity of the following investment-grade bond categories:

S&P Corporate Composite Bond Yield Average—AAA

S&P Corporate Composite Bond Yield Average—AA

S&P Corporate Composite Bond Yield Average—A

S&P Corporate Composite Bond Yield Average—BBB

S&P Industrial Bond Yield Average—AAA

S&P Industrial Bond Yield Average—AA

S&P Industrial Bond Yield Average—A

S&P Industrial Bond Yield Average—BBB

The bonds underlying each of the four corporate composite averages are typically divided evenly between industrial and utility issues. All averages have been calculated weekly since 1971 as arithmetic averages of the yield to maturity on bond prices supplied by Salomon Brothers.

Standard & Poor's Municipal Bond Indexes

Standard & Poor's maintains two indexes for municipal bonds, based on price and yield. The S&P Municipal Bond Price Index is derived from 15 issues rated AAA to A whose maturity is typically 20 years. Since 1971, the prices have been obtained in a weekly telephone survey of municipal bond dealers; the yields to maturity of the underlying components are converted to a selling price equivalent to that of a standard 4 percent, 20-year bond and then averaged.

On the other hand, the S&P Municipal Bond Yield Index is based on 15 general-obligation bonds, rated AAA to A. The yield index is also based on a weekly telephone survey of municipal bond dealers and is an arithmetic average of the yield to maturity of the 15 issues.

Standard & Poor's Government Bond Averages and Indexes

Since January 1942, Standard & Poor's has maintained averages and indexes for U.S. Treasury bonds based on both price and yield, as follows:

S&P Long-Term Government Yield Average

S&P Intermediate-Term Government Yield Average

S&P Short-Term Government Yield Average

S&P Long-Term Government Price Index

S&P Intermediate-Term Government Price Index

S&P Short-Term Government Price Index

The terms to maturity are different for long-term, intermediate-term, and short-term issues and are defined by Standard & Poor's for both the Government Price Indexes and Government Yield Averages as follows:

| | Term to Maturity | |
Issue	Price Index	Yield Average
Long-term	15 years	10 years
Intermediate-term	7.5 years	6–9 years
Short-term	3.5 years	2–4 years

Since 1971, all three yield averages have been calculated as arithmetic averages of the prices of four representative issues from prices published in *The Wall Street Journal*. Each of the three yield indexes is computed on the basis of the bid price of its four component issues, which are converted from yield to maturity quotations published in *The Wall Street Journal* based on 3½% coupons and the respective maturities of 15, 7½, and 3½ years.

Standard & Poor's Junk Bond Indexes

In response to the tremendous growth in the market for low-quality, high-yield corporate bonds, Standard & Poor's in 1988 created two junk bond indexes. The BB Rated Junk Bond Index measures the average yield for those six bond issues rated BB by S&P (Exhibit 3.8). The B Rated Junk Bond Index measures the average yield for the seven issues listed in Exhibit 3.9.

EXHIBIT 3.8   Standard & Poor's BB Rated Junk Bond Index as of July 26, 1988

Issuer	Rate	Maturity
Bally's Grand, Inc.	11½% notes	1996
Caesar's World, Inc.	13½% notes	1997
FMC Corporation	9½% debentures	2000
Heritage Communications, Inc.	12% notes	1998
Phillips Petroleum Company	8⅞% notes	2000
Union Carbide Corporation	8½% debentures	2005

Source: *Investor's Daily.*

EXHIBIT 3.9 Standard & Poor's B Rated Junk Bond Index as of July 26, 1988

Issuer	Rate	Maturity
Armco, Inc.	9.2% debentures	2000
BCI Holdings Corp.	12¾% debentures	2001
Burlington Holdings, Inc.	15¼% debentures	2003
Colt Industries, Inc.	12½% debentures	2001
Harte-Hanks Comm., Inc.	14⅜% debentures	2000
Holiday Inns, Inc.	11% debentures	1999
Supermarkets General Holdings Corp.	14½% notes	1997

Source: *Investor's Daily.*

Chapter

4 Mutual Funds and Money Market Funds

A mutual fund is an investment fund that pools investors' money to invest in securities; it may be either open-ended or closed-ended. An *open-ended* mutual fund continuously issues new shares when investors want to invest in the fund, and it redeems shares when investors want to sell. For no-load (no sales charge) funds, the buying or selling price is pegged at the fund's current net asset value. On the other hand, a *closed-end* fund issues only a fixed number of shares, which usually trade at a discount from the net asset value.

Money market funds invest in short-term money market instruments, such as certificates of deposit, Treasury bills, banker's acceptances, and reverse purchase agreements, all of whose maturities are generally less than 180 days. This chapter discusses those major barometers that track the mutual fund and money market industries.

Lipper Mutual Fund Indexes

Lipper Analytical Services is a publisher of statistical data covering the investment company industry in the United States and overseas. The firm tracks the performance of the indexes covering six equity mutual fund categories, a municipal bond index, as well as a price index covering the stock prices of a group of mutual fund management companies, as follows:

- Equity Fund Indexes
    Balanced Fund Index
    Gold Fund Index
    Growth Fund Index
    Growth & Income Fund Index
    International Fund Index
    Science & Technology Fund Index
- General Municipal Bond Index
- Mutual Fund Management Company Stock Price Index

The values of most of these indexes are periodically published in *The Wall Street Journal,* as shown in Figure 4.1.

FIGURE 4.1 Lipper Mutual Fund Indexes

LIPPER INDEXES

Thursday, March 9, 1989

Indexes	Close	Percentage chg. since		
		Dec. 31	Wk ago	Yr ago
Growth Fund	406.01	+ 7.44	+ 1.45	+ 13.44
Growth & Income ...	656.22	+ 6.07	+ 1.07	+ 15.78
Balanced Fund	494.44	+ 4.49	+ 1.00	+ 9.67
Gold Fund	149.90	+ 7.87	– 2.17	– 1.77
Science & Tech Fd .	150.31	+ 5.05	+ 0.63	+ 4.77
International Fund ..	284.30	+ 3.76	+ 0.28	+ 13.98

Source: Lipper Analytical Services

Balanced Fund Index

The Lipper Balanced Fund Index is a narrow-based index of the 10 largest funds; its primary objective is the stability of net asset value, achieved by maintaining a balanced portfolio of stocks and bonds. Typically, the stock/bond ratio is approximately 60/40. The underlying component funds for the Balanced Fund Index—as well as the Gold Fund, Growth Fund, Growth & Income Fund, International Fund, Science & Technology Fund, and General Municipal Bond Indexes—are summarized in Exhibit 4.1.

The index is net-asset-value weighted, and its level is calculated weekly from Thursday's closing prices and at the end of each month with adjustments for income, dividends, and capital gains distributions as of the ex-dividend dates. The index level was set at 100 on December 27, 1982. The underlying mutual funds represent approximately 75 percent of the total assets of all balanced mutual funds and account for about 2 percent of the combined assets of all equity mutual funds.

Gold Fund Index

The Lipper Gold Fund Index is a narrow-based index of the 10 largest funds for which at least 65 percent of the assets consist of shares of gold mining companies and gold-mining–oriented finance houses, gold coins, or bullion. The index is net-asset-value weighted, and its value is calculated weekly from Thursday's closing prices and at the end of each month with adjustments for income, dividends, and capital gains distributions as of the ex-dividend dates. The index level was set at 100 on December 31, 1984, and the underlying mutual funds represent approximately 75 percent of the total assets of all gold mutual funds.

Growth Fund Index

The Lipper Growth Fund Index is a narrow-based index of the 30 largest funds that invest in companies whose long-term earnings are expected to grow significantly faster than the earnings of the stocks

EXHIBIT 4.1   Lipper Mutual Fund Indexes as of August 16, 1988

1. **Growth Fund Index (30)**

   Alliance Fund   Merrill Lynch Fund for Tomorrow
   American Capital Fund   New Economy Fund
   Elfun Trusts   Nicholas Fund
   Evergreen Fund   Oppenheimer Special
   Fidelity Destiny I   Partners Fund
   Fidelity Magellan Fund   Phoenix Growth
   Fidelity Trend   Prudential Bache Equity Fund
   General Electric S&S Program   Putnam Investors
   Growth Fund of America   Seligman Growth
   Hutton Investor Series-Growth   Sequoia Fund
   IDS Growth Fund   T. Rowe Price Growth Stocks
   IDS New Dimensions   Twentieth Century Select
   Legg Mason Value Trust   United Accumulative
   Massachusetts Capital Development   United Vanguard Fund
   Massachusetts Investors Growth   WL Morgan Growth

2. **Growth & Income Fund Index (30)**

   Affiliated Fund   Merrill Lynch Retirement Equity
   American Mutual   Mutual Qualified Income
   Dean Witter Dividend Growth   Mutual Shares
   Dreyfus Fund   Paine Webber Assets Allocation
   Federated Stock Trust   Pioneer Fund
   Fidelity Fund   Pioneer II
   Fidelity Growth & Income   Pioneer III
   Fundamental Investors   Putnam Growth & Income
   IDS Managed Retirement   Seligman Common Stock
   Massachusetts Investors Trust   Vanguard Index-500 Portfolio
   Merrill Lynch Basic Value   Washington Mutual Investors
   Merrill Lynch Capital   Windsor Fund
   Merrill Lynch Retirement Benefit   Windsor II

3. **Balanced Fund Index (10)**

   George Putnam Fund of Boston   Massachusetts Financial Total Return
   IDS Mutual   Phoenix Balanced
   Investors Portfolio-Total Return   United Continental Income
   Kemper Total Return   Vanguard Star
   Loomis Sayles Mutual   Wellington Fund

4. **Gold Fund Index (10)**

   Fidelity Select-American Gold   Keystone Precious Metals
   Fidelity Select-Precious Metals   U.S. Gold Shares
   Franklin Gold Fund   USAA Gold
   Hutton Investor Series-Precious Metals   Van Eck Gold/Resources
   International Investors   Vanguard Special-Gold

5. **International Fund Index (10)**

   Alliance International   T. Rowe Price International Fund
   Fidelity Overseas   Templeton Foreign
   IDS International Fund   United International Growth
   Scudder International   Vanguard World-International Growth

6. **Science & Technology Index (10)**

   Alliance Technology   National Telecommunications & Technology
   Explorer Fund   Putnam Information Science
   Fidelity Select-Technology   Science/Technology Holdings
   Kemper Technology Fund   Seligman Communications & Information
   National Aviation & Technology   United Science & Energy

7. **General Municipal Bond Index (10)**

   Dreyfus Tax Exempt Bond Fund   Merrill Lynch Insured Portfolio
   Fidelity Mutual Bond Fund   Nuveen Municipal Bond Fund
   IDS Tax Exempt Bond Fund   T. Rowe Price Tax Free Income Fund
   Kemper Municipal Bond Fund   Scudder Managed Municipal Bond Fund
   MFS Managed Municipal Bond Fund   Vanguard Long-Term Municipal Bond Fund

Source: Lipper Analytical Services, Inc.

FIGURE 4.2   Comparison of Lipper Balanced Fund Index with S&P 500 and DJIA

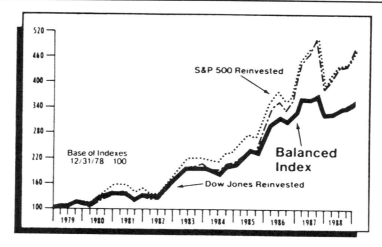

Reprinted by permission of Lipper Analytical Services Corporation.

represented in the major unmanaged stock averages—such as the Dow Jones Industrial Average, S&P 500, NYSE Composite Index, AMEX Market Value Index—or even the Consumer Price Index. The index is net-asset-value weighted, and it is calculated daily from the closing prices of its underlying components with adjustments for income, dividends, and capital gains distributions as of the ex-dividend dates. The index level was set at 100 on December 31, 1968. The underlying mutual funds represent approximately 64 percent of the total assets of all growth mutual funds and account for about 8 percent of the combined assets of all equity mutual funds.

FIGURE 4.3   Comparison of Lipper Gold Fund Index with S&P 500 and DJIA

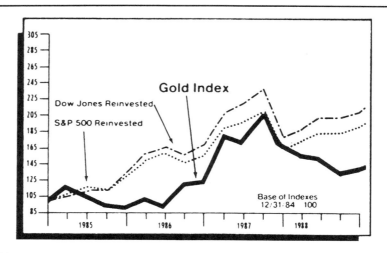

Reprinted by permission of Lipper Analytical Services Corporation.

FIGURE 4.4   Comparison of Lipper Growth Fund Index with S&P 500 and DJIA

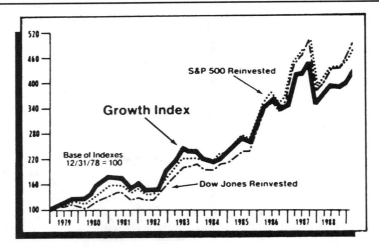

Reprinted by permission of Lipper Analytical Services Corporation.

Growth & Income Fund Index

The Lipper Growth and Income Fund Index is a narrow-based index of the 30 largest funds; it combines an objective of earnings growth with a requirement for level and/or rising dividends. The index is net-asset-value weighted, and its level is calculated weekly from the closing prices of its underlying components and at the end of each month with adjustments for income, dividends, and capital gains distributions as of the ex-dividend dates. The index level was set at 100 on December 31, 1968. The underlying mutual funds represent approximately 77 percent of the total assets of all growth and income mutual funds and account for about 12 percent of the combined assets of all equity mutual funds, excluding money market and municipal bond funds.

FIGURE 4.5   Comparison of Lipper Growth & Income Fund Index with S&P 500 and DIJA

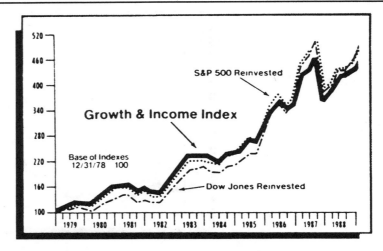

Reprinted by permission of Lipper Analytical Services Corporation.

International Fund Index

The Lipper International Fund Index is a narrow-based index of the 10 largest funds that invest more than 50 percent of their assets in securities whose primary trading markets are outside of the United States. The index is net-asset-value weighted; its level is calculated weekly from the closing prices of its underlying components and at the end of each month with adjustments for income, dividends, and capital gains distributions as of the ex-dividend dates. The index level was set at 100 on December 31, 1984. The underlying mutual funds represent approximately 64 percent of the total assets of all growth mutual funds and account for about 2 percent of the combined assets of all equity mutual funds.

Science & Technology Fund Index

The Lipper Science & Technology Fund Index is a narrow-based index of the 10 largest funds that invest more than 65 percent of their equity portfolio in science and technology stocks. The index is net-asset-value weighted, and it is calculated weekly from the closing prices of its underlying components and at the end of each month with adjustments for income, dividends, and capital gains distributions as of the ex-dividend dates. The index level was set at 100 on December 31, 1984. The underlying mutual funds represent approximately 83 percent of the total assets of all growth mutual funds and account for about 1 percent of the combined assets of all equity mutual funds.

General Municipal Bond Index

The Lipper General Municipal Bond Index is a narrow-based index of the 10 largest mutual funds. The index is a principal-only index on a

FIGURE 4.6 Comparison of Lipper International Fund Index with S&P 500 and DJIA

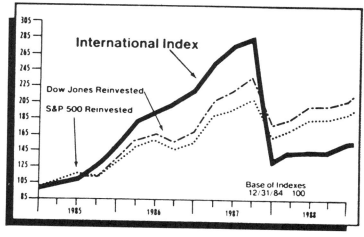

FIGURE 4.7   Comparison of Lipper Science & Technology Index with S&P 500 and DJIA

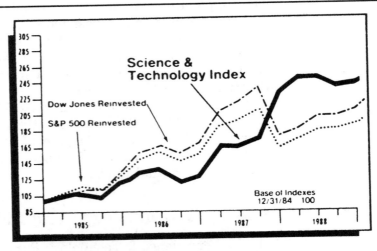

Reprinted by permission of Lipper Analytical Services Corporation.

dollar-weighted basis. The index level was set at 100 on December 31, 1980.

Mutual Fund Management Company Stock Price Index

The Lipper Mutual Fund Management Company Stock Price Index is composed of the stocks of the 10 publicly owned mutual fund management companies traded on the NYSE and OTC whose business is predominantly that of portfolio management (Exhibit 4.2). The index level was set at 100 on December 31, 1982, by combining equal dollar amounts of each of the five stocks that made up the original index. At the end of each year, the index is reweighted retroactively to give each of the component companies equal weight. In addition, the number of shares of the component stocks is periodically adjusted for stock splits and dividends.

EXHIBIT 4.2   Lipper Mutual Fund Management Company Stock Price Index Components as of August 16, 1988

Company	Exchange	Ticker Symbol
American Capital Management Research	NYSE	ACA
Bull & Bear Group	OTC	BNBGA
Colonial Group, Inc.	OTC	COGRA
Criterion Group, Inc.	OTC	CRITA
Dreyfus Corporation	NYSE	DRY
Eaton Vance Corporation	OTC	EAVN
Franklin Resources, Inc.	NYSE	BEN
Pioneer Group	OTC	PIOG
T. Rowe Price Associates	OTC	TROW
Thompson McKinnon/United, Inc.	NYSE	TMA

Source: Lipper Analytical Services, Inc.

Investor's Daily Fund Index

The Investor's Daily Fund Index is a narrow-based index of 20 mutual funds (Exhibit 4.3) whose investment objectives include growth, capital appreciation, international companies, and natural resources.[1] The distribution of the component funds on the basis of investment objective is as follows:

Fund Objective	Percentage Composition
Capital appreciation (11)	55%
Growth (7)	35
International companies (1)	5
Natural resources (1)	5

Prior to September 12, 1988, the Investor's Daily Fund Index was composed of only six mutual funds: Fidelity Magellan Fund, Lehman Capital Fund, Loomis Sales Capital Development Fund, Seligman Capital Fund, Twentieth Century Select Investors, and the Weingarten Equity Fund.

The index is computed by *Investor's Daily* as a total return index

EXHIBIT 4.3   Investor's Daily Fund Index Components as of March 28, 1989

Fund	Objective
Alliance Quasar Associates	Growth
Dreyfus Leverage Fund	Capital appreciation
Fidelity Magellan Fund	Growth
Founders Growth Fund	Growth
Franklin Equity Fund	Growth
IDS Aggressive Equity Fund	Capital appreciation
Integrated Resources Aggressive Growth	Capital appreciation
Loomis Sales Capital Development	Growth
Merrill Lynch Pacific Fund	International countries
Oppenheimer Time Fund	Capital appreciation
Pacific Horizons Aggressive Growth	Capital appreciation
Prudential Bache Reseach Fund	Growth
Putnam Vogager Fund	Capital appreciation
Scudder Capital Growth Fund	Growth
Shearson Aggressive Growth Fund	Capital appreciation
Strong Opportunity Fund	Capital appreciation
T. Rowe Price New Era Fund	Natural resources
Twentieth Century Vista Fund	Capital appreciation
Vanguard Primecap Fund	Capital appreciation
Weingarten Equity Fund	Capital appreciation

Source: *Investor's Daily.*

---

[1] A capital appreciation mutual fund meets at least two of the following criteria: (1) the investment objective stated in the prospectus is capital appreciation; (2) a turnover rate of 100 percent or more is either expected or realized; (3) the fund is permitted to borrow more than 10 percent of its portfolio value; and (4) the prospectus permits short selling, purchases of options, or investing in common stock or unregistered securities. A natural resource mutual fund is one that typically invests more than 65 percent of its equity in natural resource stocks.

FIGURE 4.8 Investor's Daily Fund Index

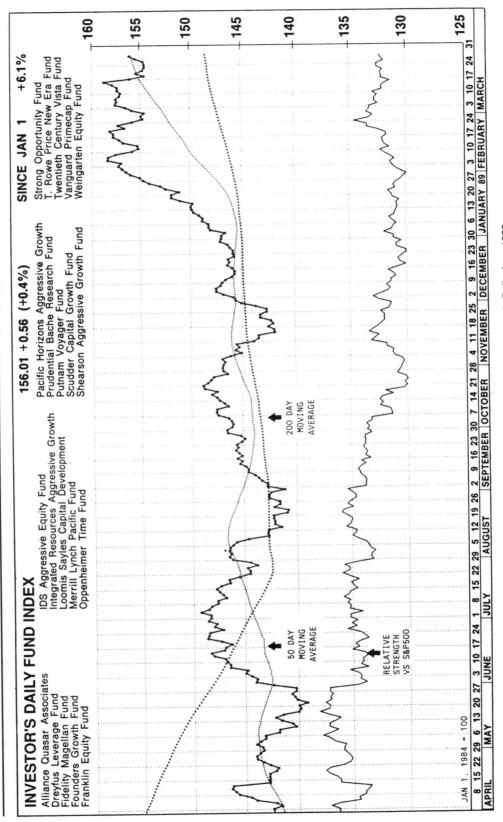

INVESTOR'S DAILY FUND INDEX

Alliance Quasar Associates
Dreyfus Leverage Fund
Fidelity Magellan Fund
Founders Growth Fund
Franklin Equity Fund

IDS Aggressive Equity Fund
Integrated Resources Aggressive Growth
Loomis Sayles Capital Development
Merrill Lynch Pacific Fund
Oppenheimer Time Fund

156.01 +0.56 (+0.4%)

Pacific Horizons Aggressive Growth
Prudential Bache Research Fund
Putnam Voyager Fund
Scudder Capital Growth Fund
Shearson Aggressive Growth Fund

SINCE JAN 1   +6.1%

Strong Opportunity Fund
T. Rowe Price New Era Fund
Twentieth Century Vista Fund
Vanguard Primecap Fund
Weingarten Equity Fund

200 DAY
MOVING
AVERAGE

50 DAY
MOVING
AVERAGE

RELATIVE
STRENGTH
VS S&P500

JAN 1, 1984 - 100

8 15 22 29 6 13 20 27 3 10 17 24 1 8 15 22 29 5 12 19 26 2 9 16 23 30 7 14 21 28 4 11 18 25 2 9 16 23 30 6 13 20 27 3 10 17 24 3 10 17 24 31

APRIL | MAY | JUNE | JULY | AUGUST | SEPTEMBER | OCTOBER | NOVEMBER | DECEMBER | JANUARY 89 | FEBRUARY | MARCH

160 155 150 145 140 135 130 125

Source: Reprinted by permission of *Investor's Daily, America's Business Newspaper* (March 30), © Investor's Daily, Inc., 1989.

based on net asset value and reinvestment of capital gains (but no dividends) of each component fund into the purchase of additional shares of that fund. The index level was set at 100 on January 1, 1984.

Herzfeld Closed-End Average

The Herzfeld Closed-End Average is based on 20 publicly traded closed-end mutual funds based in the United States that invest principally in domestic securities (Exhibit 4.4). Maintained and published by Thomas J. Herzfeld Advisors of Miami, Florida, it represents approximately half the capitalization of all closed-end funds.

The barometer is computed on the basis of a hypothetical portfolio that invests the same dollar amount in each of the 20 component funds and reinvests capital gains only in additional shares of the fund (dividends are not reinvested).

EXHIBIT 4.4 Herzfeld Closed-End Average Components as of July 1, 1988

1. Adams Express Corporation
2. Baker, Fentress & Company
3. Blue Chip Value Fund
4. Central Securities
5. Claremont Capital Corporation
6. Cypress Fund
7. Financial News Composite Fund
8. Gabelli Equity Fund
9. General American Investors
10. Growth Stock Outlook Trust
11. Lehman Corporation
12. Liberty All-Start Equity Fund
13. Morgan Grenfell SMALLCap Fund
14. Nicholas Applegate Growth Equity
15. Niagara Share Corporation
16. Royce Value Trust
17. Schafer Value Trust
18. Source Capital
19. Tri-Continental Corporation
20. Zweig Fund

Source: Thomas J. Herzfeld Advisors, Inc.

Donoghue's Money Fund Averages

The Donoghue's Money Fund Averages are based on the yields of all taxable money market funds reported in Donoghue's *MONEYFUND Report* and in many local and national newspapers. These simple arithmetic averages—of the (1) average maturity, (2) 7-day average percent yield, (3) 7-day compounded percent yield, and (4) 30-day average percent yield—are calculated for the portfolios of all the mutual funds

FIGURE 4.9   Herzfeld Closed-End Average

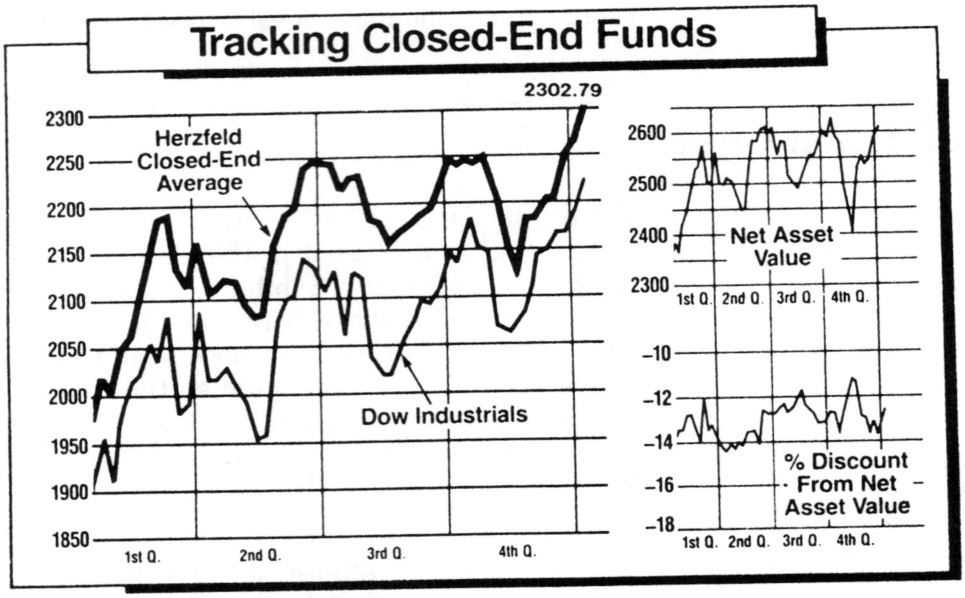

Tracking Closed-End Funds

Reprinted by permission of Thomas J. Herzfeld Advisors, Inc., The Herzfeld Building, P.O. Box 161465, Miami, FL 33116. (305) 271-1900.

reported. They are valuable in making week-to-week comparisons of the average maturity of the portfolio. In general, an increasing trend in the average maturity over several weeks indicates that money managers expect interest rates to decline and are lengthening the maturity of their portfolio. On the other hand, a decreasing trend over several weeks suggests that the managers expect interest rates to rise.

5 Commodities

Commodity indexes have long been the most reliable and timely of the economic indicators. Among the indicators surveyed in this chapter are the Baltic Freight Index, Commodity Research Bureau Spot Price and Futures Indexes, Dow Jones Commodity Spot Price Index, the Economist Indicators, and the Reuters Daily Index of United Kingdom Staple Commodity Prices. Strongly associated with commodity indexes is the Consumer Price Index.

Baltic Freight Index

In 1984, the London Commodity Exchange, the Baltic Exchange, and the Grain and Feed Association formulated a method to enable businesses that trade internationally to hedge commercial shipping costs. The result was the creation of a cash-settled tradable futures contract, called the Baltic Freight Index (BFI). Traded on the Baltic International Freight Futures Market (BIFFEX), the BFI is the first index based on a specific service, rather than a commodity.

The index is a weighted average of the costs of shipping standard cargoes over 13 well-defined worldwide trading routes; it gives a reasonably accurate composite of world prices of shipping dry cargo on a daily basis (Exhibit 5.1). Each of the 13 prices is weighted according to its influence on the shipping market. The grain routes (Routes 1–5) dominate the weighting at 65 percent of the index because grain is the dominant cargo of the spot market.

The BFI is published daily on the basis of information supplied by eight leading London shipbrokers concerning current voyage charter rates. The index has a base level of 1000 as of January 4, 1985.

Commodity Research Bureau Index

As the best-known commodity index, the Commodity Research Bureau (CRB) Index originated in the Tuesday Index of Spot Market Prices

EXHIBIT 5.1   Baltic Freight Index Components as of November 4, 1988

Route	Ports	Cargo	Percent Index Weight
1	1 port US Gulf/Antwerp (Belgium)	50,000 tons grain	20%
2	1 port US Gulf/1 port South Japan	52,000 tons grain	20
3	1 port US North Pacific/1 port South Japan	52,000 tons grain	15
4	1 port US Gulf/Venezuela	21,000 tons grain	5
5	Antwerp (Belgium)/Jeddah (Saudi Arabia)	35,000 tons barley	5
6	1 port Hampton Roads + Richards Bay (UK)/1 port South Japan	120,000 tons coal	7.5
7	1 port Hampton Roads (US), excluding Baltimore/ 1 port Amsterdam, Rotterdam, or Antwerp (Netherlands)	65,000 tons coal	5
8	Queensland (Australia)/Rotterdam (Netherlands)	110,000 tons coal	5
9	US West Coast (San Diego–Vancouver)/Rotterdam (Netherlands)	55,000 tons petroleum coke	5
10	Monrovia (Liberia)/Rotterdam (Netherlands)	90,000 tons iron ore	5
11	Casablanca (Morocco)/West Coast India	15,000–20,000 tons phosphate rock	2.5
12	Aqaba (Jordan)/1 port West Coast India	14,000 tons phosphate rock	5

Sources: The Baltic Exchange; Baltic International Freight Futures Exchange.

computed since January 1934 by the Bureau of Labor Statistics (BLS). In 1939 the index was based on 28 commodities; in 1952 the number was reduced to 22 commodities and the index related to a 1947–49 base period. The index has been rebased several more times; the most recent base period was set at 1967 to be consistent with other federal government indexes, such as the Consumer Price Index. Daily computation was discontinued in 1969; the index was thereafter computed

FIGURE 5.1   Baltic Freight Index (Feb. 3, 1986–Dec. 31, 1987)

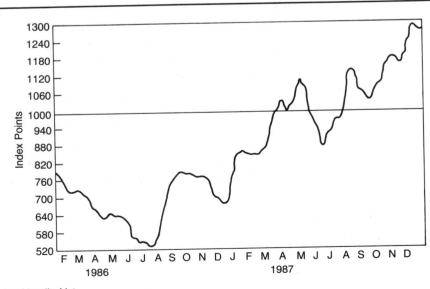

Source: *Lloyd's List.*

weekly on the basis of Tuesday's prices, which gave the index its name. Since May 26, 1981, however, the Tuesday Index of Spot Market Prices has no longer been published by the BLS; with some modifications, it is now maintained and published by the CRB.

Before being taken over by the BLS index, the original CRB index was created in 1957 by William Jiler, whose brother, Milton, founded the CRB in 1934. He had become dissatisfied with the Dow Jones Commodity Index, which had not been updated since 1925. As is summarized in Exhibit 5.2, the current CRB Spot Price Index is a merger of the old BLS and CRB index, and is often referred to as the CRB-BLS Spot Market Index. The index is based on prices of 23 different commodities, representing livestock and products, fats and oils, metals, and textiles and fibers, and it serves as the continuation of the BLS index as an indicator of inflation.

Besides the CRB Spot Price Index, CRB also maintains a CRB Futures Index, based on 21 commodities, including fibers, metals, livestock and meats, petroleum, and wood. The index serves as the basis for cash-settled futures contracts that are traded on the New York Futures Exchange (NYFE) under the commodity code CR. Exhibit 5.3 summarizes the components of the Futures Index along with their underlying futures contract specifications. Prior to 1984, gold was not included in the index because its price was controlled by the federal government for a long time at $35 per ounce. After the government

EXHIBIT 5.2   Commodity Research Bureau–Bureau of Labor Statistics Spot Price Index Component Commodities as of December 31, 1988

Foodstuffs (10)
   Butter AA, 93 (Chicago)
   Cocoa Beans (Ivory Coast)
   Corn, No. 2 Yellow (Chicago)
   Hogs, average weight (Omaha)
   Lard (Chicago)
   Soybean oil crude (Decatur)
   Steers, choice (Texas/Oklahoma)
   Sugar, raw (New York)
   Wheat, No. 1, hard winter (Kansas City)
   Wheat, No. 1, spring (Minneapolis)
Raw industrials (13)
   Burlap, 10 oz., 40″ (New York)
   Copper scrap, No. 2 (New York)
   Cotton, 1 1/16″ (7-market average)
   Hides, heavy native (Central U.S.)
   Lead scrap, heavy soft
   Print cloth, 48″ 78 × 78 (New York)
   Rosin window glass (New York)
   Rubber, #1 ribbed smoked sheets (New York)
   Steel scrap, No. 1 heavy melt (Chicago)
   Tallow, prime (Chicago)
   Tin, grade A (New York)
   Wool tops, nominal (Boston)
   Zinc, prime western (New York, delivered)

Source: Commodity Research Bureau.

EXHIBIT 5.3   Commodity Research Bureau Futures Price Index Component Commodities—Underlying Contract Specifications

Group/Commodity	Exchange*	Contract Size	Minimum Movement†	Daily Limit†
Grain and oilseed (6)				
Corn	CBOT	5,000 bushels	0.25¢/bu	10¢/bu
Oats	CBOT	5,000 bushels	0.25¢/bu	6¢/bu
Soybeans	CBOT	5,000 bushels	0.25¢/bu	30¢/bu
Soybean meal	CBOT	100 tons	10¢/ton	$10/ton
Soybean oil	CBOT	60,000 pounds	0.01¢/lb	1¢/lb
Wheat	CBOT	5,000 bushels	0.25¢/bu	20¢/bu
Food and fiber (5)				
Cocoa	CSCE	10 metric tons	$1/ton	$88/ton
Coffee	CSCE	37,500 pounds	0.01¢/lb	4¢/lb
Cotton, #2	NYCE	50,000 pounds	0.01¢/lb	2¢/lb
Orange juice	NYCE	15,000 pounds	0.05¢/lb	5¢/lb
Sugar, #11 world	CSCE	112,000 pounds	0.01¢/lb	0.5¢/lb
Metals (4)				
Copper	COMEX	25,000 pounds	0.05¢/lb	5¢/lb
Gold	COMEX	100 troy ounces	10¢/oz	$25/oz
Platinum	NYMEX	50 troy ounces	10¢/oz	$25/oz
Silver	COMEX	5,000 ounces	0.1¢/oz	50¢/oz
Livestock and Meats (3)				
Cattle, live	CME	40,000 pounds	0.025¢/lb	1.5¢/lb
Hogs	CME	30,000 pounds	0.025¢/lb	1.5¢/lb
Pork bellies	CME	40,000 pounds	0.025¢/lb	2¢/lb
Petroleum (2)				
Crude oil, light	NYMEX	1,000 barrels	1¢/bbl	$1/bbl
Heating oil, #2	NYMEX	1,000 barrels	0.01¢/gal	2¢/gal
Wood (1)				
Lumber	CME	130,000 board ft	10¢/1000 bd ft	$5/1000 bd ft
Total: 21 commodities, as of 12/31/88				

* Exchange abbreviations:
  CBOT—Chicago Board of Trade
  CME—Chicago Mercantile Exchange
  COMEX—Commodity Exchange (New York)
  CSCE—Coffee, Sugar & Cocoa Exchange (New York)
  NYCE—New York Cotton Exchange
  NYMEX—New York Mercantile Exchange
† Per contract
Source: Commodity Research Bureau.

lifted its restriction against private ownership of gold, which had been in force from 1933 to 1974, its price did not immediately stabilize and tended to be volatile. As a comparison, Figure 5.2 graphs the movements of both the spot and futures indexes.

The CRB Futures Index can be thought of as a three-dimensional index. In addition to averaging the prices of all 21 components, the index also incorporates an average of prices over time for each commodity. The price for each commodity is the simple average of the futures prices for a nine-month period.[1] For example, the average price for

---

[1] Prior to July 20, 1987, the CRB Futures index was composed of 26 commodities, for each of which the average price was based on a 12-month period. Certain commodity contracts, such as heating oil and sugar, cease trading the month prior to delivery.

FIGURE 5.2   CRB Spot and Futures Indexes

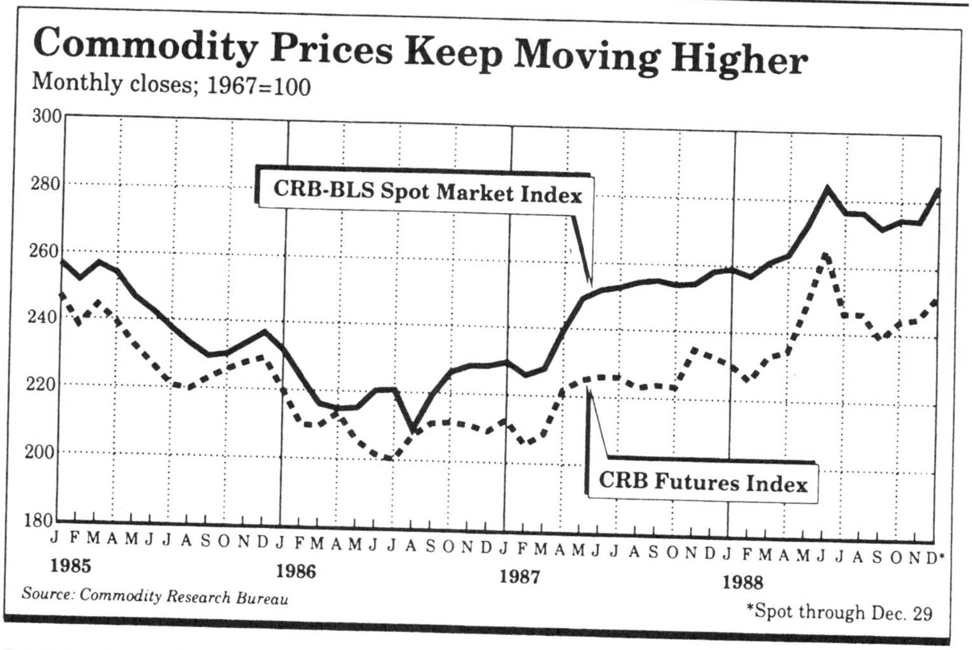

Commodity Prices Keep Moving Higher

Monthly closes; 1967=100

CRB-BLS Spot Market Index

CRB Futures Index

Source: Commodity Research Bureau

*Spot through Dec. 29

live cattle contracts traded on the Chicago Mercantile Exchange in July 1988 would be determined as the average for the following five contract months: August, October, and December, 1988, and February and April, 1989. Mathematically,

$$\frac{\text{Wheat}}{\text{average}} = \frac{\text{Aug '88 + Oct '88 + Dec '88 + Feb '89 + Apr '89}}{5} \qquad \textbf{(5.1)}$$

For other commodities, there may be more or less than five contract months in the average.

The average prices of the 21 component commodities are then geometrically averaged and the result is divided by 53.0615 (the 1967 base-year average for these commodities); multiplied by 0.95035 and by 100. Mathematically,

$$\begin{array}{l}\text{CRB} \\ \text{Futures} \\ \text{Index} \end{array} = \frac{\sqrt[21]{\text{Cattle avg.} \times \cdots \times \text{Wheat avg.}}}{53.0615} \times (0.95035) \times (100) \qquad \textbf{(5.2)}$$

The factor 0.95035 accounts for an adjustment necessitated by the index's changeover (July 20, 1987) from 26 commodities averaged over 12 months to 21 commodities averaged over 9 months. The index is multiplied by 100 in order to convert its level into percentage terms. In other words, the CRB Futures Index involves both geometric and arithmetic averaging techniques.

In addition to the CRB Futures Index, nine subindexes are maintained for baskets of commodities representing currencies, energy, interest rates, imported commodities, industrial commodities, grains, oilseeds, livestock and meats, and precious metals (Exhibit 5.4). All indexes have a base level of 100 as of 1967, except the currencies, energy, and interest rate indexes, which were set at 100 as of 1977.

EXHIBIT 5.4   Commodity Research Bureau Futures Subindexes as of December 31, 1988

Subindex/Commodities	Exchange of Underlying Contract*
1. Currencies (5)	
British pound	IMM
Canadian dollar	IMM
Deutsche mark	IMM
Japanese yen	IMM
Swiss franc	IMM
2. Energy (3)	
Crude oil	NYMEX
Heating oil, #2	NYMEX
Unleaded gasoline	NYMEX
3. Interest rates (3)	
T-Bills	IMM
T-Notes	CBOT
T-Bonds	CBOT
4. Imported commodities (3)	
Cocoa	CSCE
Coffee	CSCE
Sugar, #11 world	CSCE
5. Industrial commodities (5)	
Cotton, #2	NYCE
Copper	COMEX
Crude oil	NYMEX
Lumber	CME
Platinum	NYMEX
Silver	COMEX
6. Grains (4)	
Corn	CBOT
Oats	CBOT
Soybean meal	CBOT
Wheat	CBOT
7. Oilseeds (3)	
Flaxseed	WCE
Rapeseed	WCE
Soybean	CBOT
8. Livestock and meats (3)	
Cattle, live	CME
Hogs, live	CME
Pork bellies	CME
9. Precious metals (3)	
Gold	COMEX
Platinum	NYMEX
Silver	COMEX

* Exchange abbreviations:
   CBOT—Chicago Board of Trade
   CME—Chicago Mercantile Exchange
   COMEX—Commodity Exchange (New York)
   CSCE—Coffee, Sugar & Cocoa Exchange (New York)
   IMM—International Money Market (Chicago)
   NYCE—New York Cotton Exchange
   NYMEX—New York Mercantile Exchange
   WCE—Winnipeg Commodity Exchange

Source: Commodity Research Bureau.

Dow Jones Commodity Spot Price Index

The Dow Jones Commodity Spot Price Index is used primarily to compare cash spot prices on commodities traded on organized exchanges with the prices of futures contracts for delivery up to six months later. Prior to January 1982, the Dow Jones Spot Price Index was based entirely on agricultural commodities, but it has been revised to include wood, livestock and meats, and metals. Exhibit 5.5 lists the current 12 underlying commodities, along with their associated futures contract specifications. The index is computed as a equal-weighted average of relative price indexes, each using a base level of 100 as of December 31, 1974, the day gold trading resumed in the U.S.

EXHIBIT 5.5 Dow Jones Commodity Index Component Commodities as of March 20, 1989—Underlying Contract Specifications

Group/Commodity	Exchange*	Contract Size	Minimum Movement†	Daily Limit†
Grain and oilseed (3)				
Corn	CBOT	5,000 bushels	0.25¢/bu	10¢/bu
Soybeans	CBOT	5,000 bushels	0.25¢/bu	30¢/bu
Wheat	CBOT	5,000 bushels	0.25¢/bu	20¢/bu
Food and fiber (3)				
Coffee	CSCE	37,500 pounds	0.01¢/lb	4¢/lb
Cotton, #2	NYCE	50,000 pounds	0.01¢/lb	2¢/lb
Sugar, #11 world	CSCE	112,000 pounds	0.01¢/lb	0.5¢/lb
Metals (3)				
Copper	COMEX	25,000 pounds	0.05¢/lb	5¢/lb
Gold	COMEX	100 troy ounces	10¢/oz	$25/oz
Silver	COMEX	5,000 ounces	0.1¢/oz	50¢/oz
Livestock and meat (2)				
Cattle, live	CME	40,000 pounds	0.025¢/lb	1.5¢/lb
Hogs	CME	30,000 pounds	0.025¢/lb	1.5¢/lb
Wood (1)				
Lumber	CME	130,000 board ft	10¢/1000 bd ft	$5/1000 bd ft

* Exchange abbreviations:
    CBOT—Chicago Board of Trade
    CME—Chicago Mercantile Exchange
    COMEX—Commodity Exchange (New York)
    CSCE—Coffee, Sugar & Cocoa Exchange (New York)
    NYCE—New York Cotton Exchange
† Per contract
Source: *Barron's*.

The Economist Commodities Indicators

The British magazine *The Economist* has since 1864 published a commodity spot price indicator. It currently is based on 28 commodities subdivided into three sectors representing foods and industrials; the latter is further broken down into metals and nonfood agricultural items (NFAS). As summarized in Exhibit 5.6, the 28 underlying compo-

EXHIBIT 5.6   The Economist Commodity Index Components

Sector/Commodity			(%) Weight (3/12/88)
Industrial materials	50.2%		
Metals (6)		29.3%	
Aluminum			12.25%
Copper			8.32
Zinc			2.90
Nickel			2.70
Tin			1.85
Lead			1.28
Nonfood agriculturals (12)		20.9	
Timber			5.60
Cotton			4.23
Rubber			2.97
Hides			2.34
Wool 64s			2.19
Wool 48s			2.19
Soybeans			0.92
Palm oil			0.15
Coconut oil			0.13
Soybean oil			0.08
Sisal			0.06
Jute			0.04
Foods (14)	49.8%		
Coffee			16.68
Cocoa			5.33
Soybeans†			5.13
Maize			4.23
Sugar			4.03
Soybean meal			3.78
Beef			3.34
Wheat			2.34
Tea			1.49
Lamb			1.05
Palm oil*			0.80
Coconut oil*			0.70
Soybean oil*			0.55
Groundnut oil			0.35
Total: 28 commodities			

* Also included in Nonfood agriculturals

Source: Reprinted with permission from *The Economist.*

nents are weighted according to the value of their imports in OECD countries for the latest three years available, so as to give a base level of 100.

The levels of all four indictors (Composite, Foods, Metals, and NFAS) are determined separately on the basis of U.S. dollars, pounds sterling, and Special Drawing Rights (SDR).[2] In turn, the four indicators collectively make up what are known as the Dollar Index, Sterling Index, and the SDR Index. The SDR index smooths out the fluctuations in

---

[2] A Special Drawing Right is a weighted average of a market basket of five currencies used by the International Monetary Fund. The currencies are: the U.S. dollar, Japanese yen, German deutsche mark, French franc, and British pound sterling.

FIGURE 5.3 Dow Jones Commodity Spot and Futures Indexes

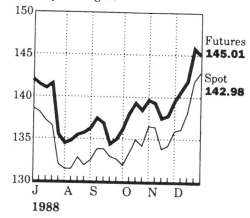

Dow Jones
Commodity Indexes
(Weekly averages)

Futures **145.01**
Spot **142.98**

J A S O N D
1988

the value of the dollar and pound sterling, and it should give a truer picture of worldwide commodity price movements.

Reuters Index

The Reuters Daily Index of United Kingdom Staple Commodity Prices is based on the prices of 17 primary commodities weighted by their relative importance in international trade (Exhibit 5.7). As the main U.K. commodity markets are international rather than domestic, this weighting helps the index to portray day-to-day changes in what may be regarded as the world commodity price level.

The index is maintained and computed by Reuters Economic Services as a geometric average of the spot prices of the underlying commodities. The basis for the spot or price quotations is either Britain or the northern European ports of Rotterdam, Hamburg, or Antwerp. The prices are given in pounds sterling or U.S. dollars, and a conversion is made at the day's prevailing exchange rate. In those cases where spot or cash quotations do not represent the market with the required accuracy, the index uses the prices of futures or forward deliveries. A "splicing" method is then used to avoid any break in continuity when an expiring or inactive futures contract quotation is replaced by a later one. The index is based on an index level of 100 as of September 18, 1931.

Even though the 17 components are weighted by their relative importance in international trade, the index generally reflects pre–World War II price patterns. Wool and cotton together represent 24 percent

EXHIBIT 5.7   Reuters Daily Index of United Kingdom Commodity Prices Component Commodities—Underlying Specifications

Commodity	Specification*	Weight (%)
1. Wheat	Canadian Western No. 1, cif U.K.	14%
2. Cotton	American New Orleans/Texas, good middling 1″	13
3. Coffee	ICO Brazilian and other Arabicas	11
4. Wool	Bradford 64's blended spot (dry combed basis)	11
5. Copper	Grade A, London metal Exchange official settlement	9
6. Sugar	No. 6 raws, cif U.K., London Daily price DLRS/tonne	7
7. Rubber	No. 1 RSS spot, London	7
8. Maize	No. 3 yellow American/French, cif U.K.	5
9. Rice	ECC milled American type No. 3 long grain, 10% broken, c & f U.K.	4
10. Beef	Scotch killed sides (ex KKCF) Smithfield	4
11. Soyabeans	American, cif Tilbury	3
12. Cocoa	Ghana, good fermented, cif U.K./N. European ports	3
13. Tin	European Free Market, spot price	2
14. Groundnutoil	Any origin, cif Rotterdam	2
15. Copra	Philippines F/M quality, delivered weight, cif N. European ports	2
16. Zinc	London Metal Exchange official settlement	2
17. Lead	London Metal Exchange official settlement	1

* cif = cost, insurance, and freight

Source: Reuters.

of the index simply because they were clothing staples in 1931, before synthetic fibers were commercially available. Furthermore, since the Reuters Index is composed of *staple commodities,* there are no energy components such as oil or gasoline, nor are there any precious metals such as silver or gold.

6

Money and the Dollar

The U.S. dollar is the principal international medium of exchange and a key reserve currency of almost every nation. Over half the world's trade is dollar-denominated, so that virtually every nation, corporation, and investor has a stake in the value of the dollar. This chapter discusses those measures by which the dollar is measured in addition to several other measures of money and interest rates.

The European Currency Unit

The European Currency Unit (ECU) is the official composite currency unit for the European Monetary System (EMS), established in 1979 to promote exchange-rate stability among the European currencies. EMS members, with the exception of Great Britain and Greece, have formally agreed to intervene in spot currency markets in order to maintain a given relationship among the currencies. The ECU is currently defined as a basket of the national currencies of the 10 member countries of the European Economic Community, or EEC (Exhibit 6.1). The weight of each currency in the ECU is the percentage share of the U.S. dollar equivalent of the prescribed amount of that currency. Because of fluctuations in exchange rates, the value of the ECU relative to the dollar also changes.

The composition of the ECU can change periodically. The currencies that make up the ECU are supposed to be reviewed every five years, or when new member countries join the EEC. This revision is made in an effort to restore the original proportion of each currency in the ECU. The original list of nine countries (excluding Greece) and their required weights in the ECU was first developed in March 1979. Five years later, on September 17, 1984, the current specifications were put into effect as a result of (1) Greece's entry into the EEC and (2) the fall of almost 25 percent in the Italian lira. The ECU has been accepted as a currency in its own right, and many bonds issued by the member countries are denominated in ECUs.

The dollar value of the ECU is determined by first multiplying the current EMS weight of each of the 10 currencies by the corresponding

EXHIBIT 6.1   European Currency Unit (ECU) Component Currencies

Country	Currency Unit	Weight (9/17/84)
West Germany	deutsche Mark	0.719
France	franc	1.31
Great Britain	pound	0.0878
Netherlands	guilder	0.256
Italy	lira	140.0
Belgium	franc	3.71
Denmark	krone	0.219
Ireland	punt	0.00871
Greece	drachma	1.15
Luxembourg	franc	0.14

Source: Federal Reserve System.

current exchange rate for that currency, and then adding the 10 values to obtain the total dollar value of one ECU. Example 6.1 illustrates this procedure.

Currently, the ECU index is the basis for 100,000 ECU cash-settled options contracts on the Philadelphia Stock Exchange, as well as futures contracts that are traded on the Philadelphia Board of Trade, International Money Market (IMM) of the Chicago Mercantile Exchange (CME), and the Financial Instrument Exchange (FINEX) under the ticker symbol EC.

FIGURE 6.1   European Currency Unit

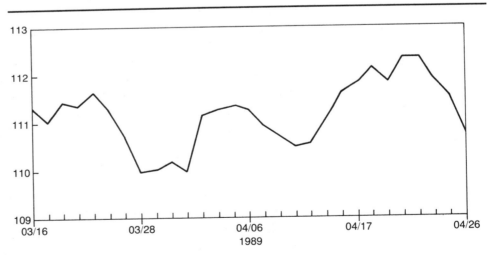

Source: Financial Instrument Exchange (FINEX).

Federal Reserve Trade-Weighted Dollar

The Federal Reserve Trade-Weighted Dollar was initially calculated by the Fed in the early 1970s to deal with numerous questions on

Example 6.1

On March 11, 1989, the dollar per unit exchange rates for the 10 EMS currencies (as obtained from *The Wall Street Journal*) were as follows:

West Germany	$0.5228/deutsche Mark
France	$0.1546/franc
Great Britain	$1.6670/pound
Netherlands	$0.4639/guilder
Italy	$0.0007173/lira
Belgium	$0.02496/franc
Denmark	$0.1344/krone
Ireland	$1.4020/punt
Greece	$0.006134/drachma
Luxembourg	$0.02496/franc

The current EMS weight from Exhibit 6.1 for West Germany is 0.719, so that the equivalent in dollars for that portion of the deutsche Mark's (DM) value that makes up the ECU is then

$$\text{Equivalent dollars} = (\text{EMS weight}) \times (\text{exchange rate})$$
$$= 0.719 \text{ DM} \times \$0.5228/\text{DM}$$
$$= \$0.3759$$

This calculation is carried out for the all 10 currencies as follows:

Country	Currency Unit	Current EMS Weight	Current Exchange Rate ($/Unit)	Equivalent Dollars
West Germany	deutsche Mark	0.719	0.5228	$0.3759
France	franc	1.31	0.1546	0.2025
Great Britain	pound	0.0878	1.6670	0.1464
Netherlands	guilder	0.256	0.4639	0.1188
Italy	lira	140.0	0.0007173	0.1004
Belgium	franc	3.71	0.02496	0.0926
Denmark	krone	0.219	0.1344	0.0294
Ireland	punt	0.00871	1.4020	0.0122
Greece	drachma	1.15	0.006134	0.0071
Luxembourg	franc	0.14	0.02496	0.0035
			Total (1 ECU)	$1.0888

The equivalent dollar values of all 10 currencies are then added up to give the total dollar value of the ECU. On March 11, 1989, 1 ECU was worth $1.0888 (or 0.9184 ECU equals $1).

foreign currency developments. The index is a market basket of the currencies of 10 countries—West Germany, Japan, France, United Kingdom, Canada, Italy, Netherlands, Belgium, Sweden, and Switzerland—that are major trading partners of the United States and account for more than half of U.S. foreign trade.

Each of the 10 currencies is weighted by the degree of its economic importance for the United States (Exhibit 6.2) and then geometrically

EXHIBIT 6.2   Federal Reserve Trade-Weighted Dollar Component Currencies

Country	Currency Unit	Base Exchange Rate ($/Unit)	Index Weight
West Germany	deutsche Mark	35.5480	0.208
Japan	yen	0.3819	0.136
France	franc	22.1910	0.131
Great Britain	pound	247.2400	0.119
Canada	dollar	100.3300	0.091
Italy	lira	0.1760	0.090
Netherlands	guilder	34.8340	0.083
Belgium	franc	2.5377	0.064
Sweden	krona	22.5820	0.042
Switzerland	franc	31.0840	0.036

Total: 10 currencies

Source: Federal Reserve System.

averaged. The calculation is compared with the base level of 100, set in March 1973. This base period marked the beginning of generalized floating foreign exchange rates. As the U.S. Dollar Index, the Federal Reserve Trade-Weighted Dollar serves as the basis of cash-settled futures contracts traded on New York's Financial Instrument Exchange (FINEX).

FIGURE 6.2   Federal Reserve Trade-Weighted Dollar (U.S. Dollar Index)

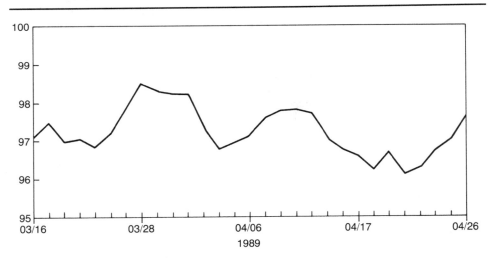

Source: Federal Reserve System.

Grant's Financial Dollar

Grant's Financial Dollar is an index developed by Gretschen Faro; it has been maintained and published by James Grant in *Grant's Interest Rate Observer* since March 1984. Unlike either the Federal Reserve

EXHIBIT 6.3   Grant's Financial Dollar Component Currencies

Country	Currency Unit	Weight
Japan	yen	0.377
West Germany	deutsche Mark	0.343
Great Britain	pound	0.189
Switzerland	franc	0.091

Source: *Grant's Interest Rate Observer.*

Trade-Weighted Dollar Index or the Morgan Guaranty Dollar Index, both of which are assigned a statistical weighting according to their relative importance in world trade, Grant's Financial Dollar can be thought of as a financial index.

Its four component currencies (Exhibit 6.3) are weighted according to the assets of their respective central banks (holdings of loans, securities, and foreign trade). These weights were assigned using the average of the 1971, 1977, and 1982 asset levels, and were converted into dollars at the then-current exchange rates.

EXHIBIT 6.4   Morgan Guaranty Dollar Index Component Currencies

Country	Currency Unit	Weight
Canada	dollar	30.3%
Japan	yen	23.2
West Germany	deutsche Mark	10.9
Great Britain	pound	9.2
France	franc	5.9
Italy	lira	4.1
Belgium	franc	3.5
Netherlands	guilder	3.0
Switzerland	franc	2.8
Australia	dollar	2.4
Sweden	krona	1.7
Spain	peseta	1.4
Denmark	krone	0.6
Norway	krone	0.6
Austria	schilling	0.4

Source: Morgan Guaranty Trust Company.

Morgan Guaranty Dollar Index

The Morgan Guaranty Dollar Index is a weighted average of 15 currencies (Exhibit 6.4). Its intent is similar to that of the Federal Reserve Trade-Weighted Dollar, but it is based on 15 currencies instead of 10. The base level of 100 was set as of the period 1980–82.

FIGURE 6.3   Morgan Guaranty Dollar Index

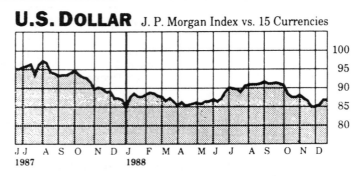

U.S. DOLLAR J. P. Morgan Index vs. 15 Currencies

BANKXQUOTE Index

The BANKXQUOTE® Index, maintained by Masterfund, Inc., is composed of 18 leading banks, 3 each from California, Florida, Illinois,
Pennsylvania, New York, and Texas (Exhibit 6.5). The index, updated
each Tuesday, is a simple algebraic average of the current interest
rates that these 18 banks pay on various fixed-rate certificates of deposits.

**EXHIBIT 6.5   BANKXQUOTE® Index
Components**

	State	Bank
1.	California	Bank of America
		Security Pacific
		Wells Fargo
2.	Florida	Florida National Bank
		NCNB Florida
		Southeast Bank
3.	Illinois	Continental Illinois
		First Chicago
		Harris Bank
4.	Pennsylvania	Mellon Bank
		Philadelphia National Bank
		Pittsburgh National Bank
5.	New York	Chase Manhattan
		Citibank
		Manufacturers Hanover
6.	Texas	First City
		NCNB Texas
		Texas Commerce

Source: Masterfund, Inc.

Money Supply Measures

Since 1960, the Federal Reserve System has attempted to define certain monetary measures. Over the years, the Fed has revised and expanded

FIGURE 6.4   Federal Reserve Money Supply Figures

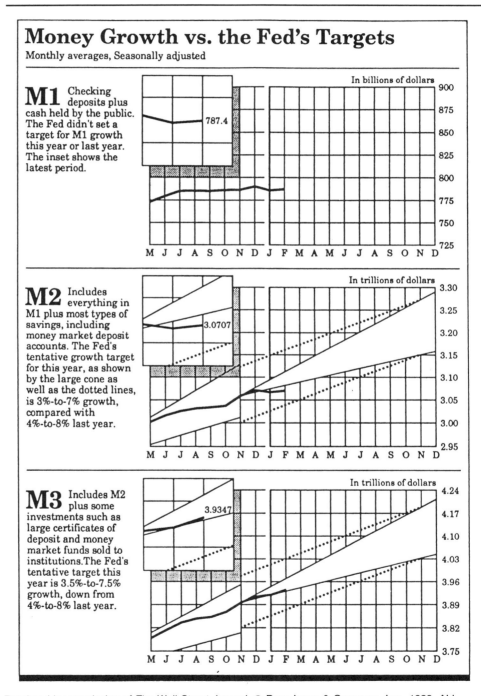

its money supply definitions to reflect the many regulatory changes and financial developments that have occurred since the introduction of its original measure.

The current money supply measures are designated M1, M2, and M3, and defined as follows:

M1: Currently the narrowest of all the monetary measures, M1 consists of noninterest-bearing sources of money. This includes all cash held by the public in currency and coins, demand deposits, notice-of-withdrawal (NOW and super-NOW) accounts, credit union share drafts, traveler's checks, and automatic transfer service (ATS) accounts. Unlike conventional NOW accounts, super-NOW accounts offer unlimited checking, third-party transfers, and an unrestricted interest rate.

M2: M2 includes all the M1 money sources plus savings and small-denomination time deposits, money market deposit accounts, shares in money market mutual funds, overnight repurchase agreements, as well as Eurodollar deposits held by U.S. residents other than banks at Caribbean branches of Federal Reserve member banks.

M3: The broadest monetary measure, M3 includes everything in M2 plus large-denomination time deposits, large-denomination term repurchase agreements, and shares in those money market mutual funds restricted to institutional investors.

Prior to 1980, the Fed released its money supply figures each Thursday afternoon. Almost as if it were a religious ritual, economists eagerly awaited these figures so as to compare them with targets proposed by the Fed. In fact, because it was the financial highlight of the week and had attracted such a large following, these figures were released after the close of the stock markets so as not to exert any undue influence on that day's trading. During the 1980–84 period, however, the weekly money supply figures were released on Friday afternoon, but the time was again shifted back to Thursday afternoons as of February 1984. Since the 1987 stock market crash, the release of the weekly money supply figures does not attract the following it once did.

7

Foreign Stocks

Since the mid-1980s, a period notable for the growth of many foreign stock markets, particularly in Japan, U.S. investors have turned a strong eye toward foreign stocks, in the form of either ADRs, mutual funds, trusts, or the foreign stocks themselves. The October 1987 worldwide stock market crash also increased the awareness of the average citizen concerning the movement of foreign markets, since those markets were open while the U.S. markets were closed, and their trends would strongly influence the movements of the U.S. markets when they reopened.

It was commonplace for early morning news broadcasts to give statements like: "The Nikkei average closed down 50 points," or, "Stocks are higher in early London trading, with the Financial Times Index up 20 points." This chapter discusses more than 75 stock market indexes and averages from 24 countries, as well as two worldwide indexes.

Australia

The Australian stock market dates back to the opening of the Sydney Stock Exchange in 1871. Today, there are six Australian stock exchanges, located in Adelaide, Brisbane, Hobart, Melbourne, Perth, and Sydney. Together, they comprise the Australian Stock Exchange (ASX), which was formed by the merger of the six exchanges on April 1, 1987. The Sydney Stock Exchange is the oldest and largest, while the Melbourne Stock Exchange ranks second, and these two account for approximately 90 percent of the total ASX trading volume.

Before 1980, several price indexes were developed by various Australian stock exchanges, banks, newspapers, brokerage houses, and governmental agencies. Prior to World War II, the Stock Exchange of Melbourne had maintained four indexes—Ordinaries, Mining, Finance, and Preference Shares—each using May 1926 as a base period. A daily index of 29 stocks continued to be calculated by the *Melbourne Herald* after the four indexes were discontinued in 1937. In the years that followed, the dramatic increase in industry required the development of a new series of indexes.

Since January 1980, the Australian Stock Exchange has maintained the All Ordinaries composite index, which is further broken down into three composite indexes—All Mining, All Resources, and All Industrials—covering 23 subindexes in addition to the Twenty Leaders Index and Fifty Leaders Index.

All Ordinaries Index

The All Ordinaries Index is a broad-based composite index of over 320 ordinary (common) shares from the 1,500+ listed companies on the ASX, and is broken down into three composite indexes (All Mining, All Resources, and All Industrials) composed of 23 subindexes (Exhibit 7.1) that represent 80 percent of the market's total capitalization. The index is capitalization-weighted according to the Paäsche formula with a base index level of 500 as of December 31, 1979.

The All Ordinaries are divided into (1) the All Industrials Index, which represents 18 industrial groups having approximately 65 percent of the market value of the All Ordinaries, (2) All Mining Index, and (3) the All Resources Index, which includes the All Mining Index as well as oil, gas, and diversified resource industries.

Since February 1983, the All Ordinaries Index has been the basis for European-style, cash-settled index option and futures options contracts that are traded on the Sydney Futures Exchange.

EXHIBIT 7.1 Australian Stock Exchange All-Ordinaries Index Components

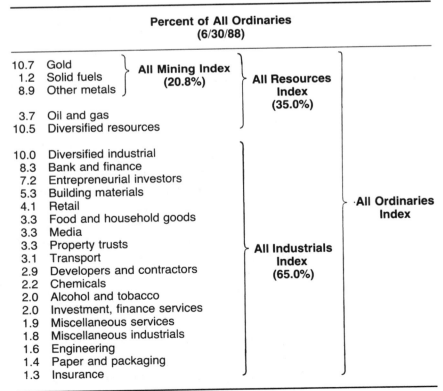

Source: Sydney Stock Exchange.

FIGURE 7.1 All Ordinaries Index

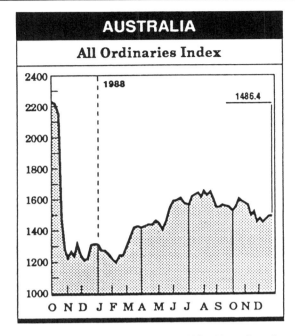

Twenty Leaders and Fifty Leaders Indexes

The Twenty Leaders Index is an index of the top 20 stocks having options contracts traded on the ASX (Exhibit 7.2), while the Fifty Leaders Index covers the top 50 stocks ranked by market size. Both indexes are capitalization-weighted by the Paäsche formula and have base levels of 500 as of December 31, 1979. The component stocks of the Twenty Leaders Index account for approximately 44 percent of the market value of the All Ordinaries Index, while the Fifty Leaders Index represents about 68 percent.

EXHIBIT 7.2 Australian Stock Exchange Twenty Leaders Index Components as of June 30, 1988

ANZ Banking	MIM
BHP	National Australian Bank
Bell Group	News Corporation
Boral	North B.H.
Bougainville	Pacific Dunlop
Coles	Pioneer Concrete
CRA	Santos
CSR	TNT
Elders	W.M.C.
I.E.L.	Westpac

Source: Sydney Stock Exchange.

Austria

The Vienna Stock Exchange *(Wiener Börsekammer)* is Austria's only stock exchange. Currently, the following two major stock indexes are used to represent trading activity:

> Vienna Stock Exchange Share Index
>
> Creditanstalt-Bankverein Index

The Vienna Stock Exchange Share Index

Of the two indexes, the major stock index is the *Wiener Börsekammer Aktienindex* (Vienna Stock Exchange Share Index), which is maintained by the stock exchange. It is a broad-based index of 54 of the 65 domestic listed companies (Exhibit 7.3). The index is capitalization-weighted by use of the Paäsche formula and has a base index level of 100 as of December 31, 1967.

Creditanstalt-Bankverein Index

The Creditanstalt-Bankverein Index is a narrow-based index based on 25 domestic companies listed on the Vienna Stock Exchange; it is maintained by Creditanstalt Bankverein, Austria's largest bank. Prior

---

EXHIBIT 7.3   Vienna Stock Exchange Index Components

AKG Holding	Montana
Allgemeine Baugesellschaft	Neusieder
Austria Email-EHT AG	ÖMV AG
Bank für Ktn und Stammaktien	ÖMV Handels-AG
Bank für Oö und Sbg	Österreicher Auto
Bank für Tirol und Vbg	Österreicher Brau
Constantia Industrie	Österreicher Brown Boveri
Creditanstalt-Bankverein	Ottakringer
Erste Allgemeine Insurance	Perimooser Cement
Gösser	Radex
Holtex	Reininghaus (Brüder)
Hunter	Schlumberger
IFE	Schwechater
Internationale Unfall	Semperit Holding
Jenbacher Werke	Stadlauer
Jungbunzlauer	Steyr-Daimler-Puch
Kabel und Drahtwerke	Styermühl
Laakirchen	Stölzle
Länderbank	Strabag
Leipnik-Lundenburger Industrie	Treibacher Chemische Werke
Lenzing	Union-Baumat
Leykam-Mürztaler Paper	Universale
Linz Textil	Veitscher Magnesit
Manner	Waagner-Biró
Mautner Markhof	Wertheim
Meinl	Wiener Allianz
MIBA	Wienerberger

Total: 54 companies

Source: Vienna Stock Exchange.

FIGURE 7.2   Vienna Stock Exchange Share Index, 1987

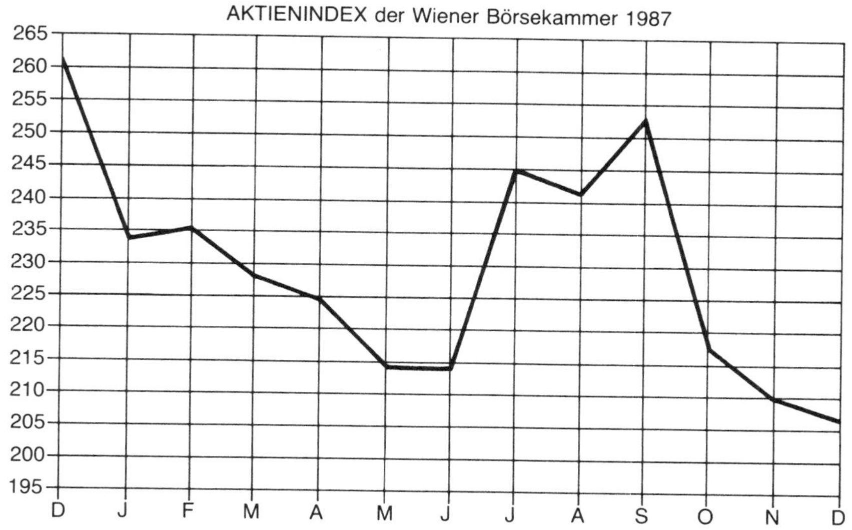

AKTIENINDEX der Wiener Börsekammer 1987

Source: Vienna Stock Exchange.

to July 1, 1986, the index was based on only 20 companies. The index is capitalization-weighted, using the Laspeyres formula, with a base index level of 100 as of December 30, 1964. The components are selected primarily on the basis of high capitalization and daily turnover.

Belgium

The Brussels Stock Exchange *(Bourse de Bruxelles)* is Belgium's only stock exchange, which lists over 430 stocks. Currently four market indexes are used:

 Cash Market All Share Price Index

 Cash Market All Share Return Index

 Forward Market Share Price Index

 Forward Market Share Return Index

The Cash Market All Share Indexes

The Cash Market All Share Index is a broad-based index based on all companies listed on the Brussels Stock Exchange (Exhibit 7.5). The index is capitalization-weighted according to the Paäsche formula and its base level of 1000 was set on January 1, 1980. Even though the Cash Market All Share Index is capitalization-weighted, there are two possible variations that depend whether or not dividends are taken into account. The Cash Market All Share Price Index does not include paid dividends, while the Cash Market All Share Return Index takes dividends into account.

EXHIBIT 7.4 Creditanstalt Share Index Components as of April 17, 1989

1. **Banks & Insurance (4)**
   Creditanstalt-Bankverein, preferred shares
   Länderbank, preferred shares
   Erste Allgemeine Insurance, common shares
   Internationale Accident and Liability
2. **Mining (1)**
   Veitscher Magnesit
3. **Chemicals (4)**
   Jungbunzlauer
   Lenzing
   Semperit Holding
   Treibacher Chemische Werke
4. **Breweries and foods (3)**
   Mautner Markhof, preferred shares
   Österreicher Brau
   Reininghaus (Brüder) Brauerei
5. **Electronics (2)**
   AKG Holding
   ASEA Brown-Boveri
6. **Construction/construction materials (4)**
   Allgemeine Baugesellschaft, common shares
   Perlmooser Cement
   Universale
   Wienerberger
7. **Machinery (3)**
   Jenbacher Werke
   Steyr-Daimler-Puch
   Waagner-Biró
8. **Paper (2)**
   Leykam-Mürztaler Paper
   Neusiedler
9. **Holding companies**
   Constantia Industrieholdung
   Leipnik-Lundenburger Industrie

   Total: 25 companies

Source: Creditanstalt-Bankverein.

The Forward Market Share Indexes

Like the Cash Market All Share Indexes, the Forward Market Share Indexes are broad-based indexes of all listed companies. The index is capitalization-weighted according to the Paäsche formula, and its base level of 1000 was defined on January 1, 1980. The Forward Market All Share Price Index does not include paid dividends, while the Forward Market All Share Return Index takes dividends into account.

Canada

Although there are five Canadian stock exchanges (Calgary, Montreal, Toronto, Vancouver, and Winnipeg), the largest is the Toronto Stock Exchange (TSE), which accounts for more than 75 percent of the total

EXHIBIT 7.5   Brussels Stock Exchange Cash Market All Share Index Components as of December 31, 1987 (Top 20 Ranked by Capitalization)

1. Petrofina
2. Intercom
3. Ebes
4. Solvay
5. Royale Belge
6. Generale Belgique
7. Tractebel
8. Generale de Banque
9. A.G.
10. G.B.L.
11. Kredietbank
12. Unreg
13. Cockerill Sambre
14. B.B.L.
15. Delhaize
16. GB-Inno-BM
17. Cobepa
18. Gevaert
19. Almanij
20. Cometra

Source: Brussels Stock Exchange.

Canadian market turnover. The TSE, founded in 1852 and incorporated in 1878, is a nonprofit corporation owned by its members. In 1934, the TSE merged with its main competitor, the Standard Stock and Mining Exchange.

Currently, three indexes reflect the price activity of the 1,400+ listed stock issues, representing over 1,000 companies, on the Toronto Stock Exchange:

TSE 300 Composite Index

TSE High-Technology Index

Toronto 35-Stock Index

FIGURE 7.3   Brussels Stock Exchange Cash Index

Reprinted by permission of *Financial Times.*

Toronto Stock Exchange 300 Composite Index—TSE 300

The TSE 300 Composite Index is the primary measure of stock activity on the TSE. The TSE used a simple arithmetic average from 1934, when Canadian stock market activity was first measured, until 1963, when a 108-stock average evolved. The current TSE-300 Composite Index, created in January 1977, is a broad-based index of 300 listed stocks that is divided into 14 industry sectors (see Exhibits 7.6 and 7.7).

The TSE 300 Index is capitalization-weighted by use of the Paäsche formula; its base level of 1000 was set in 1975. On the basis of market capitalization, British Columbia Telephone, Alcan Industries, and the Toronto Dominion Bank currently account for approximately 14 percent of the index's value. To be included in the index, the underlying stocks are selected on the following criteria:

- In most cases, only common shares are included.
- Company must be incorporated in Canada or be substantially Canadian-owned.
- Stock must be listed for at least 12 consecutive months prior to consideration.
- Capitalization must be at least C$3 million.
- Stock must trade at least 25,000 shares for a value of C$1 million in the year prior to consideration.

Since its formation, the index has been the basis for European-style, cash-settled index option contracts that are traded on the TSE.

EXHIBIT 7.6   Toronto Stock Exchange 300 Composite Index Industry Sectors

Industry Sector	Capitalization Weight (%) (8/31/88)
1. Financial services (37)	17.59%
2. Industrial products (41)	10.74
3. Utilities (18)	10.63
4. Metals and minerals (15)	10.56
5. Gold and silver (34)	9.34
6. Oil and gas (34)	8.95
7. Consumer products (26)	7.08
8. Management companies (10)	6.90
9. Communications and media (20)	5.16
10. Merchandising (29)	5.06
11. Paper and forest products (16)	3.03
12. Transportation (7)	2.05
13. Pipelines (4)	1.53
14. Real estate and construction (9)	1.36
Total: 300 companies	

Source: Toronto Stock Exchange.

EXHIBIT 7.7 Toronto Stock Exchange 300 Composite Index Components (Top 20 Ranked by Capitalization)

Company	Capitalization Weight (%) (8/31/88)
1. British Columbia Telephone	7.17%
2. Canam Manac "A"	4.47
3. Alcan Aluminum	4.01
4. Toronto-Dominion Bank	3.44
5. Royal Bank	2.92
6. Canadian Imperial Bank of Commerce	2.71
7. Seagrams	2.61
8. INCO Ltd.	2.60
9. Bank of Montreal	1.96
10. Imperial Oil "A"	1.80
11. Nova Corporation of Alberta	1.76
12. Moore Corporation	1.72
13. Bank of Nova Scotia	1.72
14. Northern Telecom	1.65
15. Echo Bay Mines	1.50
16. Laidlaw "B"	1.36
17. Transalta Utilities "A"	1.24
18. IMASCO	1.19
19. International Thomson	1.05
20. Canadian Tire Corp "A"	1.01
Total	47.89%

Source: Toronto Stock Exchange.

FIGURE 7.4 Toronto Stock Exchange 300 Composite Index

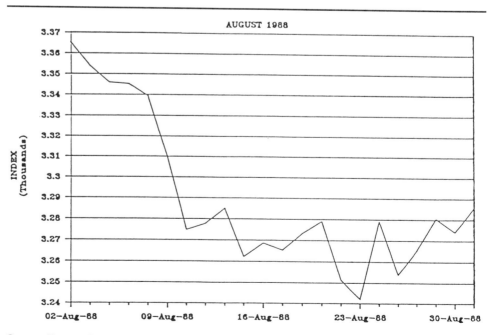

Source: Toronto Stock Exchange.

Toronto Stock Exchange High-Technology Index

The TSE High-Technology Index is a narrow-based index of 27 Canadian high-technology companies, 12 of which are included in the TSE 300 Index (Exhibit 7.8). The index is capitalization-weighted according to the Paäsche formula, and its base level was set at 100 on December 31, 1974.

To be included in the index, stocks are selected on the basis of the following criteria:

- Stock must be listed on the TSE (common shares only).
- Company must be incorporated in Canada.
- Company receives at least 50 percent of aggregate gross operating profit from high-technology industry.
- Capitalization must be at least C$5 million.

**EXHIBIT 7.8   Toronto Stock Exchange
High-Technology Index**

Industry Sector/Company	Weight (%) (12/31/86)	
1. **Communications (7)**	**62.13%**	
Northern Telecom		54.51
Mitel		5.36
Gandalf Technologies		0.87
Glenayre Electronics		0.74
Futurtek		0.26
Develcon Electronics		0.19
TIE/Telecommunications		0.19
2. **Electronics (13)**	**30.67%**	
CAE		17.38
Canadian Marconi		4.81
Spar Aerospace		2.69
Lumonics		1.46
Leigh Instruments		1.30
Fleet Aerospace		1.22
Meridian Technologies		0.47
Circo Craft		0.43
Linear Technology		0.39
Helix Circuits		0.34
Fathom Oceanology		0.07
Siltronics		0.07
Triple Crown Electronics		0.05
3. **Computer Industry (7)**	**7.20%**	
SHL Systemhouse		5.49
Computer Innovations		0.93
Comterm		0.32
Lanpar Technologies		0.20
Geac		0.13
BMB Compuscience		0.08
Zavitz Technology		0.05
Total: 27 companies		

Source: Toronto Stock Exchange.

The Toronto 35-Stock Index

The Toronto 35-Stock Index is a narrow-based index of the share prices of 35 Canadian blue-chip companies (Exhibit 7.9). Its changes closely parallel those in the TSE 300 Composite Index. Developed in May

EXHIBIT 7.9   Toronto 35-Stock Index Components

Industry Sector/Company	Ticker Symbol	Weight (%) (8/31/88)
1. **Financial services (7)**		17.93%
Toronto-Dominion Bank	TD	3.93
Royal Bank	RY	3.80
Bank of Montreal	BMO	3.15
Canadian Imperial Bank	CM	2.78
Bank of Nova Scotia	BNS	1.61
Power Financial Corporation	POW	1.42
National Bank of Canada	NA	1.24
2. **Metals and minerals (4)**		15.77%
Alcan Aluminum	AL	6.45
INCO Ltd.	N	4.20
Noranda Mines	NOR	2.60
Falconbridge Nickel	FL	2.52
3. **Industrial products (5)**		14.14%
Nova Corporation of Alberta	NVA	4.23
Moore Corporation	MCL	3.15
Steel Company of Canada, Series A	STE.A	2.65
Northern Telecom	NTL	2.47
CAE Industries	CAE	1.64
4. **Utilities (2)**		9.48%
Bell Canada Enterprises	B	6.37
Transalta Utilities "A"	TAU.A	3.11
5. **Oil and gas (4)**		9.15%
Imperial Oil "A"	IMO.A	3.08
Ranger Oil	RGO	2.46
Gulf Canada Resources	GOU	2.04
Bow Valley Industries	BVI	1.57
6. **Gold and silver (3)**		7.61%
Pacer Dome	PDG	3.84
Echo Bay Mines	ECO	2.58
LAC Minerals	LAC	1.19
7. **Transportation (2)**		7.49%
Canadian Pacific	CP	4.81
Laidlaw, Class B	LDM.B	2.68
8. **Consumer products (2)**		6.69%
Seagrams	VO	3.78
IMASCO	IMS	2.91
9. **Merchandising (2)**		5.95%
Canadian Tire Corp "A"	CTR.A	3.88
Sears Canada	SCC	2.07
10. **Communications and media (2)**		2.74%
International Thomson	ITO	1.55
Southam Press	STM	1.19
11. **Paper and forest products (1)**		1.58%
MacMillan Bloedel	MB	1.58
12. **Pipelines (1)**		1.47%
Transcanada Pipelines	TRP	1.47
Total: 35 companies		

Source: Toronto Stock Exchange.

FIGURE 7.5   Toronto 35-Stock Index

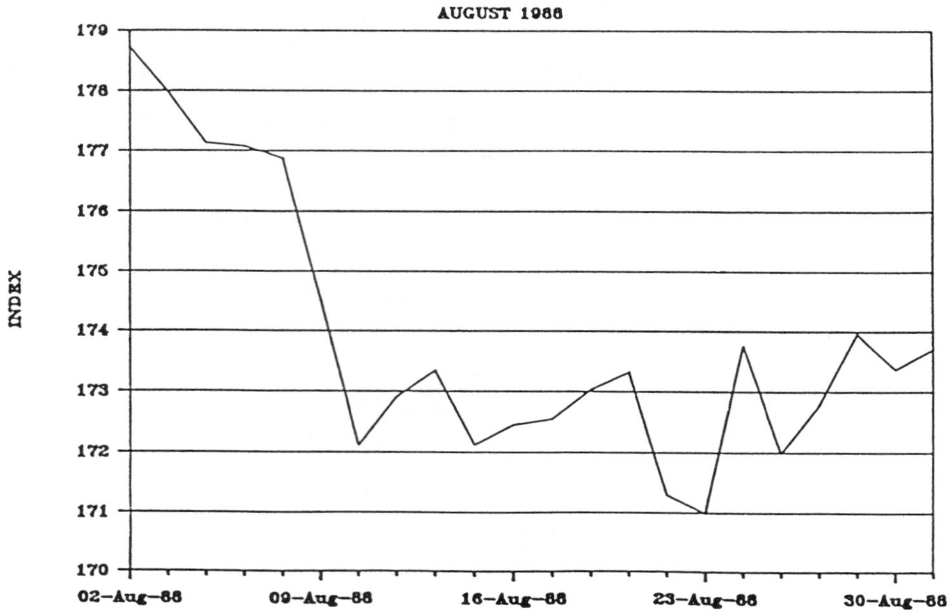

Source: Toronto Futures Exchange.

1987, the index is capitalization-weighted by the Paäsche formula, and its base level was set at 100 as of 1987. Based on market capitalization, Alcan Industries, Bell Canada Enterprises, and the Bank of Montreal currently account for over 15 percent of the index's value.

Since its formation, the index has been the basis for European-style, cash-settled index option contracts that are traded on the TSE under the ticker symbol TXO, while similarly based futures contracts are traded on the Toronto Futures Exchange under the ticker symbol TXF.

Denmark

The Copenhagen Stock Exchange *(Københavns Fondsbørs)* is Denmark's only stock exchange, and the General Share Index *(Københavns Fondsbørs Aktienindeks)* is the only index computed for its listed stocks. It is a broad-based composite index of all the 430+ listed companies, but it excludes foreign companies, unit trusts, and two specific companies: EAC Holding and GN Holding (Exhibit 7.10). The two holding companies, as well as unit trusts, are both excluded as their purpose is the holding of shares of single companies that are already included in the index.

The index is capitalization-weighted according to the Paäsche formula, and its base level was set at 100 as of January 2, 1983. Based on market capitalization, Electrolux "B" free, Skandinaviska Enskilda

**EXHIBIT 7.10   Copenhagen Stock Exchange
General Share Index Components as of October 17,
1988 (Top 10 Ranked by Capitalization)**

1. Superfos
2. Ostasiatiske Kompagni
3. Den Danske Bank
4. H + H Industri
5. Dampshipseelkapet of 1912
6. Novo B
7. Andelsbanken EM
8. Cheminova
9. Top-Denmark
10. Schades Papir nye

Source: Copenhagen Stock Exchange.

FIGURE 7.6   Copenhagen Stock Exchange General Share Index

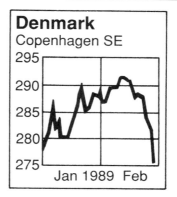

Reprinted by permission of *Financial Times.*

Banken "A" restricted, and Skanska "B" restricted shares account for
approximately 25 percent of the index's value.

Finland

The Helsinki Stock Exchange *(Helsingin Arvopaperipörssi)* is Finland's
only stock exchange. Currently, there are two indexes that reflect the
price activity of the listed stocks on the Exchange—the Unitas Share
Index and the Kansallis-Osake-Pankki Index.

Unitas Share Index

The Unitas Share Index is a broad-based composite index of 69 stocks
covering 125 classes, or series of stock issues, and is subdivided into
four main groups—Industrial, Banks, Trade and Transport, and Insurance (Exhibit 7.11). The index, maintained by Unitas Ltd., a major
Finnish brokerage firm, is capitalization-weighted by the Paäsche for-

EXHIBIT 7.11   Unitas Share Index Components

Sector/Company/Share Series*	Capitalization Weight (%) (12/31/88)
1. Industrial (37/79)	**60.89%**
Kymmene	5.28%
Nokia	3.68
Outokumpu "A"	3.31
Partek	2.99
Rauma-Repola	2.93
Valmet "A"	2.93
United Paper Mills	2.25
Sponsor	2.11
Lohja "A"	2.11
Enzo-Gutszeit "A"	2.00
Amer Group "A"	1.72
Instrumentarium "A"	1.72
Finnish Sugar "I"	1.63
Wärtsilä "I"	1.59
Spontel	1.52
Kajaani	1.44
Huhtamäki "K"	1.35
Asko "A"	1.19
Kymmene, nonrestricted	1.14
Tampella	1.12
Metsä-Serla "A"	1.10
Finkars "K"	0.97
Nokia, preferred	0.90
Enzo-Gutszeit "R"	0.84
Metsä-Serla "B"	0.83
United Paper Mills, preferred	0.77
Kone "B"	0.71
Nokia, nonrestricted	0.63
Kemi	0.58
Rauma-Repola, nonrestricted	0.53
Werner Söderström "A"	0.52
Enzo-Gutszeit "A", nonrestricted	0.45
Amer Group "A," nonrestricted	0.43
Tamfelt	0.43
Wärtsilä "II"	0.43
Lohja "B"	0.42
Nokia, preferred, nonrestricted	0.41
Farmos Group "I"	0.40
Werner Söderström "B"	0.32
Lassila & Tikanoja	0.30
Enzo-Gutszeit "R," nonrestricted	0.29
Huhtamäki "I"	0.27
Wärtsilä "II," nonrestricted	0.25
United Paper Mills, preferred, nonrestricted	0.24
Finkars "K," nonrestricted	0.24
Otava	0.24
Kajanni, nonrestricted	0.22
Kone "B," nonrestricted	0.21
Finkars "A"	0.21
Finvest "A"	0.20
Otava, preferred	0.20
Raision Margariini	0.18
Metsä-Serla "B," nonrestricted	0.18
Tampella, nonrestricted	0.18
Instrumentarium "B," nonrestricted	0.18
Finnish Sugar "II," nonrestricted	0.17
Finnish Sugar "II"	0.14

EXHIBIT 7.11 *(continued)*

Sector/Company/Share Series*	Capitalization Weight (%) (12/31/88)
Asko "B," nonrestricted	0.12%
Instrumentarium "B"	0.12
Huhtamäki "I," nonrestricted	0.11
Finkars "A," nonrestricted	0.10
Volvo "B," nonrestricted	0.10
Virke	0.09
Mancon "B"	0.09
Suomen Trikoo "A"	0.09
Farmos Group "IIA"	0.08
Metsä-Serla "A," nonrestricted	0.08
Partek, nonrestricted	0.08
Tamfelt, preferred	0.08
Wärtsilä "I," nonrestricted	0.07
Itikka "A"	0.06
Finvest "B"	0.05
Tamfelt, preferred, nonrestricted	0.03
Asea "B," nonrestricted	0.03
AGA "B," nonrestricted	0.02
Huhtamäki "K," nonrestricted	0.02
Suomen Trikoo "A," nonrestricted	0.01
Suomen Trikoo "B"	0.00†
Suomen Trikoo "B," nonrestricted	0.00†
2. Banking and finance (7/12)	**18.13%**
Union Bank of Finland "A"	7.92
Kansallis-Osake-Pankki	6.15
Union Bank of Finland "B"	0.81
Union Bank of Finland "C," nonrestricted	0.68
Kansallis-Osake-Pankki, nonrestricted	0.62
Finnish Corporate Finance	0.50
Säastöpankkien Keskus-Osake-Pankki Bank "A"	0.48
Säastöpankkien Keskus-Osake-Pankki-Finance	0.37
Alandsbanken	0.37
Op-Finance Centre "C"	0.17
Säastöpankkien Keskus-Osake-Pankki-Finance, nonrestricted	0.04
Alandsbanken, preferred, nonrestricted	0.02
3. Investment and insurance (16/21)	**10.97%**
Pohjola "A," nonrestricted	3.82
Sampo "A," nonrestricted	3.04
Pohjola "B," nonrestricted	1.44
Jämerä-Kiinteistöt "B"	0.29
SP-Sijoitus "B"	0.27
Suomen Pörssikiinteistöt	0.26
Castrum	0.25
YIT-Kiinteistöt	0.24
Intervanti	0.23
Suomen Kiinteistö	0.20
SYS-Invest "B"	0.18
Citycon	0.15
J. Tallberg Kiinteistöt "B"	0.10
Medical Investment Trust "A"	0.10
Siltasaari-Invest "B"	0.09
STS-Invest "B"	0.08
SP-Sijoitus "B," nonrestricted	0.07
Op-Sijoitus	0.06
Castrum, nonrestricted	0.05
SYS-Invest "C," nonrestricted	0.04
Medical Investment Trust "A," nonrestricted	0.01

EXHIBIT 7.11 *(concluded)*

Sector/Company/Share Series*	Capitalization Weight (%) (12/31/88)	
4. Trade and transport (9/13)	**10.01%**	
Kesko		2.75%
Stockmann "A"		2.03
Rautakirja "A"		1.65
Effoa "K"		1.50
Leipurien Tukku		0.64
TOK		0.45
Ford, nonrestricted		0.39
Effoa "A"		0.19
Stockmann "B," nonrestricted		0.12
Rautakirja "B"		0.10
Stockmann "A," nonrestricted		0.09
Tietotehdas "B"		0.09
Kuusinen "B"		0.01
Total: 69 companies/125 share series		

* All shares are ordinary except for class A/B/C/K/R/I/II/IIA/and preferred shares.
† Less than 0.01%.
Source: UNITAS Ltd.

mula and its base level of 100 refers to 1975. On the basis of market capitalization, the industrial companies account for most of the index's value.

Kansallis-Osake-Pankki Index—KOP

The Kansallis-Osake-Pankki (KOP) Index is a broad-based composite index covering all companies and classes of stock listed on the Helsinki Stock Exchange; it is maintained by Kansallis-Osake-Pankki, a major Finnish national bank. Published since 1977, the KOP index is capital-ization-weighted according to the Paäsche formula and currently uses a base level of 100, set in 1970.

France

There are seven French stock exchanges (bourses): the Paris Bourse *(Bourse de Paris)* and the six regional bourses, located in Bordeaux, Lille, Lyons, Marseilles, Nancy, and Nantes. Of these, the Paris bourse is the largest and accounts for over 95 percent of the total turnover of the French stock exchanges. Currently, there are two indexes that reflect the price activity of the 700+ listed stocks on the Paris bourse: CAC-240 and the CAC-40 Indexes.

FIGURE 7.7   Unitas Share Index

Source: Unitas Ltd.

FIGURE 7.8   Unitas and KOP Indexes

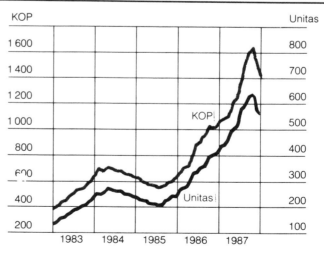

Source: Helsinki Stock Exchange.

The CAC-240 Index

The CAC-240 *(Compagnie des Agents de Change)*[1] Index is the major French stock index. It is a broad-based index composed of the 240 companies having the highest capitalization of those listed on the Paris bourse (Exhibit 7.12). The index is capitalization-weighted according to the Paäsche formula and its base level was set at 100 as of December 31, 1981.

EXHIBIT 7.12   CAC-240 Index Components as of December 30, 1988 (Top 10 Ranked by Capitalization)

1. Elf-Aquitaine
2. Peugeot SA
3. Air Liquide
4. BSN-Gervais Danone
5. Cie. de Saint Gobain
6. Paribas (Cie. Financiere)
7. Louis Vuitton Moet-Hennessy (LVMH)
8. Sté. Général
9. Cie. du Midi
10. Cie. Générale d'Electricité

Source: Société des Bourses Françaises.

FIGURE 7.9   CAC-240 General Index

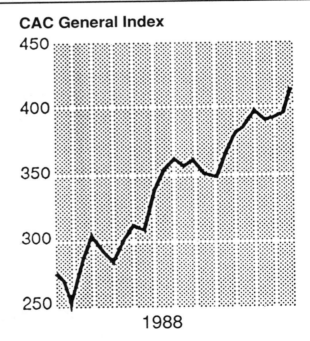

Reprinted by permission of *Financial Times.*

---

[1] *Agents de Change* are member firms of a bourse through which all security transactions must be passed. In effect, they are stockbrokers, acting as the middlemen between buyer and seller. The *Compagnie des Agents de Change* (CAC) is the National Broker's Association.

CAC-40 Index

The CAC-40 Index is a narrow-based index of 40 companies listed on the Paris Bourse that are also traded on the monthly settlement market[2] (Exhibit 7.13). Compiled by the *Société des Bourses Françaises* and managed by its Scientific Advisory Commission, it was developed as a French counterpart to other market indexes like the S&P 100, Major Market Index, and FT-100 which allow for options trading and a man-

EXHIBIT 7.13   CAC-40 Index Components

Company	Capitalization Weight (%) (12/30/88)
1. Elf-Aquitaine	6.02%
2. Peugeot SA	5.73
3. Air Liquide	5.27
4. BSN-Gervais Danone	5.20
5. Cie. de Saint Gobain	4.89
6. Paribas (Cie. Financiere)	4.67
7. Louis Vuitton Moet-Hennessy (LVMH)	4.53
8. Sté. Général	4.35
9. Cie. du Midi	4.33
10. Cie. Générale d'Electricité	4.06
11. Lafarge Coppée	3.96
12. Générale des Eaux	3.95
13. Thompson-CSF	3.62
14. L'Oréal	3.56
15. Michelin "B"	3.25
16. The Carrefour Group	2.94
17. Pernod-Ricard	1.90
18. Sanofi SA	1.89
19. Crédit Foncier de France	1.66
20. Alcatel (Cie. Financiere)	1.59
21. Lyonnaise des Eaux	1.46
22. Havas	1.36
23. Bouygues	1.35
24. Générale Occidentale	1.32
25. Darty et Fils	1.31
26. Legrand	1.31
27. Cie. Bancaire	1.27
28. Saint Louis	1.27
29. Télémécanique Electric	1.22
30. Pechelbronn	1.18
31. Chargeurs SA	1.13
32. Navigation Mixte	1.12
33. CGIP	1.11
34. Economiques du Casino	1.09
35. Accor	1.05
36. Club Méditerranée	0.91
37. Dumez	0.80
38. Arjomari-Prioux	0.77
39. Essilor Internationale	0.81
40. Hachette	0.80

Source: Société des Bourses Françaises.

---

[2] The monthly settlement market, *Règlement Mensuel* (RM), is similar to the U.S. options market.

FIGURE 7.10   CAC-40 and CAC-240 Indexes

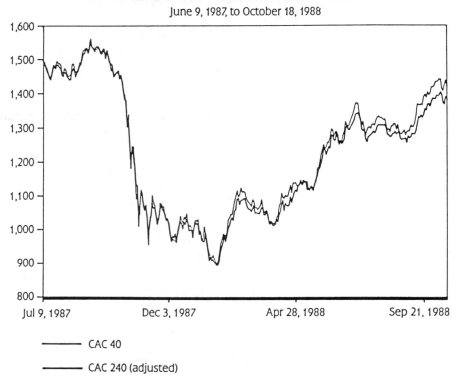

THE CAC 40 VERSUS THE CAC 240
June 9, 1987, to October 18, 1988

——— CAC 40

——— CAC 240 (adjusted)

Source: Société des Bourses Françaises.

ageable number of shares against which arbitrage opportunities could be created. The CAC-40 is capitalization-weighted according to the Paäsche formula and has a base value of 1000 as of December 31, 1987.

Since June 15, 1988, the CAC-40 Index has been the basis for European-style, cash-settled index option contracts that are traded on MONEP (France's Options Market), while similarly based futures contracts are traded on the *Marché à Terme International de France* (MATIF), France's International Futures Market.

Great Britain

Since the early 1700s, the major equity marketplace in Great Britain was London. In 1973, a merger of the regional exchanges located in Belfast, Birmingham, Bristol, Dublin, Glasgow, Leeds, Liverpool, London, Manchester, and Newcastle created a large single marketplace, known as The Exchange. As a result of the merger, the London Stock Exchange has the largest turnover and is now officially known as The

EXHIBIT 7.14 Financial Times 30-Share Index Components as of March 31, 1988

Group/Company	Ticker Symbol
1. Banks, hire, purchase, and leasing (1)	
National Westminster Bank*	NWB
2. Beers, wines, and spirits (2)	
Allied-Lyons*	ALLD
Guinness*	GUIN
3. Building, timber, and roads (1)	
Blue Circle Industries*	BCI
4. Chemicals and plastics (1)	
Imperial Chemical Industries*	ICI
5. Drapery and stores (1)	
Marks & Spencer*	MKS
6. Electricals (5)	
BICC	BICC
British Telecommunications*	BTA
General Electric Corporation-Elliot Automation*	GEC
Plessy*	PLES
Thorn EMI*	THN
7. Engineering (2)	
GKN	GKN
Hawker Siddeley Group*	HSID
8. Food and groceries (3)	
ASDA-MFI Group*	ASSD
Cadbury Schweppes*	CBRY
Tate & Lyle*	TATE
9. Hotels and caterers (2)	
Grand Metropolitan*	GMET
Trusthouse Forte*	TRST
10. Industrials (6)	
BOC Group*	BOC
BTR*	BTR
Beecham Group*	BCHM
The Boots Company*	BOOT
Glaxo Holdings*	GLXO
Hanson Trust*	HNSN
11. Oil and gas (2)	
British Gas*	GASR
British Petroleum*	BP
12. Insurances (1)	
Royal Insurance*	ROYL
13. Motors (1)	
Lucas Industries	LUCS
14. Shipping (1)	
Peninsular & Orient Steam Navigation, defd*	PO
15. Textiles (1)	
Courtaulds*	CTLD

* Also components of the FT-SE 100 Index (26).
Source: *Financial Times.*

International Stock Exchange of the United Kingdom and the Republic of Ireland (ISE).

Currently, the following indexes track the price movements of the 2,500+ stocks listed on the ISE:

Financial Times All-Share Index

Financial Times 30 Index

Financial Times–Stock Exchange 100-Share Index

Financial Times 30 Index

The Financial Times 30 (FT-30) Index is a narrow-based index of 30 leading industrial companies (Exhibit 7.14). Maintained by the *Financial Times,* London's leading daily financial newspaper, the index is a price-weighted geometric average of the prices of the 30 stocks with a base level of 100 as of July 1, 1935. Like the Value Line Index, each stock price therefore has the same weight, regardless of size and value.

Financial Times–Stock Exchange 100-Share Index—FT–SE 100

The Financial Times–Stock Exchange 100-Share Index (FT–SE 100) is affectionately known as the "Footsie." It was developed jointly by the *Financial Times* and The Exchange as a British counterpart to other market indexes like the S&P 100, Major Market Index, and CAC-40, which allow for options trading and a manageable number of shares against which arbitrage opportunities could be created. Since its creation in 1984, it has enjoyed a wider popularity than the older FT-30 Index.

FIGURE 7.11   Financial Times Share Indexes

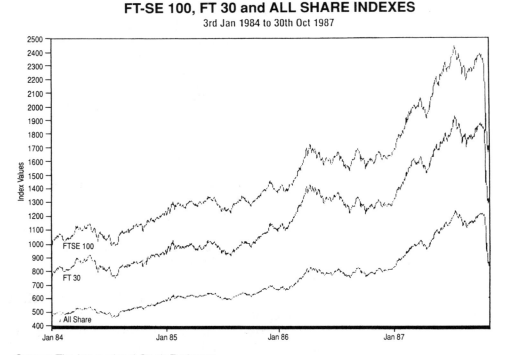

Source: The International Stock Exchange.

The FT–SE 100 is a narrow-based index of the stock prices of the 100 companies listed on the ISE that have the largest capitalization (Exhibit 7.15). Unlike the FT-30, the FT–SE is capitalization-weighted according to the Paäsche formula and has a base index level of 1,000

EXHIBIT 7.15   Financial Times–Stock Exchange 100-Share Index Components as of March 31, 1988 (Ranked by Capitalization)

Rank	Company	Ticker Symbol	Rank	Company	Ticker Symbol
1.	British Petroleum	BP	51.	Dee Corporation	DEE
2.	British Telecommunications	BTA	52.	Rank Organisation	RNK
3.	Shell Transport & Trading	SHEL	53.	Pearson	PSON
4.	Glaxo Holdings	GLXO	54.	Cadbury Schweppes	CBRY
5.	British Gas	GASR	55.	Maxwell Communication	MWC
6.	Imperial Chemical Industries	ICI	56.	Racal Electronics	RCAL
7.	BAT Industries	BATS	57.	Guardian Royal Exchange	GARD
8.	Hanson Trust	HNSN	58.	Whitbread & Company	WHIT
9.	Marks & Spencer	MKS	59.	Commercial Union Assurance	CUAC
10.	National Westminster Bank	NWB	60.	Burton Group	BRTO
11.	BTR	BTR	61.	Associated British Foods	ABF
12.	Grand Metropolitan	GMET	62.	Standard Telephone & Cables	STC
13.	General Electric	GEC	63.	Legal & General Group	LGEN
14.	Wellcome	WCM	64.	BAA	BAA
15.	Unilever	ULVR	65.	British Airways	BAY
16.	Barclays Bank	BARC	66.	Woolworth Holdings	WLTH
17.	Beecham Group	BCHM	67.	Courtaulds	CTLD
18.	J. Sainsbury	SBRY	68.	Coats Viyella	CVY
19.	Cable & Wireless	CW	69.	Smith & Nephew Associated	SN
20.	Prudential Corporation	PRU	70.	Fisons	FISN
21.	Bass	BASS	71.	Reckitt & Colman	RCOL
22.	Allied-Lyons	ALLD	72.	BPB Industries	BPB
23.	RTZ Corporation	RTZ	73.	Plessy	PLES
24.	Great Universal Stores 'A'	GUSA	74.	British & Commonwealth Hldgs	BCH
25.	Land Securities	LAND	75.	Hillsdown Holdings	HLD
26.	Guinness	GUIN	76.	Redland	RDLD
27.	Tesco	TSCO	77.	Blue Circle Industries	BCI
28.	Peninsular & Oriental Steam	PO	78.	Rothmans International 'B'	RINT
29.	Lloyds Bank	LLOY	79.	Ranks Hovis McDougall	RHM
30.	Reed International	REED	80.	Storehouse	SHS
31.	Midland Bank	MID	81.	Rowntree	RWTN
32.	The Boots Company	BOOT	82.	United Biscuits Holdings	UBIS
33.	ASDA-MFI Group	ASSD	83.	Cookson Group	CKSN
34.	Consolidated Gold Fields	CGLD	84.	Royal Bank of Scotland Gr.	RBOS
35.	Royal Insurance	ROYL	85.	Next	NXT
36.	Sears	SEAR	86.	Scottish & Newcastle	SCTN
37.	Trusthouse Forte	TRST	87.	British & Aerospace	BAS
38.	MEPC	MEPC	88.	Enterprise Oil	ETP
39.	BOC Group	BOC	89.	Hammerson Property	HMSN
40.	Argyll Group	AYL	90.	Hawker Siddeley Group	HSID
41.	Sun Alliance & London Insurance	SUN	91.	RMC Group	RMC
42.	Tarmac	TARM	92.	Rolls-Royce	RR
43.	General Accident Fire & Life	GACC	93.	Williams Holdings	WLM
44.	Thorn EMI	THN	94.	Lonrho	LRHO
45.	Ladbroke Group	LADB	95.	Burmah Oil	BMAH
46.	BET	BET	96.	Amstrad Consumer Electronics	ATD
47.	Trafalgar House	TRAF	97.	Granada Group	GAA
48.	Reuters Holdings 'B'	RTR	98.	English China Clays	ECC
49.	Pilkington Brothers	PILK	99.	Blue Arrow	BAW
50.	TSB Group	TSB	100.	Globe Investment Trust	GLOB

Source: *Financial Times*; London International Financial Futures Exchange.

as of January 3, 1984. Currently, 26 of the underlying companies are also included in the FT-30 Index.

For various reasons, some companies with large market values are excluded from the index because of the following criteria:

- The company is regarded for tax purposes as "resident overseas."
- The company is a subsidiary of one already included in the index.
- The company does not intend to pay a dividend.
- The company has one or more very large static shareholdings, the vast majority held by the Secretary of State.

Since January 1984, the FT-SE 100 has been the basis for European-style, cash-settled index option contracts that are traded on the London Traded Options Market (a division of the ISE), while similarly based futures and futures options contracts have been traded on the London International Financial Futures Exchange (LIFFE) since May 3, 1984.

Hong Kong

The forerunners of the present-day stock market in Hong Kong began trading in 1891. In 1986, The Stock Exchange of Hong Kong Ltd. (SEHK) was formed by the unification of the Far East, Kim Ngan, Hong Kong, and Kowloon stock exchanges. Currently there are two indexes that reflect the major price activity of the 320+ listed stocks on the SEHK: the Hong Kong Index and the Hang Seng Index.

The Hong Kong Index

The Hong Kong Index is a narrow-based index of 49 companies that represent approximately 75 percent of the total market capitalization of the SEHK (Exhibit 7.16). Compiled by the SEHK, the index is capitalization-weighted and its base level of 1,000 was set on April 2, 1986.

Stocks are selected for the list on the basis of the following criteria:

- Trading activity—The top 62 stocks are selected, the turnover of which covers 94.993 percent of the total market.
- Market capitalization—The top 79 stocks are selected, the market capitalization of which covers 95.0516 percent of the total market. From these two lists, 49 stocks common to both lists are chosen for the index. Certain stocks in the index are not from the two lists but are sometimes selected on the basis of their performance in their respective industrial sectors.
- Past company financial performance.
- Quotation for not less than two years.

The components of the Hong Kong Index are divided into six subindexes: Finance, Utilities, Properties, Industrials, Hotels, and Consolidated Enterprises.

EXHIBIT 7.16   Hong Kong Index Components

1. **Properties (14)**
   Cheung Kong (Holdings) Ltd.*
   The Great Eagle Co. Ltd.
   Hang Lung Development Co. Ltd.*
   Henderson Land Development Ltd.*
   The Hongkong Land Co. Ltd.*
   Hongkong Realty & Trust Co. Ltd. 'A'*
   Hopewell Holdings Ltd.
   Hsin Chong Holdings (H.K.) Ltd.
   Hysan Development Co. Ltd.*
   New Town (N.T.) Properties Ltd.
   New World Development Co. Ltd.*
   Sino Land Co. Ltd.
   Sun Hung Kai Properties Ltd.*
   Tai Cheung Properties Ltd.*

2. **Consolidated enterprises (10)**
   Cathay Pacific Airways Ltd.*
   Cavendish International Holdings Ltd.*
   Dairy Farm International Holdings Ltd.*
   HK-TVB Ltd.*
   Hutchison Whampoa Ltd.*
   Jardine Matheson Holdings Ltd.*
   Lane Crawford Holdings Ltd. 'A'
   Swire Pacific Ltd. 'A'*
   The Warf (Holdings) Ltd.*
   World International (Holdings) Ltd.*

3. **Industrials (9)**
   Chung Wah Shipbuilding & Engineering Co. Ltd.
   Conic Investment Co. Ltd.
   Green Island Cement (Holdings) Ltd.*
   Hong Kong Aircraft Engineering Co. Ltd.*
   Johnson Electric Industrial Manufactory Ltd.
   Nan Fung Textiles Consolidated Ltd.
   Paul Y. Construction Co. Ltd.
   San Miguel Brewery Ltd.
   Winsor Industrial Corp. Ltd.*

4. **Finance (6)**
   The Bank of East Asia Ltd.*
   Hang Seng Bank Ltd.*
   The Hongkong & Shanghai Banking Corp.*
   Jardine Strategic Holdings Ltd.*
   Sun Hung Kai & Co. Ltd.
   Wing Lung Bank Ltd.

5. **Hotels (5)**
   Harbour Centre Development Ltd.
   The Hongkong & Shanghai Hotels Ltd.*
   Mandarin Oriental International Ltd.*
   Miramar Hotel & Investment Co. Ltd.*
   Regal Hotels (Holdings) Ltd.

6. **Utilities (5)**
   China Light & Power Co. Ltd.*
   Hongkong Electric Holdings Ltd.*
   The Hong Kong & China Gas Co. Ltd.*
   Hong Kong Telecommunications Ltd.*
   The Kowloon Motor Bus Co. (1933) Ltd.*

   Total: 49 companies as of 5/2/88

* Components of the Hang Seng Index (33).
Source: Hong Kong Stock Exchange.

FIGURE 7.12   Hong Kong Index

Hong Kong Index Weekly Chart

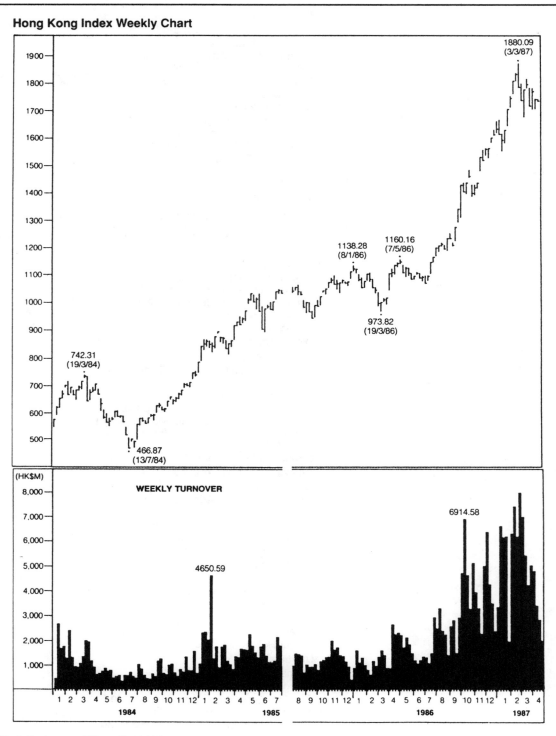

Source: Stock Exchange of Hong Kong Ltd.

FIGURE 7.13   Hong Kong Stock Exchange Sector Indexes

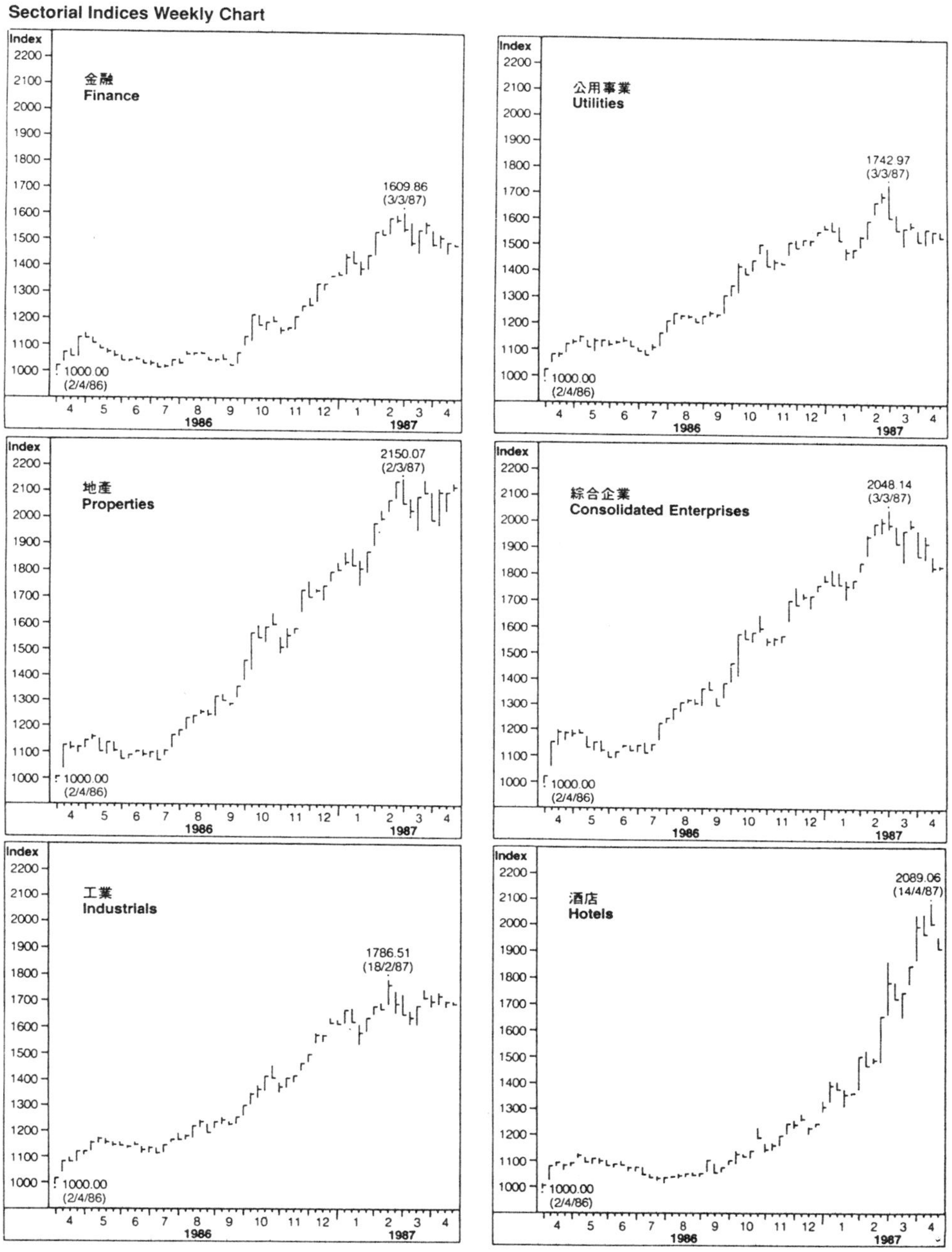

Sectorial Indices Weekly Chart

Source: Stock Exchange of Hong Kong Ltd.

The Hang Seng Index

The Hang Seng Index[3] is a narrow-based index of 33 companies that represent approximately 70 percent of the total market capitalization of the SEHK (Exhibit 7.17). Compiled by HSI Services Ltd., a wholly owned subsidiary of Hang Seng Bank Ltd., and first published in Novem-

---

[3] *Hang Seng* is Chinese for "evergrowing."

EXHIBIT 7.17   Hang Seng Index Components

1. **Commerce and industry (15)**
   Cathay Pacific Airways Ltd.
   Cavendish International Holdings Ltd.
   Dairy Farm International Holdings Ltd.
   Green Island Cement (Holdings) Ltd.
   Hong Kong Aircraft Engineering Co. Ltd.
   The Hongkong & Shanghai Hotels Ltd.
   Hong Kong-TVB Ltd.
   Hutchison Whampoa Ltd.
   Jardine Matheson Holdings Ltd.
   Mandarin Oriental International Ltd.
   Miramar Hotel & Investment Co. Ltd.
   Swire Pacific Ltd. 'A'
   The Warf (Holdings) Ltd.
   Winsor Industrial Corp. Ltd.
   World International (Holdings) Ltd.

2. **Properties (9)**
   Cheung Kong (Holdings) Ltd.
   Hang Lung Development Co. Ltd.
   Henderson Land Development Ltd.
   The Hongkong Land Co. Ltd.
   Hongkong Realty & Trust Co. Ltd. 'A'
   Hysan Development Co. ltd.
   New World Development Co. Ltd.
   Sun Hung Kai Properties Ltd.
   Tai Cheung Properties Ltd.

3. **Utilities (5)**
   China Light & Power Co. Ltd.
   Hongkong Electric Holdings Ltd.
   The Hong Kong & China Gas Co. Ltd.
   Hong Kong Telecommunications Ltd.
   The Kowloon Motor Bus Co. (1933) Ltd.

4. **Finance (4)**
   The Bank of East Asia Ltd.
   Hang Seng Bank Ltd.
   The Hongkong & Shanghai Banking Corp.
   Jardine Strategic Holdings Ltd.

   Total: 33 companies as of 2/2/88

Source: Stock Exchange of Hong Kong Ltd.

ber 1969, the Hang Seng Index is the most widely used indicator of the Hong Kong Stock market. It is capitalization-weighted and its base level of 100 was set on July 31, 1964. All 33 stocks are also components of the Hong Kong Index.

Hong Kong Telecommunications, created in a merger on January 22, 1988, between Hong Kong Telephone and the local operations of Cable and Wireless, constitutes approximately 19 percent of the index's capitalization; Hongkong & Shanghai Banking Corporation is second at 9 percent. Prior to this merger, The Hongkong & Shanghai Banking Corporation was the leader, with 11 percent of the index's capitalization.

Stocks are selected for the index according to the following criteria:

- The issuing company must be incorporated in Hong Kong or use Hong Kong as its principal base.

FIGURE 7.14   Hang Seng Index

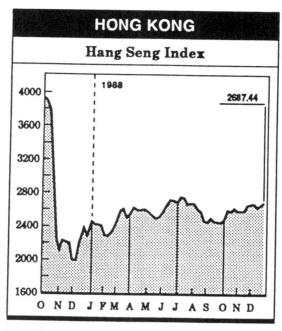

- The stock must maintain a minimum average monthly market value for a specified period, usually the latest 12 months.
- The stock must satisfy a minimum average monthly turnover value for a specified period, usually the latest 24 months.
- Past company financial performance.
- Earning records and growth prospects of the company.
- Management qualities of the company.

The components of the Hang Seng Index are divided into four subindexes: Commerce and Industry, Finance, Utilities, and Properties. To facilitate the introduction of these four subindexes, the base level for the Hang Seng Index was changed to 975.47 on January 13, 1984. The index is the basis for cash-settled index futures contracts traded on the Hong Kong Futures Exchange.

Italy

Italy currently has 10 stock exchanges *(Borsa Valori),* located in Bologna, Florence, Genoa, Milan, Naples, Palermo, Rome, Trieste, Turin, and Venice. Of these, the Milan Stock Exchange *(Borsa Valori di Milano)*—which was founded in 1801 by a decree of Viceroy Eugene Napoleon and modeled after the Paris Stock Exchange—is the principal market, with approximately 90 percent of total trading volume. The two major stock indexes, reflecting the activity of over 320 stocks, listed on the Milan Stock Exchange, are the MIB General Index and the Banca Commerciale Italiana All-Share Index.

MIB General Index

The MIB *(indice Borsa Valori di Milano)* General Index is a broad-based index of all stocks listed on the Milan Stock Exchange (Exhibit 7.18). It is a weighted arithmetic average, based on elementary price indexes calculated by using the following formula:

$$I_{\text{MIB}} = \frac{\sum C_{0i}\dfrac{P_{ti}}{P_{0i}}}{\sum C_{0i}} \times 1000 \qquad (7.1)$$

where

C_{0i} = Market capitalization at base period
P_{0i} = Average price of the ith stock at the base period
P_{ti} = Average price of the ith stock at the current period.

Its base level has been 1,000 since January 1, 1985.

Banca Commerciale Italiana All-Share Index

The Banca Commerciale Italiana All-Share Index (BCI) is a broad-based index of the stock prices of all the approximately 320 companies listed on the Milan Stock Exchange (Exhibit 7.19). Maintained and computed by Banca Commerciale Italiana, one of Italy's major banks,

**EXHIBIT 7.18   MIB Index Components
(Top 20 Ranked by Capitalization)**

Company	Approximate Weight (%) (1/4/88)
1. Stet, ordinary shares	1.79%
2. SIP, ordinary shares	1.56
3. Montedison	1.50
4. Fiat	1.00
5. SIP, savings shares	0.85
6. Stet, savings shares	0.82
7. Banca Commerciale Italiana	0.60
8. Silos Genova	0.54
9. Banco di Roma	0.50
10. Credit Italiano	0.47
11. Autostrade PTC, preferred shares	0.42
12. Italgas	0.35
13. Ferruzzi Agricola Financiaria	0.34
14. Snia BPD	0.33
15. Olivetti	0.32
16. Assicurazioni Generali	0.30
17. Pirelli SPA	0.28
18. Nuovo Banco Ambrosiano	0.28
19. Sabaudia	0.25
20. Immobliare matanopoli	0.25
Total: 308 companies	12.79%

Source: Milan Stock Exchange.

FIGURE 7.15   MIB Index

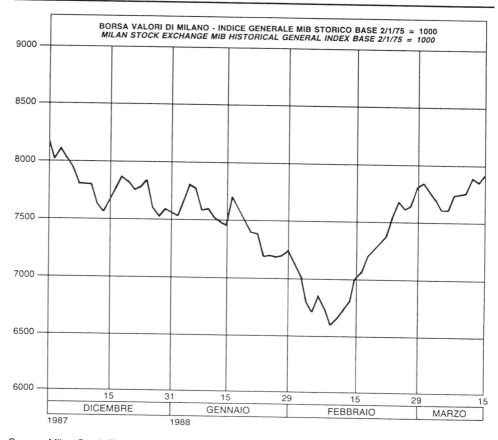

BORSA VALORI DI MILANO - INDICE GENERALE MIB STORICO BASE 2/1/75 = 1000
MILAN STOCK EXCHANGE MIB HISTORICAL GENERAL INDEX BASE 2/1/75 = 1000

Source: Milan Stock Exchange.

the BCI is capitalization-weighted by the Paäsche formula, and its base level of 100 was set on December 31, 1972. Besides the composite all-share index, Banca Commerciale Italiana calculates seven sectorial indexes—Banking, Financial, Insurance, Communications, Property, Industrial, and Miscellaneous—in a similar manner.

EXHIBIT 7.19   Banca Commerciale Italiana All-Share Index Components

Industry Sector	Approximate Capitalization Weight (%) (6/30/88)
1. Industrial (157)	36.98%
2. Insurance (25)	28.06
3. Finance (51)	11.37
4. Banks (29)	10.13
5. Communications (15)	9.68
6. Property (7)	0.62
7. Other (30)	3.16
Total: 314 companies	

Source: Banca Commerciale Italiana.

FIGURE 7.16   Banca Commerciale Italiana Index

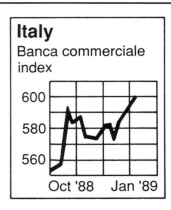

Reprinted by permission of *Financial Times*.

Japan

The first Japanese stock exchanges were established as profit-making corporations on May 15, 1878, in both Tokyo (Tokyo Stock Exchange Company, Ltd.) and Osaka (Osaka Stock Exchange).[4] These exchanges served as marketplaces for the trading of public bonds that were issued to the deposed feudal lords and samurai. Within three years, over 130 such stock exchanges had opened throughout Japan.

On June 30, 1943, as an emergency measure to control the wartime economy, Japan's then-existing 11 stock exchanges were consolidated into one semigovernmental company, the Japan Securities Exchange. However, its operation was suspended in August 1945 following Japan's defeat in World War II, and it was finally dissolved on April 16, 1947.

In 1948, a new Securities and Exchange Law (*Shoken Torihiki Ho*) was enacted, which allowed the reestablishment, on April 1, 1949, of those exchanges located in Tokyo, Osaka, and Nagoya as nonprofit companies. Later that year, six additional regional exchanges were established in Fukuoka, Hiroshima, Kobe, Kyoto, Niigata, and Sapporo. The Kobe Stock Exchange was merged with the Osaka Securities Exchange on October 31, 1967, giving the current eight exchanges. Of these, the Tokyo Stock Exchange (TSE) is by far Japan's largest and accounts for over 85 percent of the trading volume, with the Osaka Securities Exchange (OSE) in second place. Based on capitalization, the TSE has replaced the New York Stock Exchange as the world's largest stock marketplace.

The following indexes are used to measure activity of Japanese stock markets:

Tokyo Price Indexes (TOPIX)
    First Section Composite Index

---

[4] In Japan, stock exchanges are technically referred to as "security exchanges."

Second Section Composite Index
Large, Medium, and Small Company Indexes

Nikkei Stock Averages
Nikkei-225 Stock Average
Nikkei-500 Stock Average

Osaka Securities Exchange
OSE First Section Adjusted Stock Price Average
OSE Second Section Adjusted Stock Price Average
OSE-300 Common Stock Index
OSF50 Average

Tokyo Price Indexes—TOPIX

Prior to July 1, 1969, the TSE computed its stock price barometer in the same manner as the Dow Jones Industrial Average. On this date, the TSE stopped using this method as unrepresentative of the market and began computing a new index, the Tokyo Price Index, or TOPIX, as it is commonly called.

Listed stocks on the TSE are classified either as being First Section *(ichibu)*, Second Section *(nibu)*, or Foreign Section. All foreign listed stocks are assigned to the Foreign Section and are not part of TOPIX. On the other hand, domestic Japanese stocks are assigned to either the First or Second Section. Other than new-issue stocks, which are first assigned to the Second Section, the top-rated and most actively traded First Section listed stocks must meet the following major criteria:

- Number of shares: 20+ million shares
- Dividends: ¥5 or more in cash per share for each of the last three years, and the ability to maintain dividends of ¥5 or more in cash per share after listing
- Trading volume: For the last six months, the average monthly trading volume on the TSE must be 200,000+ shares.

TOPIX is a broad-based composite index that includes all those 1,100+ domestic stocks listed in the First Section of the TSE (Exhibit 7.20) and is Japan's second major stock price measure after the Nikkei Stock Average. It is capitalization-weighted by the Paäsche formula and has a base index level of 100 as of January 4, 1968, which is the same as for the Nikkei-225 Stock Average. From time to time, as with any index, adjustments to the base market value must be made for any one of the following eight situations:

- Transfer of company between the First Section and the Second Section
- Delisting
- Rights offering
- Public offering
- Private placement
- Merger
- Exercise of stock subscription warrant
- Conversion of convertible bond or preferred stock into common stock

EXHIBIT 7.20   Tokyo Price Index (TOPIX) Components (Top 20 Ranked by Capitalization)

	Company	Approximate Weight (%) (1/1/87)
1.	Tokyo Electric Power	3.63%
2.	Toyota Motor	2.05
3.	Sumitomo Bank	1.97
4.	Nomura Securities	1.89
5.	Industrial Bank of Japan	1.79
6.	Dai-Ichi Kangyo Bank	1.64
7.	Fuji Bank	1.51
8.	Mitsubishi Bank	1.51
9.	Matsushita Electric Industrial	1.30
10.	Kansai Electric Power	1.27
11.	Sanwa Bank	1.22
12.	Hitachi	1.09
13.	Tokyo Gas	1.07
14.	Mitsubishi Estate	1.06
15.	Nippon Electric Corporation	1.01
16.	Chibu Electric Power	0.97
17.	Sumitomo Trust & Banking	0.94
18.	Mitsubishi Trust & Banking	0.94
19.	Tokio Marine & Fire Insurance	0.86
20.	Long-Term Credit Bank of Japan	0.76
	Total	28.48%

Note: List does not include Nippon Telegraph & Telephone (NTT), the world's largest capitalized company, whose shares were being auctioned over a three-year period.
Source: Tokyo Stock Exchange.

The composite index is supplemented by subindexes of 28 industry sectors as well as subindexes for large, medium, and small companies, defined as follows:

Large—Companies with 200+ million shares

Medium—Companies with 60–200 million shares

Small—Companies with less than 60 million shares

The TSE also computes a Second Section Price Index, which is a composite broad-based index of all the 425+ stocks traded on the Second Section of the TSE. Like the First Section TOPIX, it is capitalization-weighted according to the Paäsche formula and was assigned a base level of 100 as of January 4, 1968.

The composite First Section TOPIX is the basis for cash-settled index futures contracts traded on the Tokyo Stock Exchange.

Nikkei Stock Averages

With the emergence of Japan's major stock markets, the Nikkei Stock Average has become the second-most quoted world stock measure after the Dow Jones Industrial Average. From May 16, 1949, until July 1, 1969, the Nikkei Stock Average was called the "Nikkei-Dow Jones Average" and was maintained by the TSE. After this period, the TSE dropped that name in favor of TOPIX because it considered the Nikkei Dow to be unrepresentative of the market. In 1975, *Nihon Keizai Shimbun Inc.,*[5] which publishes a daily financial newspaper of the same name, acquired the right to calculate and publish the old Nikkei-Dow Jones Average. In 1985, the average was renamed the Nikkei Stock Average.

The Nikkei Stock Average is composed of the stocks of 225 companies listed in the First Section of the TSE (Exhibit 7.21). These stocks are highly liquid and account for approximately 60 percent of the total market value of the 1,100+ issues listed in the First Section. There are notable inclusions and omissions, however. For example, Nippon Telephone and Telegraph (NTT) is part of the Nikkei Stock Average and is the world's biggest stock in terms of capitalization. Once wholly owned by the Minister of Finance, the company went public[6] in 1986 when the government began selling approximately 2 million shares over a period of three years. At its peak, NTT's share price reached almost ¥3.2 million, and its capitalization (approximately 10 percent of the TSE) was estimated to exceed the combined total capitalization of both the German and Hong Kong stock markets. On the other hand, well-known companies like Victor Corporation of Japan (JVC), Daiwa Bank, and Sanwa Bank are conspicuously absent from the list.

Like the Dow Jones Industrial Average, the Nikkei Stock Average is a price-weighted average, but of 225 stocks. When the Nikkei Stock Average was first published on May 16, 1949, the average price was ¥176.21 with an original divisor of 225. Also like the Dow, the Nikkei's divisor is adjusted either when the composition of the 225 underlying companies is changed, or when any company has exercised its rights for stock splits or gratis issues (ex-rights).

When a right is exercised, the new divisor is calculated from the following formula:

$$D_{\text{new}} = \frac{TP_{\text{old}} - W}{TP_{\text{cum}}} \times D_{\text{old}} \qquad (7.2)$$

where

D_{new} = New divisor
D_{old} = Old divisor
TP_{old} = Total price of the 225 shares prior to ex-rights.
TP_{cum} = Total price of the 225 shares on closing day of cum rights
W = Value of rights

Since September 3, 1986, the Nikkei Stock Average has been the basis for European-style, cash-settled index futures contracts traded on the Singapore International Monetary Exchange (SIMEX) as well as the Chicago Mercantile Exchange under the commodity code NK.

Besides the Nikkei Stock Average of 225 stocks, the *Nihon Keizai Shimbun* also calculates and publishes the Nikkei-500 Average. This is an average price of 500 stocks listed on the First Section of the TSE, calculated in a manner similar to that used for the more famous 225-stock average.

---

[5] Translated from Japanese as "Japan Economic Journal."
[6] Although NTT's shares are traded on the Tokyo Stock Exchange, foreign investors are currently prohibited from owning them.

EXHIBIT 7.21   Nikkei 225 Index Components as of January 1, 1989

1. **Fisheries (3)**
   Kyokuyo   Nippon Suisan
   Nichiro Gyogyo
2. **Mining (3)**
   Mitsui Mining   Teikoku Oil
   Sumitomo Coal Mining
3. **Construction (10)**
   Daiwa House Industry   Shimizu
   Fujita   Taisei
   Kajima Corporation   Tekken
   Ohbayashi   Toa
   Sato Kogyo   Toboshima
4. **Foods (18)**
   Anjinomoto   Nichirei
   Asahi Breweries   Nippon Beet Sugar
   Godo Shusei   Nippon Flour Mills
   Hohnen Oil   Nisshin Flour Milling
   Kikkoman   The Nisshin Oil Mills
   Kirin Brewery   Sanraku
   Meiji Milk Products   Sapporo Breweries
   Meiji Seika   Taito
   Morianga   Takara Shuzo
5. **Textiles (16)**
   Asahi Chemical Industry   Nisshinbo Industries
   Daito Woolen Spinning & Weaving   Nitto Boseki
   Fuji Spinning   Teijin
   Japan Wool Textile   Teikoku Sen-i
   Kanebo   Toho Rayon
   Katakura Industries   Toray Industries
   Kuraray   Toyobo
   Mitsubishi Rayon   Unitika
6. **Pulp and paper (6)**
   Hokuetsu Paper Mills   Mitsubishi Paper
   Honsu Paper   Oji Paper
   Jujo Paper   Sanyo-Kokusaku Pulp
7. **Chemicals (21)**
   Asahi Denka Kogyo   Nippon Oil & Fats
   Denki Kagaku Kogyo   Nippon Soda
   Fuji Photo Film   Nissan Chemical Industrial
   Japan Synthetic Chemical Industry   Rasa Industries
   Konica   Shin-Etsu Chemical
   Kyowa Hakko Kogyo   Showa Denko
   Mitsubishi Chemical Industry   Sumitomo Chemical
   Mitsui Toatsu Chemicals   Toagosei Chemical Industry
   Nippon Carbide Industries   Tosoh Corporation
   Nippon Chemical Industrial   Ube Industries
   Nippon Kyaku
8. **Pharmaceuticals (4)**
   Dai Nippon Pharmaceutical   Takeda Chemical Industries
   Sankyo   Yamanouchi Pharmaceutical
9. **Oil products (4)**
   Mitsubishi Oil   Showa Shell Sekiyu
   Nippon Oil   Toa Nenryo Kogyo
10. **Rubber products (2)**
    Bridgestone   Yokohama Rubber
11. **Glass and ceramics (12)**
    Asahi Glass   Noritake
    Mitsubishi Mining & Cement   Onoda Cement
    NGK Insulators   Shinagawa Refractories
    Nihon Cement   Sumitomo Cement
    Nippon Carbon   Tokai Carbon
    Nippon Sheet Glass   Toto

EXHIBIT 7.21 *(continued)*

12. **Iron and steel (11)**

The Japan Steel Works	Nippon Metal Industry
Kawasaki Steel Corporation	Nippon Stainless Steel
Kobe Steel	Nippon Steel Corporation
Mitsubishi Steel Manufacturing	Nippon Yankin Kogyo
Nippon Denko	Sumitomo Metal Industries
Nippon Kokan	

13. **Nonferrous metals (15)**

Dowa Mining	Shimura Kako
Fujikura	Showa Electric Wire & Cable
Furukawa	Sumitomo Electric Industries
Furukawa Electric	Sumitomo Metal Mining
Mitsubishi Metal Corporation	Toho Zinc
Mitsui Mining & Smelting	Tokyo Rope Manufacturing
Nippon Light Metal	Toyo Seikan
Nippon Mining	

14. **Machinery (11)**

Chiyoda	Niigata Engineering
Ebara	Nippon Piston Ring
Komatsu	Nippon Seiko
Koyo Seiko	NTN Toyo Bearing
Kubota	Okuma Machinery Works
Nachi-Fujikoshi	

15. **Electric machinery (15)**

Fuji Electric	Oki Electric Industry
Fujitsu	Sanyo Electric
Hitachi	Sharp Corporation
Matsushita Electrical Industrial	Sony
Meidensha	Toshiba
Mitsubishi Electric	Yokogawa Electric
Nippon Electric Corporation	Yusasa Battery
Nippondenso	

16. **Shipbuilding (4)**

Hitachi Zosen	Mitsubishi Heavy Industries
Ishikawajima-Harima Heavy Industries	Mitsui Engineering & Shipbuilding

17. **Automobiles (7)**

Hino Motors	Nissan Motor
Honda Motor	Suzuki Motor
Isuzu Motors	Toyota Motor
Mazda Motor	

18. **Transport equipment (1)**

Nippon Sharyo

19. **Precision instruments (4)**

Canon	Nikon
Citizen Watch	Ricoh

20. **Trading companies (6)**

C. Itoh	Mitsubishi
Iwantani International	Mitsui
Marubeni	Somitumo

21. **Retail (5)**

Maruzen	Takashimaya
Matsuzakaya	Tokyu Department Store
Mitsukoshi	

22. **Banking (8)**

Bank of Tokyo	Mitsubishi Trust & Banking
Dai-Ichi Kangyo Bank	Mitsui Bank
Fuji Bank	Mitsui Trust & Banking
Mitsubishi Bank	Sumitomo Bank

23. **Other financial institutions (2)**

Japan Securities Finance	Nippon Shinpan

24. **Insurance (2)**

Nikko Securities	Nomura Securities

EXHIBIT 7.21 *(concluded)*

25. **Nonlife insurance (3)**
    Taisho Marine & Fire Insurance   Yasuda Fire & Marine Insurance
    Tokio Marine & Fire Insurance
26. **Real estate (3)**
    Heiwa Real Estate   Mitsui Real Estate
    Mitsubishi Estate
27. **Rail and bus companies (6)**
    Keio Electric Railway   Odakyu Electric
    Keihin Electric Express Railway   Tobu Railway
    Keisei Electric Railway   Tokyu
28. **Land transportation (1)**
    Nippon Express
29. **Marine transportation (6)**
    Japan Line   Nippon Yusen
    Kawasaki Kisen   Showa Line
    Mitsui O.S.K. Lines   Yamashita-Shinnihon Steamship
30. **Air transportation (1)**
    All Nippon Airways (1)
31. **Warehousing (2)**
    Mitsubishi Warehouse & Transportation   Mitsui Warehouse
32. **Communication (1)**
    Nippon Telegraph & Telephone
33. **Electric power (2)**
    Kansai Electric Power   Tokyo Electric Power
34. **Gas (2)**
    Osaka Gas   Tokyo Gas
35. **Services (5)**
    Korakuen   Toei
    Nikkatsu   Toho
    Shochiku
36. **Other products (3)**
    Dai Nippon Printing   Yamaha
    Toppan Printing

Source: Osaka Securities Exchange.

Osaka Securities Exchange Indexes

The Osaka Securities Exchange (OSE) publishes several stock-price indicators. The OSE Adjusted Price Averages are computed for both the First and Second Sections. The 250 Osaka Stock Exchange Average, often referred to as the Osaka Dow-Jones Average among Japanese investors, is based on 250 of the over 800 listed stocks on the OSE's First Section and has been maintained on a closing-price basis since the opening of the Exchange on May 16, 1949 (Exhibit 7.22). It is a price-weighted average that is calculated in the same manner as the Nikkei and Dow Jones Averages.

The OSE Second Section Adjusted Price Average is a price-weighted arithmetic average based on 40 of the 270+ listed stocks. It has been published daily since Second Section trading began, on October 2, 1961. For either average, adjustment of the divisor as a response to nonmarket factors, such as ex-rights, is accomplished in the same manner as for the Nikkei Stock Average (Equation 7.2), but no adjustment in the divisor is made for dividends paid.

FIGURE 7.17   Nikkei Stock Average

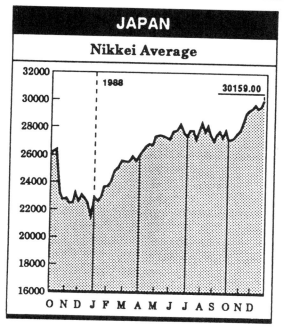

Like all arithmetic averages, both the First and Second Section Averages have shortcomings. In order to provide a more comprehensive measure of the Osaka market, the OSE on August 1, 1969, introduced the OSE-300 Common Stock Index. It is a broad-based index based on 300 First Section listed stocks, and it represents approximately 60 percent of the total capitalization. The OSE-300 is capitalization-weighted by the Paäsche formula and has a base index level of 100 as of January 4, 1968.

The Osaka Securities Futures 50 Average (OSF50) is a narrow-based average based on 50 stocks traded on the OSE that have a parallel link with the Nikkei Stock Average (i.e., the price movements of a basket of 50 stocks will closely resemble that of 225 stocks (Exhibit 7.23). Of its 50 components, 46 are included in the Nikkei Stock Average and 43 in the 250 OSE Average. Unlike most price-weighted arithmetic averages, the OSF50 is the average capitalization of the 50 issuing companies, calculated by the following formula:

$$\text{OSF50 Average} = \frac{\dfrac{\text{Total current capitalization}}{1,000}}{50} \tag{7.3}$$

The 1,000 in the above formula is a scaling factor that accounts for the fact that Japanese stocks are traded in 1,000-share units. Since June 9, 1987, the OSF50 has been the basis for cash-settled index futures contracts traded on the OSE.

EXHIBIT 7.22 Osaka Securities Exchange 250 Adjusted Stock Price Average Components as of January 1, 1989

1. **Fisheries (3)**
   Nichiro Gyogyo
   Nippon Suisan
   Sumitomo Forestry

2. **Mining (2)**
   Mitsui Mining
   Teikoku Oil

3. **Construction (14)**
   Asanuma Gumi
   Chugai Ro
   Daisue Construction
   Daiwa House Industry
   Fudo Construction
   Fujita
   Kinki Electrical Construction
   Ohbayashi
   Okumura
   Penta-Ocean Construction
   Sato Kogyo
   Taisei
   Toyo Construction
   Zenitaka

4. **Foods (10)**
   Anjinomoto
   Asahi Breweries
   Ezaki Gurico
   Fuji Oil
   Itoham Foods
   Kirin Brewery
   Marudai Food
   Nichirei
   Nisshin Food Products
   Takara Shuzo

5. **Textiles (19)**
   Asahi Chemical Industry
   Daiwabo
   Fukusuke
   Gunze
   Japan Wool Textile
   Kanebo
   Kobe Kitto
   Kurabo Industries
   Kuraray
   Nitto Boseki
   Omikenshi
   Sakai Textile
   Shikibo
   Teijin
   Teikoku Sangyo
   Toa Wool Spinning & Weaving
   Toray Industries
   Toyobo
   Unitika

6. **Pulp and paper (6)**
   Jujo Paper
   Kanzaki Paper Manufacturing
   Kishu Paper
   Oji Paper
   Sanyo-Kokusaku Pulp
   Rango

7. **Chemicals and pharmaceuticals (41)**
   Central Glass
   Daicel Chemical Industries
   Daido Sanso
   Dai-ichi Kogyo Seiyaku
   Dainippon Pharmaceutical
   Dai Nippon Toryo
   Fuji Photo Film
   Fujisawa Pharmaceutical
   The Green Cross
   Ishihara Sangyo Kaisha
   Kanegafuchi Chemical Industry
   Kansai Paint
   Konica
   Kyowa Hakko Kogyo
   Mitsubishi Chemical Industry
   Mitsui Toatsu Chemicals
   Nippon Kyaku
   Nippon Oil & Fats
   Nippon Paint
   Nippon Shinyaku Kagaku Kogyo
   Nippon Shokubai
   Nippon Soda
   Nissan Chemical Industries
   Okura Industrial
   Ono Pharmaceutical
   Osaka Sanso
   Osaka Soda
   Rasa Industries
   Rohto Pharmaceutical
   Sakai Chemical Industry
   Seikisui Chemical
   Shin-Etsu Chemical
   Shionogi
   Showa Denko
   Sumitomo Chemical
   Sunstar
   Takeda Chemical Industries
   Tanabe Seiyaku
   Tokuyama Soda
   Tosoh Corporation
   Ube Industries

8. **Oil products (3)**
   Cosmo Oil
   Nippon Oil
   Showa Shell Sekiyu

9. **Rubber products (2)**
   Mitsuboshi
   Toyo Tire & Rubber

EXHIBIT 7.22 *(continued)*

10. **Glass and ceramics (7)**
    Asahi Glass
    Danto
    Nihon Cement
    Nippon Sheet Glass
    Onoda Cement
    Osaka Cement
    Sumitomo Cement

11. **Iron and steel (13)**
    Godo Steel
    The Japan Steel Works
    Kawasaki Steel Corporation
    Kobe Cast Iron
    Kobe Steel
    Kurimoto
    Nippon Kokan
    Nippon Steel Corporation
    Nippon Yankin Kogyo
    Nisshin Steel
    Sumitomo Metal Industries
    Yamato Kogyo
    Yodogawa Steel

12. **Nonferrous and metal products (11)**
    Dowa Mining
    Furukawa Electric
    Matsuo Bridge
    Mitsubishi Metal Corporation
    Mitsui Mining & Smelting
    Nippon Light Metal
    Nippon Mining
    Showa Aluminum
    Sumitomo Electric Industries
    Sumitomo Metal Mining
    Toho Zinc

13. **Machinery (22)**
    Chiyoda
    Daikin Industries
    Daido Kogyo
    Daifuku
    Iseki
    Koyo Seiko
    Komatsu
    Kubota
    Morita Fire Pump Manufacturing
    Nachi-Fujikoshi
    Niigata Engineering
    Nikko
    NTN Toyo Bearing
    O-M
    Osaka Kiko
    Sumitomo Heavy Industries
    Takuma
    Teijin Seiki
    Toyo Umpanki
    Tsubakimoto Chain
    Tsudakoma
    Tsugami

14. **Electric machinery (24)**
    Daihen
    Fujitsu
    Hitachi
    Hoshiden Electronics
    Japan Storage Battery
    Matsushita Electric Works
    Matsushita Electrical Industrial
    Matsushita-Kotobuki Electronics
    Matsushita Refrigeration
    Meidensha
    Mitsubishi Electric
    Nichicon
    Nippon Electric Corporation
    Nippon Electric Industry
    Nissin Electric
    Nitto Electric Industrial
    Oki Electric Industry
    Omron Tateishi Electronics
    Sanyo Electric
    Sharp Corporation
    Shinko Electric
    Toshiba
    Yuasa Battery
    Yasukawa Electric Manufacturing

15. **Transport equipment (15)**
    Daihatsu Motor
    Hitachi Zosen
    Honda Motor
    Ishikawajima-Harima Heavy Industries
    Isuzu Motors
    Kawasaki Heavy Industries
    Mazda Motor
    Mitsubishi Heavy Industries
    Mitsui Engineering & Shipbuilding
    Namura Shipbuilding
    Nippon Yusoki
    Nissan Motor
    Shin Meiwa Industry
    Suzuki Motor
    Toyota Motor

16. **Precision instruments (5)**
    Canon
    Minoruta
    Nikon
    Ricoh
    Shimadzu

17. **Trading companies (14)**
    Chori
    C. Itoh
    Daimaru
    Mitsui
    Nichimen
    Nissho Iwai

EXHIBIT 7.22 *(concluded)*

Hankyu Department Stores
Iwantani International
Marubeni
Mitsubishi

Shinsho
Sogo
Somitumo
Takashimaya

18. **Banking and nonlife insurance (9)**
Daiwa Bank
Dowa Fire & Marine Insurance
Hyogo Sego Bank
Sanwa Bank
Sumitomo Bank

Sumitomo Trust & Banking
Taiyo Kobe Bank
Tokio Marine & Fire Insurance
Yasuda Fire & Marine Insurance

19. **Real estate (3)**
Heiwa Real Estate
Keihanshin Real Estate

Mitsubishi Estate

20. **Land transportation (6)**
Hankyu
Hanshin Electric Railway
Keihin Electric Express Railway

Kinki Nippon Railway
Nankai Electric Railway
Nippon Express

21. **Marine transportation (6)**
Japan Line
Kansai Kisen Kaisha
Kawasaki Kisen

Mitsui O.S.K. Lines
Nippon Yusen
Yamashita-Shinnihon Steamship

22. **Air transportation (1)**
All Nippon Airways

23. **Warehousing (2)**
Kamigumi

Sumitomo Warehouse

24. **Electric power and gas (3)**
Chugoku Electric Power
Kansai Electric Power

Osaka Gas

25. **Services (4)**
Nippon Dream Kanko
Shochiku

Toei
Yoshimoto Kogyo

26. **Other products (5)**
Daiken Trade & Industry
Nintendo
Takara Standard

Toppan Printing
Toyo Linoleum

Source: Osaka Securities Exchange.

**EXHIBIT 7.23 Osaka
Securities Futures 50
Average Components
as of January 1, 1989**

1. **Construction (2)**
Daiwa House Industry
Kajima Corporation

2. **Foods (3)**
Anjinomoto
Kirin Brewery
Meiji Seika

3. **Textiles (4)**
Asahi Chemical Industry
Teijin
Toray Industries
Toyobo

EXHIBIT 7.23 *(concluded)*

4. **Pulp and paper (1)**
   Oji Paper
5. **Chemicals (8)**
   Denki Kagaku Kogyo
   Fuji Photo Film
   Kanegafuchi Chemical Industry
   Kyowa Hakko Kogyo
   Mitsubishi Chemical Industry
   Sumitomo Chemical
   Takeda Chemical Industries
   Tosoh Corporation
6. **Oil and coal (1)**
   Nippon Oil
7. **Glass and ceramics (3)**
   Mitsubishi Mining & Cement
   Nippon Sheet Glass
   Onoda Cement
8. **Iron and steel (3)**
   Kawasaki Steel Corporation
   Nippon Steel Corporation
   Sumitomo Metal Industries
9. **Nonferrous metals (3)**
   Mitsubishi Metal Corporation
   Nippon Mining
   Sumitomo Electric Industries
10. **Machinery (2)**
    Komatsu
    Nippon Seiko
11. **Electric machinery (3)**
    Hitachi
    Matsushita Electrical Industrial
    Sharp Corporation
12. **Transportation equipment (3)**
    Mitsubishi Heavy Industries
    Nissan Motor
    Toyota Motor Corporation
13. **Precision instruments (1)**
    Canon
14. **Commerce (3)**
    Mitsubishi Corporation
    Mitsui
    Mitsukoshi
15. **Banking and insurance (3)**
    Sumitomo Bank
    Tokio Marine & Fire Insurance
    Yasuda Fire & Marine Insurance
16. **Real estate (1)**
    Mitsubishi Estate
17. **Land transportation (2)**
    Kinki Nippon Railway
    Nippon Express
18. **Marine transportation (1)**
    Nippon Yusen
19. **Electricity and gas (2)**
    Kansai Electric Power
    Osaka Gas
20. **Other products (1)**
    Dai Nippon Trading

Source: Osaka Securities Exchange.

FIGURE 7.18   Nikkei and OSF50 Stock Averages

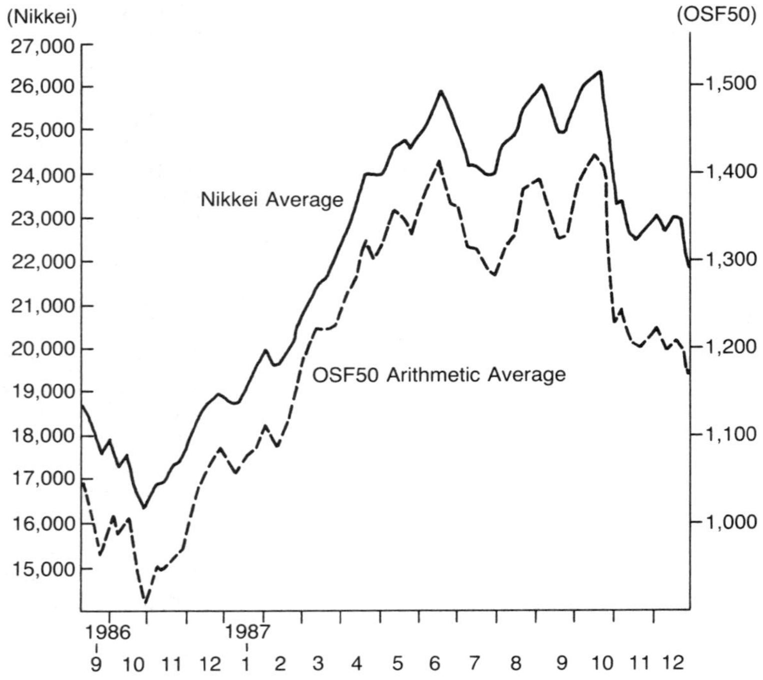

Source: Osaka Securities Exchange.

Korea

The first Korean stock market existed as far back as 1911 but was closed during World War II. Since the war, it existed informally until 1956, when the present Korea Stock Exchange (KSE) was founded in Seoul as a nonprofit corporation whose capital stock was owned by the government and member firms. The KSE Composite Stock Price Index, the only barometer of activity on the KSE, is a broad-based index composed of all 240+ listed companies (Exhibit 7.24). The index is capitalization-weighted by the Paäsche formula and has a base level of 100 as of January 4, 1980.

Luxembourg

The Luxembourg Stock Exchange *(Bourse de Luxembourg)* is the country's only stock exchange; it lists over 230 issues. It was incorporated in 1927 and is operated by a state-owned stock company, *Société Anonyme de la Bourse de Luxembourg.* Currently, there are two indexes that reflect the price activity of listed stocks on the Exchange: the Luxembourg Shares Index and the Luxembourg Shares Return Index.

EXHIBIT 7.24 Korea Stock Exchange Composite Index Components as of December 31, 1987 (Top 20 Ranked by Capitalization)

Company

1. Yu Kong
2. Gold Star
3. Hun Dai Motor
4. Korea First Bank
5. The Hanil Bank
6. The Bank of Seoul
7. The Cho Heung Bank
8. The Commercial Bank of Korea
9. Kin Industrial
10. Sam Sung Electronics
11. Dae Woo Securities
12. Hyun Dai Engineering & Construction
13. Dae Woo
14. Lucky Securities
15. Korean Air
16. Dai Shin Securities
17. Dong Suh Securities
18. Sam Sung Semiconductor & Telecommunications
19. Dae Woo Electronics
20. Lucky

Source: Korea Stock Exchange.

FIGURE 7.19 Korea Stock Exchange Composite Index

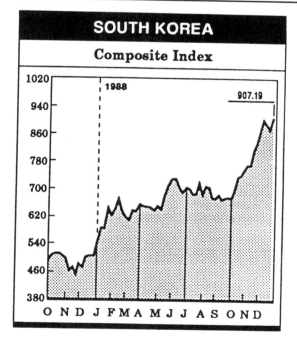

**EXHIBIT 7.25   Luxembourg Shares Index
Components as of September 15, 1988**

ARBED
Audiofina
Banque Générale du Luxembourg
Banque Internationale à Luxembourg
Bil Participations
Cegedel
Kreditbank S.A. Luxembourgeoise
Kreditbank S.A. Luxembourgeoise, private Series A
Rodange-Athus
SEO, private "B"
SEO, ⅕ private "B"

Source: Luxembourg Stock Exchange.

The Luxembourg Shares Index

The Luxembourg Shares Index is a narrow-based index of 11 listed industrial and commercial companies (Exhibit 7.25). The index is capitalization-weighted according to the Paäsche formula and has a base level of 1,000 as of January 2, 1985. On the basis of capitalization, the index is dominated by bank issues, led by Banque Générale du Luxembourg and Banque Internationale à Luxembourg.

The Luxembourg Shares Return Index

Until January 1988, the Luxembourg Stock Exchange published only the Luxembourg Shares Index. Since then, a second index, the Luxembourg Shares Return Index, has also been available. Both indexes are calculated for the same 11 issues and have the same base period and base price. However, the Return Index also includes the dividends that are paid by each company in addition to its market capitalization value. The return is assessed by (1) adding the aggregate amount of dividends paid to the current market capitalization and (2) taking the ex-dividend day into account.

The Netherlands

The Amsterdam Stock Exchange *(Vereniging voor de Effechtenhandel),* founded in 1876 as a private association, is The Netherlands' only stock exchange. Currently, two major stock indexes are used to represent trading activity of the 570+ stocks listed on the Amsterdam Stock Exchange (ASE): the CBS Tendency Index and the EOE Index.

CBS Index

The *Centraal Bureau voor de Statistiek* (Netherlands Central Bureau of Statistics, CBS) has calculated price indexes since 1925. After several interim changes in the method of calculation, a new index was started on April 1, 1955, and published daily in cooperation with the ANP

(General Dutch Press Association) and the *Vereniging voor de Effecten-handel*. Called the ANP-CBS General Index, it was based on the prices of 43 issues traded on the ASE (Exhibit 7.26). Over the years, however, the index failed to keep pace with Amsterdam's stock market and was phased out as the major daily indicator on the last trading day of

EXHIBIT 7.26   ANP-CBS General Index Components as of September 1, 1988

1. **Industrial (20)**
   ACF Holding
   Berkel's Patent Maatschappij
   Bols (Lucas)
   Boskalis Westminster
   Bührmann-Tetterode
   Caland Holdings
   Desseaux, Tapijtfabriek
   Fokker Vliegtuigenfabrik
   Gamma Holding
   Gist-Brocades
   Heineken
   Holec
   Hollandsche Beton Groep
   Koninklijke Nederlandse Papierfabrieken
   Koninklijke Wessanen
   Nijverdal Ten Cate
   Nutricia
   Océ-van der Grinten
   Twentsche Kabel Holdings
   Ver Machinfabrieken Stork

2. **Nonfinancial (8)**
   Hagemeyer
   Internatio Müller
   Koninklijke Ahold
   Koninklijke Bijenkorf Beheer
   Pakhoed Holding
   VNU
   Weyers
   Wolters-Kluwer

3. **International concerns (5)**
   Akzo
   Koninklijke Nederland Hoogovens en Staalfabrieken
   Koninklijke Nederlandsche Petroleum Maatschappij
      (Royal Dutch Petroleum)
   Philips Gloeoilampenfabrieken
   Unilever

4. **Insurance (4)**
   AEGON
   AMEV
   Assurance Concern Stad Rotterdam
   Nationale Nederlanden

5. **Banks (3)**
   Algemene Bank Nederland
   Amsterdam-Rotterdam Bank
   Nederland Middenstandsbank

6. **Shipping and aviation (3)**
   Koninklijke Luchtvaart Maatschappij (KLM)
   Koninklijke Nedlloyd Groep
   Van Ommeren Ceteco

   Total: 43 companies

Source: Netherlands Central Bureau of Statistics.

1986. Even so, it is still maintained on a weekly basis for purposes of historical continuity.

In its place, CBS introduced the CBS Tendency Index on January 2, 1985, in order to provide a more effective short-term barometer of Dutch stocks. This index existed side by side with the ANP-CBS index for two years. Originally, the CBS Tendency Index was a narrow-based index of 29 stocks traded on the ASE; this number was increased to the current 34 components on July 1, 1986 (Exhibit 7.27). In general, stocks of investment and property funds are excluded from the index as the former's prices are thought to be partly determined by those of other stocks, while the latter generally exhibit erratic price behavior.

The composite index is calculated for all 34 stocks which are divided into two groups: International Concerns (5 companies) and Local Enterprises (29 companies). The latter group is broken down further into Financial (Banking, Insurance) and nonfinancial (Industry, Transportation and Storage) subgroups. The price of each stock is converted into a price relative index (I_i) by expressing it as a percentage of the base-period price (P_0), as follows:

$$I_i = \frac{\text{Current stock price}}{\text{Base stock price}} \times 100 \qquad \textbf{(7.4a)}$$

or, in a more compact form,

$$I_i = \frac{P_i}{P_0} \times 100 \qquad \textbf{(7.4b)}$$

If a "stock factor" is defined for each stock, each price relative index can be expressed alternatively as follows:

$$I_i = (\text{Stock factor}) \times (\text{Current stock price}) \qquad \textbf{(7.5a)}$$

or

$$I_i = Z_i P_i \qquad \textbf{(7.5b)}$$

where the stock factor Z_i, equal to 100/base-period price, remains constant except for changes in capitalization. All base prices are those of December 31, 1984.

Example 7.1

The stock factor for AEGON is determined from its closing price at the end of 1984. If this closing price is 148.80 guilders, the stock factor is then 100/148.80, or 0.672943. If AEGON shares are currently quoted at 162.00 guilders, the relative price index for AEGON is:

$$I_{\text{AEGON}} = (0.672943) \times (162.00)$$
$$= 108.90$$

As the computation of the CBS Tendency Index is different from that of any other currently used stock index, it is examined in detail. The computation is affected by dividends paid (either in cash or stock), changes in capital, and changes in component stocks.

**EXHIBIT 7.27 CBS Tendency Index
Components as of September 1, 1988**

1. **Industrial (15)**
   Bols (Lucas)
   Bührmann-Tetterode
   CSM
   Elsevier-NDU
   Fokker Vliegtuigenfabrik
   Gist-Brocades
   Heineken
   Hunter-Douglas
   Koninklijke Nederlandse Papierfabrieken
   Koninklÿke Wessanen
   Nijverdal Ten Cate
   Océ-van der Grinten
   Ver Machinfabrieken Stork
   VNU
   Wolters-Kluwer
2. **International concerns (5)**
   Akzo
   Koninklijke Nederland Hoogovens en Staalfabrieken
   Koninklijke Nederlandsche Petroleum Maatschappij
     (Royal Dutch Petroleum)
   Philips Gloeoilampenfabrieken
   Unilever
3. **Insurance (4)**
   AEGON
   AMEV
   Assurance Concern Stad Rotterdam
   Nationale Nederlanden
4. **Transportation and storage (4)**
   Koninklijke Luchtvaart Maatschappij (KLM)
   Koninklijke Nedlloyd Groep
   Pakhoed Holding
   Van Ommeren Ceteco
5. **Banks (3)**
   Algemene Bank Nederland
   Amsterdam-Rotterdam Bank
   Nederland Middenstandsbank
6. **Nonfinancial (3)**
   Borsumij Wehry
   Internatio Müller
   Koninklijke Ahold

   Total: 34 companies

Source: Netherlands Central Bureau of Statistics.

1. Basic Formula. The CBS Index is calculated as the algebraic mean of 34 individual price relative indexes, as follows:

$$I_{CBS} = \frac{\text{Sum of price relative indexes}}{34} \times 100 \qquad \textbf{(7.6a)}$$

or, in a more compact form,

$$I_{\text{CBS}} = \frac{\Sigma I_i}{34} \times 100 \qquad \textbf{(7.6b)}$$

Example 7.2

On January 31, 1985, an index for the group of three bank stocks can be calculated as follows:

Stock	Stock Factor	Current Price	Relative Index
Algemene Bank Nederland	0.276243	393.00	108.56350
Amsterdam-Rotterdam Bank	1.582278	75.00	118.67085
Nederland Middenstandsbank	0.694444	174.00	120.83326

Total = 348.06761

Group Average = 116.03

2. Effect of Payment of Cash Dividends. The payment of a dividend in cash will decrease the share price on the day that it is paid, and the CBS Index is not corrected for the ex-dividend price. In order to have a meaningful index, however, the effect of the dividend payment is also calculated and published. This negative dividend effect is calculated by using Equations 7.5 and 7.6 by replacing the share price by the amount of the dividend.

Example 7.3

Suppose that on May 2, 1987, Ahold shares (stock factor = 0.538213) were quoted at ex 6.59 guilders, while Algemene Bank Nederland shares (stock factor = 0.276243) were priced at ex 15.00 guilders. As a result, the composite index as well as the Bank (ABN), Financial (ABN), Nonfinancial (Ahold), and Local Enterprises (ABN + Ahold) indexes are affected.

Using Equation 7.5, the dividend effects on the price relative indexes of both stocks are then:

$$\text{Ahold: } -0.538213 \times 6.59 = -3.55$$
$$\text{ABN: } -0.276243 \times 15.00 = -4.14$$

The dividend effects on the four subindexes and the general index are calculated as follows:

Index	1/shares	Decrease	Dividend Effect
Bank (ABN)	1/3	−4.14	−1.38
Financial (ABN)	1/9	−4.14	−0.46
Nonfinancial (Ahold)	1/15	−3.55	−0.24
Local enterprises (ABN + Ahold)	1/24	−(4.14 + 3.55)	−0.32
Composite index (ABN + Ahold)	1/34	−(4.14 + 3.55)	−0.23

3. Effect of Changes in Capital. The capital of a given stock can be changed in a number of ways—designations of rights or stocks, repayment or share splits—any of which will decrease the share price of a given stock. To eliminate this decrease from the index, the stock factor is corrected in a manner similar to that used for the Dow Jones Averages:

$$\text{New factor} = \frac{\text{Closing price before change in capital}}{\text{Theoretical share price after change in capital}} \times \text{Old factor}$$

(7.7a)

or, in a more compact form,

$$Z_t = \frac{P_0}{P_t} \times Z_0$$

(7.7b)

Example 7.4

Suppose that on June 25, 1985, Amsterdam-Rotterdam Bank (AMRO) was quoted ex-right in connection with an issue of new shares with a right of preference in a ratio of 1 new share for 10 old shares at a price of 70.00 guilders per share. The new shares entitled the holders to the final dividend in 1985. If an interim dividend of 2.00 guilders per share, still to be paid, is taken into account, the value of the right, assuming a closing price of 78.00 guilders, is 0.545 guilder. The theoretical ex-right price is then $78.00 - 0.545$, or 77.455 guilders. If the stock factor for AMRO stock on this date was 1.588374, then the new stock factor is:

$$\text{New factor} = \frac{78}{77.455} \times (1.588374)$$
$$= 1.599550$$

EOE Index

Besides the ASE, Amsterdam is the home of the European Options Exchange (EOE), which as its name implies, restricts its activity to the trading of options contracts. The EOE Index is a narrow-based index of 20 leading Dutch stocks traded on the ASE (Exhibit 7.28), whose options are traded on the EOE. The market value of these stocks amounts to approximately 80 percent of the total market value of all shares listed on the ASE. Currently, 16 of the component stocks of the ANP-CBS index are included in the EOE Index, while all 20 stocks of the EOE Index are included in the CBS Tendency Index. Exhibit 7.29 compares the components stocks of the ANP-CBS, CBS, and EOE stock indexes.

Initially, the EOE Index was an "equal-investment" index (the original index level was based on an equal investment in each of the component companies). As of September 1983, the index has been capitalization-weighted by using the Paäsche formula and its base level is 100. The EOE Dutch Stock Index is the basis for European-style, cash-settled option contracts traded on the EOE using the ticker symbol EOE; futures contracts are traded on the *Financiele Termijnmarkt Amsterdam* (Financial Futures Market Amsterdam) using the code FTA.

**EXHIBIT 7.28   European Options Exchange
Index Components as of January 26, 1989**

1. **Industrial (6)**
   Bührmann-Tetterode
   Elsevier-NDU
   Gist-Brocades
   Heineken
   Koninklijke Nederlandse Papierfabrieken
   Koninklijke Wessanen
2. **International concerns (5)**
   Akzo
   Koninklijke Nederland Hoogovens en Staalfabrieken
   Koninklijke Nederlandsche Petroleum Maatschappij
       (Royal Dutch Petroleum)
   Philips Gloeoilampenfabrieken
   Unilever
3. **Insurance (3)**
   AEGON
   AMEV
   Nationale Nederlanden
4. **Transportation and storage (3)**
   Koninklijke Luchtvaart Maatschappij (KLM)
   Koninklijke Nedlloyd Groep
   Van Ommeren Ceteco
5. **Banks (2)**
   Algemene Bank Nederland
   Amsterdam-Rotterdam Bank
6. **Nonfinancial (1)**
   Koninklijke Ahold

   Total: 20 companies

Source: European Options Exchange.

New Zealand

There are four regional stock exchanges in New Zealand—Auckland, Christchurch-Invercargill, Dunedin, and Wellington—that are linked together to form the New Zealand Stock Exchange (NZSE). Currently, there are four indexes that reflect the price activity of the 350+ listed stocks on the NZSE:

NZSE Capital Index

NZSE Gross Index

Barclays Industrial Index

Barclays Mining Share Index

New Zealand Stock Exchange Indexes

The New Zealand Stock Exchange compiles two broad-based indexes. The NZSE Capital Index is composed of all the NZSE-listed stocks. The index is capitalization-weighted by using the Paäsche formula and

EXHIBIT 7.29 Comparison of Dutch Stock Indexes

Company	Index		
	ANP-CBS	CBS	EOE
ACF Holding	x		
AEGON	x	x	x
Akzo	x	x	x
Algemene Bank Nederland	x	x	x
AMEV	x	x	x
Amsterdam-Rotterdam Bank	x	x	x
Assurance Concern Stad Rotterdam	x	x	
Berkel's Patent Maatschappij	x		
Bols (Lucas)	x	x	
Borsumij Wehry		x	
Boskalis Westminster	x		
Bührmann-Tetterode	x	x	
Caland Holdings	x		
CSM		x	
Desseaux, Tapijtfabriek	x		
Elsevier-NDU		x	x
Fokker Vliegtuigenfabrik	x	x	x
Gamma Holding	x		
Gist-Brocades	x	x	x
Hagemeyer	x		
Heineken	x	x	x
Holec	x		
Hollandsche Beton Groep	x		
Hunter-Douglas		x	
Internatio Müller	x		
Koninklijke Ahold	x	x	x
Koninklijke Bijenkorf Beheer	x		
Koninklijke Luchtvaart Maatschappij (KLM)	x	x	x
Koninklijke Nederland Hoogovens en Staalfabrieken	x	x	x
Koninklijke Nederlandsche Petroleum Maatschappij (Royal Dutch Petroleum)	x	x	x
Koninklijke Nederlandse Papierfabrieken	x	x	x
Koninklijke Nedlloyd Groep	x	x	x
Koninklijke Wessanen	x	x	x
Nationale Nederlanden	x	x	x
Nederland Middenstandsbank	x	x	
Nijverdal Ten Cate	x	x	
Nutricia	x		
Océ-van der Grinten	x	x	
Pakhoed Holding	x	x	
Philips Gloeoilampenfabrieken	x	x	x
Twentsche Kabel Holdings	x		
Unilever	x	x	x
Van Ommeren Ceteco	x	x	x
Ver Machinfabrieken Stork	x	x	
VNU	x	x	
Weyers	x		
Wolters-Kluwer	x	x	
Totals	43	34	20

has a base level of 1,000 as of July 31, 1986. Since it is a capital index, no adjustments are made for dividends.

On the other hand, the NZSE Gross Index is a total return index: it is adjusted for dividends on the ex-dividend date. Otherwise both indexes have the same composition, base period, and base price.

Barclays Industrial Share Index

The Barclays Industrial Share Index is a narrow-based index of the top 40 capitalized companies listed on the NZSE; it is maintained daily by Barclays Bank (Exhibit 7.30). It is the major index used for measuring stock activity of the NZSE, and its components account for more than 75 percent of the aggregate market value of all the shares traded.

The index is capitalization-weighted by using the Paäsche formula and has a base level of 100 as of January 31, 1957. The top four companies—Fletcher Challange, Goodman Fielder, Brierley Investments, and

EXHIBIT 7.30 Barclays Industrial Share Index Components

	Company	Capitalization Weight (%) (1/12/89)
1.	Fletcher Challange	22.55%
2.	Goodman Fielder	11.91
3.	Brierley Investments	10.84
4.	New Zealand Forest Products Elders	9.87
5.	Bank of New Zealand	5.36
6.	Lion Nathan	4.80
7.	Magnum Investments	4.80
8.	Carter Holt Harvey	4.65
9.	NZI Corporation	3.03
10.	Robert Jones Investments	2.89
11.	Wilson and Horton	1.86
12.	Chase Corporation	1.63
13.	Fisher and Paykel	1.58
14.	Independent News	1.10
15.	Bank of New Zealand Finance	0.99
16.	Capital Markets Ltd.	0.88
17.	FERNZ Corporation	0.80
18.	Jarden Morgan	0.80
19.	Corporate Investments	0.80
20.	Wilson Neill	0.79
21.	Countrywide Bank	0.61
22.	CERAMCO Ltd.	0.59
23.	National Pacific	0.59
24.	Pacer Kerridge	0.55
25.	McKechnie Brothers	0.50
26.	Steel and Tube	0.50
27.	ICI NZ Ltd.	0.45
28.	Newmans Group	0.43
29.	Mair Astley	0.42
30.	Baycorp	0.40
31.	Wellesley Resources	0.39
32.	Sanford Limited	0.39
33.	Mainzeal Properties	0.36
34.	Mainzeal Corporation	0.35
35.	New Zealand Refining	0.33
36.	Kingsgate	0.31
37.	City Realties	0.26
38.	Lane Walker Rudkin	0.25
39.	Waitaki New Zealand	0.20
40.	Smith City Group	0.19

Source: Barclays Bank New Zealand.

FIGURE 7.20 Barclays Industrial Share Index

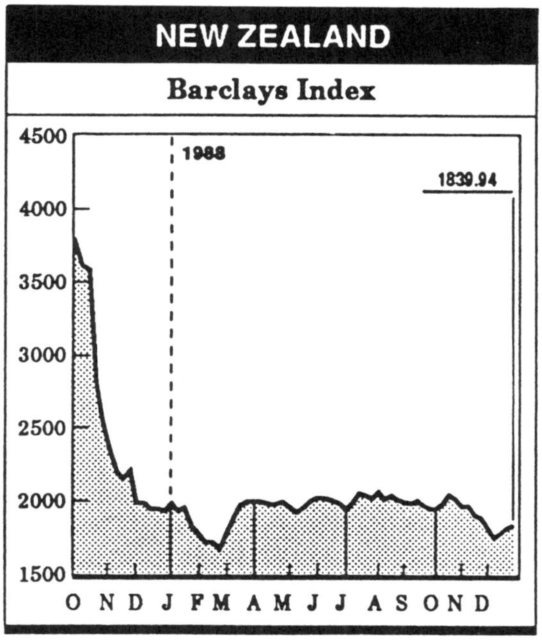

Reprinted by permission of *The Asian Wall Street Journal Weekly,*

New Zealand Forest Products Elders—account for approximately 55 percent of the index's value. The index is the basis for cash-settled index futures contracts that are traded on the New Zealand Futures Exchange.

Barclays Mining Share Index

The Barclays Mining Share Index is a narrow-based index of the 12 largest mining companies on the basis of capitalization (Exhibit 7.31). The index is capitalization-weighted by using the Paäsche formula and has a base level of 100 as of August 31, 1981. Based on capitalization, New Zealand Oil and Gas and Southern Petroleum together account for approximately 53 percent of the index's value.

Norway

The Oslo Stock Exchange *(Oslo Børs),* which was founded in 1819 for the foreign exchange market, is Norway's only stock exchange. The Exchange has two equity markets, defined by capitalization and the number of stockholders. The Børs 1 (1st Section) includes those companies having at least NKr 10 million in share capital and a minimum of 500 stockholders. Established in 1984, the 2nd Section (Børs 2) includes companies with at least NKr 2 million in share capital and a minimum of 200 stockholders.

**EXHIBIT 7.31 Barclays Mining Share
Index Components**

	Company	Capitalization Weight (%) (1/18/89)
1.	New Zealand Oil and Gas	33.37%
2.	Southern Petroleum	20.21
3.	Mineral Resources	8.90
4.	United Resources	8.21
5.	L & M Mining	7.70
6.	Restech International	7.57
7.	Spectrum Resources	4.98
8.	New Zealand Petroleum	4.72
9.	Kiwi Gold NL	2.79
10.	Gold Resources Limited	2.11
11.	Striker	2.36
12.	Platinum Group Metals	1.90

Source: Barclays Bank New Zealand.

Currently, there are two indexes that reflect the price activity of the 200+ stocks listed on the Exchange: The Oslo Stock Exchange General Index, and the Custos Finansanalyse Index.

The Oslo Stock Exchange General Index

The Oslo Stock Exchange General Index is a broad-based composite index of 44 of the 150+ listed companies on Børs 1 of the Oslo Stock Exchange (Exhibit 7.32). The index is capitalization-weighted and has a base level of 100 as of January 2, 1983. Based on market capitalization, Norske Hydro is the index's largest component. The component compa-

FIGURE 7.21 Oslo Stock Exchange General Index

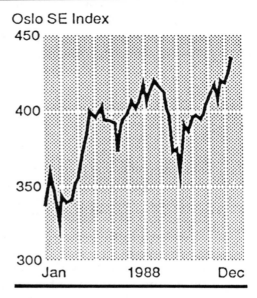

Reprinted by permission of *Financial Times*.

EXHIBIT 7.32   Oslo Stock Exchange General Index Components as of August 31, 1988

Company	Ticker Symbol
Aker Norcem	ANO
Autotransport	AUT
Bergen Bank	BBA
Bergesen "A"	BEA
Bjolvefossen	BJF
Borgestad	BOR
Den Norske Creditbank	DNC
Det Norske Oljeselskap	DNO
Dyno Industrier	DYN
Eidsiva	EID
Electrisk Bureau	ELB
Elkem	ELK
Fokus Bank	FOB
Follum Fabrikker	FOL
Forenede-Gruppen	FGR
Freia "B"	FRB
G. Block Watne	GBW
Ganger Rolf	GRO
Grand Hotel	GHO
Hafslund Nycomed "A"	HAF
Ivarans Rederi, Oslo	IVA
Jonas Oglaend	JON
Kosmos	KOS
Kreditkassen	CBK
Kvaener Industrier	KVI
Laboremus	LAB
Nobo Fabrikker	NOB
Nora Industrier	NOI
Norsk Data "A"	NDA
Norske Hydro	NHY
Norske Skogindustrier	NSK
Orkla-Borregaard	OBG
Rogalandsbanken	RBK
Rosshavet, Sandefjord	ROS
Saga Petroleum	SAG
Scanvest-Ring "A"	SRA
Simrad	SMD
Storebrand	STB
Storli	STO
Tofte Industrier	TOF
Tomra Systems	TOM
Vard	VAR
Veidekke	VEI
Wilh. Wilhelmsen Ltd.	WWI
Total: 44 companies	

Source: Oslo Stock Exchange.

nies of the General Index are assigned to Banks, Insurance, Industrial, Oil, and Shipping subindexes.

The Custos Finansanalyse Index

The Custos Finansanalyse Index (CFX) is a narrow-based index of the 30 most-traded issues on the Oslo Stock Exchange (Exhibit 7.33). The CFX was developed by A/S Custos Finansanalyse before being acquired by the Oslo Stock Exchange on January 1, 1988, and is main-

**EXHIBIT 7.33   Custos
Finansanalyse Index (CFX)
Components as of March 6, 1989**

Company	Ticker Symbol
Aker Norcem*	ANO
Bergen Bank*	BBA
Bergesen "A"*	BEA
Bergesen "B"	BEB
Bjolvefossen*	BJF
Bonheur	BON
Den Norske Creditbank*	DNC
DNL "B"	DNL
Dyno Industrier*	DYN
Electrisk Bureau*	ELB
Elkem*	ELK
Fokus Bank*	FOB
Hafslund Nycomed "A"*	HAF
HCA Melbye	MEL
Kosmos*	KOS
Kreditkassen*	CBK
Kvaener Industrier*	KVI
Laboremus*	LAB
Leif Hoegh & Co. A/S	LHO
Nora Industrier*	NOI
Norske Hydro*	NHY
Norske Skogindustrier*	NSK
Orkla-Borregaard*	OBG
Saga Petroleum*	SAG
Storebrand*	STB
Storli*	STO
Tofte Industrier*	TOF
Unitor Ships Service	UTO
Vard*	VAR
Wilh. Wilhelmsen Ltd.*	WWI

Total: 30 companies

* Components of the Oslo Stock Exchange
General Index (24).
Source: A/S Oslo Børs Informasjon.

tained by A/S Oslo Børs Informasjon. The index is capitalization-weighted and has a base level of 100 as of January 1, 1987. On the basis of market capitalization, Norske Hydro is the index's largest component.

Singapore/Malaysia

The stock exchanges of Singapore and Malaysia have a common origin. In 1957, Singapore became self-governing, as did several other former British colonies in the Malay Peninsula, nine of which were organized into the Federation of Malaya. Singapore remained independent until 1963, when it became part of the new Federation of Malaysia (along with Malacca, Sarawak, Sabah, and the nine states of the Federation of Malaya). In 1965 Singapore seceded from Malaysia and became an independent republic, although the two nations retained a common currency until 1967. In 1973 the Malaysian government stopped allowing conversion of the two nations' currencies.

As early as 1964, the Stock Exchange of Malaysia and Singapore was in existence, but upon the currency-conversion decision of 1973, the two nations formed their own exchanges, the Stock Exchange of Singapore (SES) and the Kuala Lumpur Stock Exchange of Malaysia (KLSE). Although separate entities since 1973, the two exchanges permit cross-listing of companies. Besides the SES, Singapore also has the Singapore International Monetary Exchange (SIMEX), which handles futures and futures options contracts. It currently trades cash-settled futures contracts based on the Nikkei 225-Stock Average.

Today, there are more Malaysian-incorporated companies than Singaporean-incorporated companies listed on the SES. The SES has approximately 315+ listed issues versus 285+ for the KLSE; the disparity is probably due to the fact that Singapore is considered to be a more efficient and highly developed financial center than Kuala Lumpur. Currently, the following indexes are used to measure price activity of both stock exchanges:

> Stock Exchange of Singapore
> > Straits Times Index
> > Business Times Composite Index
>
> Kuala Lumpur Stock Exchange
> > Kuala Lumpur Stock Exchange Composite Index
> > Industrials Index
> > Finance Index
> > Properties Index
> > Tins Index
> > Plantations Index
> > Hotels Index

Straits Times Index

The Straits Times Index is the best-known of Singapore's stock market indexes. It is a narrow-based index of 30 companies (Exhibit 7.34) listed on the SES. The underlying portfolio for the index is compiled by the *Straits Times,* the leading newspaper in Singapore.

The Straits Times Index is capitalization-weighted by using the Paäsche formula and has a base level of 100 as of December 31, 1966. Currently, 16 of the underlying stocks of the Straits Times Index are also part of the Kuala Lumpur Stock Exchange Composite Index.

Business Times Index

The Business Times Index, published in Singapore by the *Business Times,* is a narrow-based index of 40 companies (Exhibit 7.35) listed on the SES. Of the underlying companies, 21 are also components of the Straits Times Index, while 20 companies are also part of the Kuala Lumpur Stock Exchange Composite Index. The index is capitalization-weighted by means of the Paäsche formula and has a base level of 100 as of December 31, 1964.

EXHIBIT 7.34 Straits Times Index Components as of September 30, 1988

Amalgamated Steel Mills*	Malaysian Tobacco Company
Boustead Holdings*	Multi-Purpose Holdings*
Cycle and Carriage Bintang*	North Borneo Timbers
Cold Storage (Malaysia)*	National Iron & Steel Mills
Chemical Company of Malaysia*	Pan Malaysia Cement Works
Cerebos	Perlis Plantations*
Esso Malaysia*	Prima
Fraser & Neave	Robinson
Genting*	SIA
Guinness Malaysia*	Selected Properties Holdings
Haw Par Brothers International	Sime Darby*
Hume Industries (Malaysia)*	Straits Trading*
Inchcape	UMW Holdings Corporation*
Keppel Shipping	Uniphone Telecommunications*
Lum Chang	Wearne Brothers*

Total: 30 companies

* Components also of Kuala Lumpur Stock Exchange Composite Index (16).
Source: Straits Times Press.

FIGURE 7.22 Straits Times Index

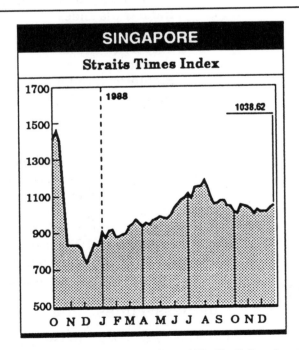

EXHIBIT 7.35   Business Times Composite Index Components as of September 30, 1988

Amalgamated Steel Mills*
Bandar Raya Development*
Berjuntai Tin*
Boustead Holdings*
Cerebos
City Developement
Cold Storage (Malaysia)*
Cycle and Carriage Bintang*
DBS
Esso Malaysia*
Fraser & Neave*
Faber Merlin*
Genting*
Haw Par Brothers International
Highlands & Lowlands*
IGB Corporation*
Inchcape
Kuala Lumpur Kepong*
Keppel Shipping
Kulim (Malaysia)*

Lum Chang
Malayan Banking*
Malaysian Mining Corporation*
Marco Polo
North Borneo Timbers
National Iron & Steel Mills
OCBC
OUE
Pan Malaysia Cement Works
Perlis Plantations*
Prima
Robinson
SIA
Selected Properties Holdings
Sime Darby*
Singapore Land
Straits Trading*
UMW Holdings Corporation*
UOB
United Plantations

Total: 40 companies

* Components also of Kuala Lumpur Stock Exchange Composite Index (20).
Source: *Business Times.*

FIGURE 7.23   Kuala Lumpur Stock Exchange Composite Index

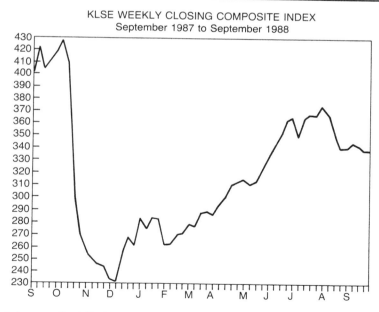

Source: Kuala Lumpur Stock Exchange.

Kuala Lumpur Stock Exchange Composite Index

The Kuala Lumpur Stock Exchange Composite Index is the major index of the stocks listed on the KLSE. It is a narrow-based index of 82 companies listed on the KLSE (Exhibit 7.36). All underlying companies are incorporated in Malaysia except for Straits Trading and Weame Brothers. The index is capitalization-weighted by the Paäsche formula and has a base level of 100 as of 1977.

The Composite Index is subdivided into six subindexes—Industrials, Finance, Properties, Tins, Plantation, and Hotels—all of which are

FIGURE 7.24   Kuala Lumpur Stock Exchange Subindexes, September 1987 to September 1988

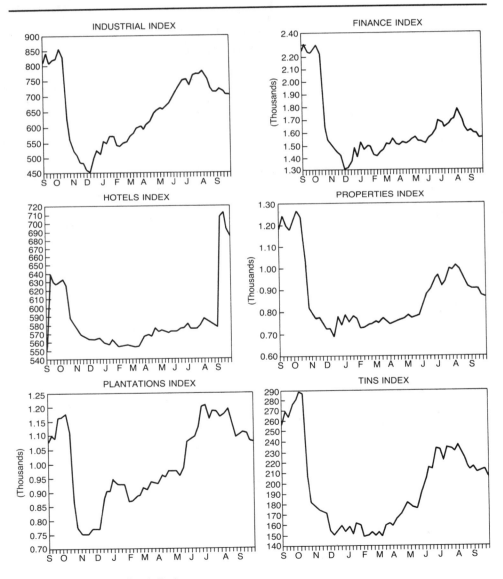

Source: Kuala Lumpur Stock Exchange.

computed in the same way as the KLSE Composite Index. The Plantation Index is composed of the companies in the Rubbers and Oil Palms industry groups.

EXHIBIT 7.36   Kuala Lumpur Stock Exchange Composite Index Components as of September 30, 1988

1. **Industrials (61)**

Aluminum Company of Malaysia	Malaysian Cement
Amalgamated Steel Mills	Malaysian International Shipping
Berjaya Corporation	Malaysian Oxygen
Boustead Holdings	Malaysian United Industries
Chemical Company of Malaysia	Multi-Purpose Holdings
CI Holdings	New Straits Times Press
Cement Industries	Oriental Holdings
Cycle & Carriage Bintang	OYL Industries
Cold Storage (Malaysia)	Palmco Holdings
Dayapai Industries	Perlis Plantations
Dragon & Phoenix	Pilecon Engineering
Dunlop Industries	Rothmans of Pall Mall
Dutch Baby Milk Industries	Samanda Holdings
The East Asiatic Co. (Malaysia)	Seal Incorporated
Esso Malaysia	Setron (Malaysia)
Ganda Holdings	Shell Refining Co. (F.O.M.)
General Corporation	Sime Darby
General Lumber (Holdings)	Sin Heng Chan (Malaysia)
Genting	Sistem Televisyen Malaysia
George Kent (Malaysia)	Sitt Tatt
Gold Coin (Malaysia)	Straits Trading
Guinness Malaysia	Sungel Way Holding
Hexza Corporation	Tan Chong Motor Holding
Hong Leong Industries	Time Engineering
Hume Industries Malaysia	Timuran Holdings
Insas	Tradewinds (Malaysia)
Kian Joo Can Factory	UMW Holdings Corporation
Kumpulan Emas	Uniphone Telecommunications
Lion Corporation	Wearne Brothers
Magnum Corporation	Yeo Hiap Seng (Malaysia)
Malaysian Airlines	

2. **Finance (7)**

Arab Malaysian Development	MBF Holdings
British-American Bank	Malayan Banking
Development & Commerical Bank	Public Bank
Kuala Lumpur Industries	

3. **Properties (4)**

Bandar Raya Development	Island & Peninsular
IGB Corporation	Selangor Properties

4. **Tins (4)**

Berjuntai Tin	Rahman Hydraulic Tin
Malaysian Mining Corporation	Selangor Dredging

5. **Oil palms (3)**

Harrisons Malaysian	TDM
Kulim (Malaysia)	

6. **Rubbers (2)**

Highlands & Lowlands	Kuala Lumpur Kepong

7. **Hotels (1)**

Faber Merlin

Total: 82 companies

Source: Kuala Lumpur Stock Exchange.

South Africa

Shortly after the discovery of the Witwatersrand goldfields in 1886, the Johannesburg Stock Exchange (JSE) was founded in November 1887 as South Africa's only stock exchange, to provide a marketplace for the stock of the many mining and financial companies that resulted. JSE-Actuaries Indexes are used to measure price activity of the listed stocks on the JSE.

EXHIBIT 7.37   Johannesburg Stock Exchange–Actuaries Indexes: Structure of Sectorial and Composite Indexes

Percent of All-Share
(12/31/86)

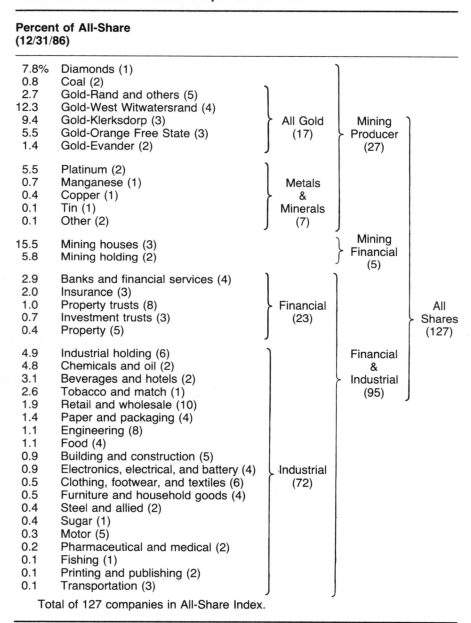

7.8%	Diamonds (1)
0.8	Coal (2)
2.7	Gold-Rand and others (5)
12.3	Gold-West Witwatersrand (4)
9.4	Gold-Klerksdorp (3)
5.5	Gold-Orange Free State (3)
1.4	Gold-Evander (2)
5.5	Platinum (2)
0.7	Manganese (1)
0.4	Copper (1)
0.1	Tin (1)
0.1	Other (2)
15.5	Mining houses (3)
5.8	Mining holding (2)
2.9	Banks and financial services (4)
2.0	Insurance (3)
1.0	Property trusts (8)
0.7	Investment trusts (3)
0.4	Property (5)
4.9	Industrial holding (6)
4.8	Chemicals and oil (2)
3.1	Beverages and hotels (2)
2.6	Tobacco and match (1)
1.9	Retail and wholesale (10)
1.4	Paper and packaging (4)
1.1	Engineering (8)
1.1	Food (4)
0.9	Building and construction (5)
0.9	Electronics, electrical, and battery (4)
0.5	Clothing, footwear, and textiles (6)
0.5	Furniture and household goods (4)
0.4	Steel and allied (2)
0.4	Sugar (1)
0.3	Motor (5)
0.2	Pharmaceutical and medical (2)
0.1	Fishing (1)
0.1	Printing and publishing (2)
0.1	Transportation (3)

Total of 127 companies in All-Share Index.

Source: The Johannesburg Stock Exchange.

EXHIBIT 7.38   Johannesburg Stock Exchange–Actuaries Sector Indexes—Component Shares

Sector Index/Companies	Percent of All-Share Index (12/31/86)	Sector Index/Companies	Percent of All-Share Index (12/31/86)
1. All Gold Index (17)	31.4%	**5. Industrial Index (72)**	25.0%
Beatrix		AECI	
Dreifontein		Abercom	
E T Cons		Adcock	
Elandsran		Afcol	
Ergo		Afrox	
Freegold		Altech	
Grootvlei		Amic	
Harmony		Amrel	
Hartebeesfontein		Anglo Alpha	
Kinross		Argus	
Kloof		BTR Dunlop	
Modderfontein		Barlows	
Randfontein		Bateman (E.L.)	
Southvaal		Blue Circle	
Vaalreefs		C-Matic	
Western Deep		CMI	
Winkelhaak		Clicks	
2. Metals & Minerals Index (7)	6.7	Consolidated Glass	
Cons Murchison		Consolidated Textiles	
Impala		De Gama	
Palamin		Dorbyl	
Rooiberg		Edgars	
Rustenberg		Ellerine	
Samancor		Everite	
Vansa		Fedfood	
3. Mining Financial Index (5)	21.3	Foschini	
Amgold		General Tyre	
Anglo American		Grinaker	
GFSA		Haggie	
Genbel		Hiveld	
Gencor		Hudaco	
4. Financial Index (23)	7.0	I & J	
Amaprop		ICS	
Barclays		Kersaf	
Barprop		Malbank	
CBD Fund		McCarthy	
Capital		Mediclinic	
Cenprop		Metair	
Fedfund		Metal Box	
Fugit		Metro	
G F Properties		Mooi River	
Industrial Selections		NEI Africa	
Liberty		Nampak	
National Selections		Natural Canvas	
Nedbank		OK	
Pioneer		Ocfish	
Prudential		P P Cement	
R M Properties		Pepcor	
Retco		Pick 'n Pay	
Southern		Plate Glass	
Stanbic		Powertech	
Stanprop		Putco	
Sycom		RIH	
Tamboti		Rembrandt Group	
Union Bank of Switzerland		Reunert	
		Rex Trueform	

EXHIBIT 7.38 *(concluded)*

Sector Index/Companies	Percent of All-Share Index (12/31/86)	Sector Index/Companies	Percent of All-Share Index (12/31/86)
Romatex		Tolgate	
S A Breweries		Tongaat	
SAAN		Toyota	
Saficon		Trencor	
Safren		Waltons	
Sappi		Wooltru	
Sasol		6. Other (3)	8.6%
Score		Amcoal	
Tedelex		De Beers	
Tiger Oats		Trans Natal	

Source: The Johannesburg Stock Exchange.

As shown in Exhibits 7.37 and 7.38, the JSE-Actuaries All-Share Index is a broad-based composite index of 127 stocks traded on the JSE and is broken down into five subindexes and two composite subindexes as follows:

Subindexes
  All Gold
  Metals and Minerals
  Mining Financial
  Financial
  Industrial
Composite Subindexes
  Mining Producer
  Financial and Industrial

All indexes are capitalization-weighted by using the Paäsche formula and their base levels of 100 were established on October 2, 1978;

FIGURE 7.25 Johannesburg Stock Exchange All Gold Index

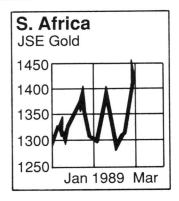

Reprinted by permission of *Financial Times*.

they are maintained by the JSE and the Actuarial Society of South Africa. Besides the All-Share Index, the other two major indexes that receive the most interest from international investors are the All Gold Index and the Mining Producer Index;[7] the latter is composed of the companies contained in both the All Gold and Mining & Minerals subindexes. The All Gold Index of seven companies accounts for approximately 31.4 percent of the All-Share Index's value, while the mining industry's production and financial companies increase the overall share to approximately 68 percent.

Sweden

The only stock exchange in Sweden is the Stockholm Stock Exchange *(Stockholms Fondbörs)*. It was founded in 1901 and is the largest equity market in Scandinavia. Swedish company stocks are divided into free and restricted shares. Free shares, which can be owned by foreign nationals, constitute up to 40 percent of a company's share capital and a maximum of 20 percent of the voting stock; the market for them is volatile and illiquid. All shares in both Atlas-Copco and Skandia are free. Approximately 25 percent of the total Stockholm market value is represented by free shares.

On the other hand, ownership of restricted shares is restricted to Swedish nationals; those shares represent the majority of the voting stock. Foreign nationals are not allowed to own common stock in Swedish banks, finance companies, or brokerage firms. Consequently, these firms have only restricted shares. In either case, companies can have Class A and B shares. Class A shares normally have a full vote, while Class B shares carry one-tenth of a vote. Exceptions to these rules are that Ericsson "B" and Electrolux "B" shares carry only a thousandth of a vote.

Stock options are traded on the Stockholm Options Market, while the Stockholm Options and Futures Exchange allows trading of both options and futures contracts. The following five indexes are currently used to measure activity of the 260+ stocks listed on the Stockholm Stock Exchange:

Stockholm Stock Exchange Composite Index

Affärsvärlden General Index

Jacobson & Ponsbach Index

Stockholm Options Market Index

SX-16 Index

A sixth index, the Alfred Berg Nordic Index, includes stock issues of other Nordic countries as well as Sweden.

---

[7] The Mining Producer Index was formerly known as the All Mining Index.

**EXHIBIT 7.39   Stockholm Stock Exchange
Composite Index Components**

Industry Sector	Approximate Capitalization Weight (%) (12/31/88)
1. Engineering industry (18)	26%
2. Forest industry (9)	11
3. Banks (10)	10
4. Real estate and building contractors (17)	10
5. Holding companies (11)	7
6. Metal and steel fabrication (6)	4
7. Mixed investment companies (13)	4
8. Retail and wholesale trade (9)	3
9. Other (68)	25
Total: 161 companies	

Source: Stockholm Stock Exchange.

Stockholm Stock Exchange Composite Index

The Stockholm Stock Exchange Composite Index is a broad-based index maintained by the Exchange; it includes all the listed stocks, covering nine major industrial groups (Exhibit 7.39). Dominated by engineering industry stocks, the index is capitalization-weighted according to the Paäsche formula and has a base level of 100 as of December 31, 1982.

Affärsvärlden General Index—AFGX

The Affärsvärlden General Index (AFGX) is the best-known performance index for stocks listed on the Stockholm Stock Exchange. It is a broad-based index of over 140 issues (Exhibit 7.40). The underlying

FIGURE 7.26   Affärsvärlden General Index

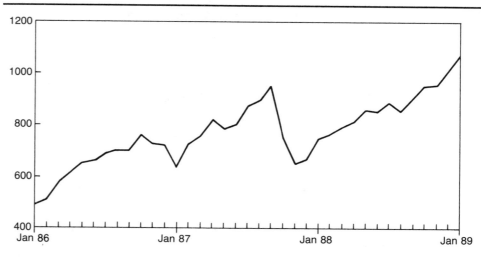

Source: Affärsvärlden.

EXHIBIT 7.40 Affärsvärlden General Index Components (Top 10 Ranked by Capitalization)

Company	Weight (%) (4/07/89)
1. Volvo	5.43%
2. Skanska	4.62
3. Asea	4.33
4. Stora Kopparberg	3.73
5. SCA	3.62
6. Skandinaviska Enskilda Banken	3.57
7. Electrolux	3.55
8. Ericsso	2.61
9. Sandvik	2.55
10. SAAB-Scania	2.55

Source: *Affärsvärlden.*

portfolio for the AFGX was compiled for *Affärsvärlden,*[8] Sweden's leading business magazine, and is computed daily by Findata Finansiell Information AB.

The AFGX is capitalization-weighted by the Paäsche formula; its base level of 100 was assigned as of December 31, 1979. On the basis of market capitalization, Electrolux "B" free, Skandinaviska Enskilda Banken "A" restricted, and Skanska "B" restricted shares account for approximately 25 percent of the index's value.

In addition to the AFGX, there are eight subindexes— Mechanical Engineering, Pulp and Paper, Retail and Wholesale, Construction and Real Estate, Mixed Investment Companies, Pure Investment Companies, Banks, and Miscellaneous—whose individual indexes have the same base period and value and are calculated in the same manner as the AFGX.

Jacobson & Ponsbach Index

The Jacobson & Ponsbach Index is a narrow-based index of 38 Swedish stocks maintained by the Hägglöf & Ponsbach Fondkommission AB (Exhibit 7.41). The index is capitalization-weighted by the Paäsche formula; its base level of 100 was set as of December 31, 1973.

There is also a capitalization-weighted 13-share Jacobson & Ponsbach Investment Index, whose components are listed in Exhibit 7.42.

Stockholm Options Market Index—OMX

The Stockholm Options Market Index (OMX) is a narrow-based index of the 30 Swedish stocks having the largest trading volume (Exhibit 7.43). The underlying portfolio for the OMX was compiled by Findata Finansiell Information AB for the Stockholms Optionsmarknad OM

---

[8] *Affärsvärlden* is Swedish for "business world."

**EXHIBIT 7.41   Jacobson & Ponsbach
Index Components**

1. **Industrial (30)**

AGA	Munksjö
Alfa Laval	NCB
Asea	Nobel Industrier
Astra	Perstorp
Atlas Copco	Pharmacia
Carnegie & Company	Procordia
Electrolux	SAAB-Scania
Ericsson, LM	Sandvik
Esselte	SCA, SV Cellulosa
Euroc	Skanska
Gambro	SKF
Incentive	Stora Kopparberg
Korsnäs Marma	Swedish Match
Marieberg	Trelleborg
Mo och Domsjö	Volvo

2. **Banking (8)**

Nordbanken	Skanska Banken
PKBanken	Svenska Handelsbanken
Skandinaviska Enskilda Banken	Wermlandbanken
Skaraborgsbanken	Östgötabanken

   Total: 38 companies

Source: Hägglöf & Ponsbach.

Fondkommission AB (Stockholm Options Market) and is computed by the same firm on days when the Stockholm Stock Exchange is open.

The index is capitalization-weighted by the Paäsche formula; its base level of 500 was set as of September 30, 1986. On the basis of market capitalization, Electrolux "B" free, Skandinaviska Enskilda Banken "A" restricted, and Skanska "B" restricted account for approximately 25 percent of the index's value. The OMX is the basis for European-style, cash-settled index option contracts that are traded on the Stockholm Options Market.

FIGURE 7.27   Jacobson & Ponsbach Index

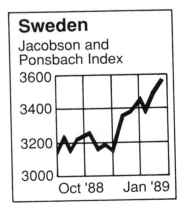

Reprinted by permission of *Financial Times*.

EXHIBIT 7.42   Jacobson & Ponsbach Investment Index Components

Asken	Latour
Bahco	Opus
Cardo	Protorp
Custos	Providentia
Export-Invest	Ratos
Industriavärden	Öresund
Investor	

Total: 13 companies

Source: Hägglöf & Ponsbach.

EXHIBIT 7.43   Stockholm Options Market Index Components

Industry Sector/Company/Share Series	Capitalization Weight (%) (11/18/87)
1. Mechanical engineering industry (11)	**44.13%**
Electrolux "B," free	8.23%
Asea "A," restricted	7.49
Ericsson "B," free	4.84
Sandvik "A," restricted	4.71
SAAB-Scania "A," restricted	4.45
Volvo "B," restricted	4.22
Volvo "B," free	3.58
Atlas Copco, free	2.56
SKF "B," free	1.58
Alfa Laval "B," free	1.39
Avesta, restricted	1.08
2. Banking (2)	**14.24%**
Skandinaviska Enskilda Banken "A," restricted	8.16
Svenska Handelsbanken, restricted	6.08
3. Forest industry (4)	**11.19%**
Stora "A," restricted	5.32
SCA "B," free	2.97
SCA "B," restricted	2.26
Munksjö "A," restricted	0.64
4. Real estate and building contractors (3)	**10.42%**
Skanska "B," restricted	8.04
Lundbergs "B," restricted	1.67
BGB, restricted	0.71
5. Other (10)	**20.03%**
Skandia, free	4.33
Astra "A," restricted	4.23
Pharmacia "B," restricted	2.65
Nobel Industrier, restricted	2.50
Trelleborg "B," restricted	1.93
Pharmacia "B," free	1.34
Astra "B," free	1.07
Esselte "B," restricted	0.68
Trelleborg "B," free	0.68
Proventus "B," restricted	0.61

Total: 30 companies

Source: Stockholm Options Market.

FIGURE 7.28   Stockholm Options Market Index

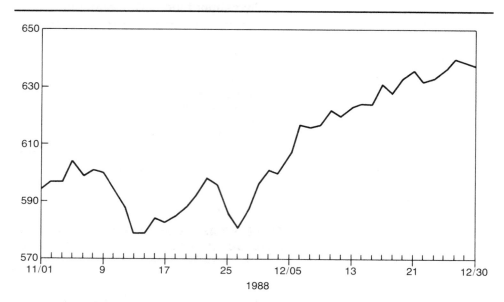

Source: Stockholm Options Market.

SX-16 Index

The SX-16 (Stockholm Stock Exchange Index-16) Index is a narrow-based index of the 16 most heavily traded stocks on the Stockholm Stock Exchange (Exhibit 7.44). The index is chain-weighted and capitalization-based, with a base value of 100 as of December 31, 1979. Each of the 16 stock issues is represented by its most liquid share class.

The composition of the index is updated every six months, and the period for which the liquidity of the shares is assessed consists

EXHIBIT 7.44   SX-16 Index Components as of November 18, 1987

AGA
Asea
Astra
Atlas Copco
Electrolux
Ericsson
Mo och Domsjö
Pharmacia
SAAB-Scania
SCA
Skandia
Skanska
SKF
Stora
Trelleborg
Volvo

Total: 16 companies

Source: Stockholm Options and Futures Exchange.

of the 12-month period ending one month before the revision. The SX-16 Index is currently the basis for European-styled, cash-settled index options contracts traded on the Stockholm Options and Futures Exchange.

Alfred Berg Nordic Index

The Alfred Berg Nordic Index is a broad-based index of over 120 Scandinavian stocks of companies in Sweden, Finland, Denmark, and Norway (Exhibit 7.45). The intent is to include those stocks that account for approximately 70 percent of the total market capitalization on each nation's stock exchange. Priority in the selection of the underlying component stocks is given to foreign investors, so that each company included in the index must meet the following criteria:

- Since all Nordic (Scandinavian) countries except Denmark have rules restricting foreign share ownership, there must be sufficient liquidity in those nonrestricted, or free component shares.
- It must be judged an "interesting" long-term investment; that is, it should be expected to yield an above-average return in a two-to-three-year time frame.
- The investment should be well timed.

The underlying index portfolio was compiled by the stockbrokerage firm Alfred Berg & Partners, which is owned by Volvo, and the index is maintained by Findata Finansiell Information AB on all days when the Stockholm Stock Exchange is open. The index is capitalization-weighted by the Paäsche formula. Before the index is calculated, the market value of each company is converted into Swedish kroner at the last known exchange rate. It has a base level of 100 as of December 31, 1986. Based on market capitalization, Swedish companies currently account for approximately 59 percent of the index's value.

EXHIBIT 7.45 Alfred Berg Nordic Index Components

Country/Company	Capitalization Weight (%) (12/21/88)
Sweden (45)	**59.00%**
Volvo	3.64%
Skanska	3.25
Asea	2.90
Skandinaviska Enskilda Banken	2.69
Electrolux	2.58
SCA	2.54
Stora	2.42
Astra	2.00
Sandvik	1.92
Svenska Handelsbanken	1.92
Sydkraft	1.84
SAAB-Scania	1.76
Ericsson	1.71
Procordia	1.67

EXHIBIT 7.45   *(continued)*

Country/Company	Capitalization Weight (%) (12/21/88)
PKBanken	1.62%
Hufvudstaden	1.60
Pharmacia	1.31
Scandia	1.31
SKF	1.30
AGA	1.26
Custos	1.19
Investor	1.14
Lundbergs	1.12
Esselte	1.09
Trelleborg	1.09
Nobel Industries	0.93
Indusrivärden	0.86
Providentia	0.84
Alfa Laval	0.82
Korsnäs	0.80
Atlas Copco	0.79
Ratos	0.75
GotaGruppen	0.61
Mo och Domsjö	0.60
Perstorp	0.58
Euroc	0.57
Marieberg	0.56
Gullspang	0.51
Protorp	0.49
Bilspedition	0.46
Cardo	0.45
Nordbanken	0.41
Incentive	0.38
Artimos	0.37
BGB	0.36
Finland (21)	**18.10%**
SYP-Invest	2.41
Kansallis-Osake-Pankki	1.53
Nokia Ab	1.50
Kymmene	1.34
Outokupmpu	0.98
Yhtyneet Paperitehtaat	0.84
Säästöpankkien Keskus-Osake-Pankki	0.84
Lohja Ab	0.77
Rauma-Repola	0.75
Partek	0.70
Sampo	0.70
Wärtsilä Marine Industries	0.67
Valmet	0.66
Vakuutus Pohjola	0.66
Enso-Gutzeit	0.64
Kesko	0.62
Amer-yhtymä	0.55
Stockmann Ab	0.54
Suomen Sokeri	0.53
Instrumentarium	0.51
Metsä-Serla	0.37
Denmark (36)	**14.38%**
Dampshipseelkapet of 1912	1.33
Dampshipseelkapet Svendborg	1.24
Forenede Bryggerier	1.17
Den Denske Bank	1.00

EXHIBIT 7.45 *(concluded)*

Country/Company	Capitalization Weight (%) (12/21/88)
Novo-Nordisk	0.74%
Handelsbanken	0.64
Baltica	0.57
Codan Forsikring	0.51
Det Östasiatiske Kompagni	0.48
Privatbanken	0.48
De Dankse Sukkerfabrikker	0.47
Provinsbanken	0.47
Baltica Holding	0.44
Andelsbanken	0.36
Hafnia Invest	0.36
F. L. Smidth & Co.	0.33
Fisker & Nielson	0.32
Aalborg Portland	0.27
Danisco	0.25
Jyske Bank	0.24
Sophus Berendsen	0.23
Nordisk Kabel-og Tradf	0.22
Danske Luftfartselskab	0.21
Superfos	0.20
ISS	0.20
Nordisk Gentofte	0.19
J. Lauritsen Holding	0.18
Top-Danmark	0.17
Potagua	0.15
DFDS	0.15
Danske Spritfabrikker	0.15
Jens Villadsens Fabrikker	0.14
H + H Industri	0.14
Korn-og Foderstofkomp	0.13
Kgl. octr. alm. Brandass.	0.13
Cheminova	0.12
Norway (21)	**8.52%**
Norske Hydro	2.73
Hafslund	1.02
Bergesen d.y.	0.68
Orkla-Borregaard	0.36
Kvaener Industrier	0.31
Saga Petroleum	0.30
Bergen Bank	0.28
Elkem	0.27
Aker Norcem	0.26
Vard & Wilhelmsen	0.26
Den Norske Creditbank	0.24
DNL	0.22
Kreditkassen	0.22
Dyno Industrier	0.20
Nora Industrier	0.20
Elektrisk Bureau	0.18
Norsk Data	0.18
Norske Skogindustrier	0.17
Storebrand	0.16
Tofte Industrier	0.14
Thon Eidendom, Olav	0.13

Total: 123 companies

Source: Alfred Berg & Partners.

FIGURE 7.29   Alfred Berg & Partners' Nordic Index

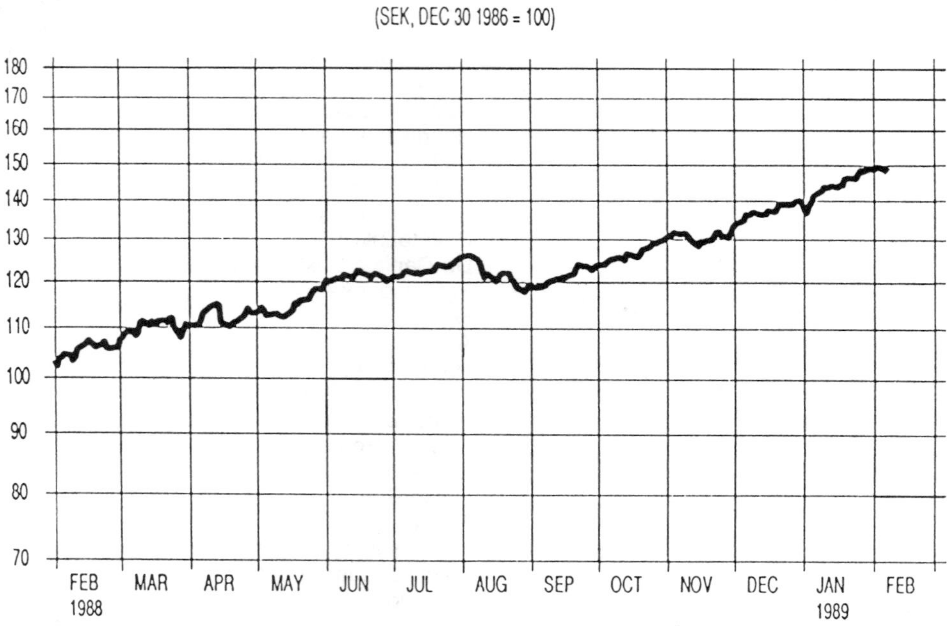

(SEK, DEC 30 1986 = 100)

Source: Alfred Berg & Partners © FINDATA.

Switzerland

Although the oldest known set of formal rules governing the brokerage trade in Switzerland, called *Sensale's Order,* dates back to 1663, it was not until 1873 that the Zurich Stock Exchange *(Effektenbörsenverein Zürich)* was founded. Currently, there are seven stock exchanges—Basel, Berne, Geneva, Lausanne, Neuchâtel (Neuenberg), Saint Gallen, and Zurich—all of which belong to the Association of Swiss Stock Exchanges. Of these, the Zurich Stock Exchange is the oldest and largest, having over 500 listed shares and accounting for over 60 percent of the total turnover.

The following major indexes are currently used to measure activity of stocks listed on the Swiss stock exchanges:

Credit Suisse Index

Swiss Market Index

Swiss Performance Index

Swiss Bank Corporation Index

Swiss National Bank Index

As Swiss company stocks are usually issued as bearer shares *(Inhaberaktien),* registered shares *(Namenaktien),* or participation certificates *(Participationsscheine),*[9] many of the Swiss stock indexes list several classes of stock for the same company.

---

[9] A participation certificate is a nonvoting class of stock, but it has the same ownership rights as bearer and registered stocks.

EXHIBIT 7.46   Credit Suisse Index Components

Industry Sector/Company/Class Share	Weight (%) (1/19/88)
1. Industrial (15)	**60.77%**
Magazine zum Globus, participation certificates	8.15%
Sandoz, registered shares	6.36
Jacobs Suchard, bearer shares	5.78
Ciba-Geigy, registered shares	5.21
Nestlé, registered shares	4.70
Jelmoli	4.39
Holderbank Financière Glarus, bearer shares	4.25
Hoffman-La Roche, deposit certificates	4.13
Aare-Tessin	3.75
Sulzer, registered shares	3.61
Landis & Gyr	3.37
Brown Boveri & Cie.	2.70
Georg Fischer, bearer shares	2.32
Aluminum Suisse, participation certificates	1.10
Oerlikon-Bührle, bearer shares	0.95
2. Insurance (3)	**15.35%**
Swiss Reinsurance, registered shares	6.18
Helvitia Unfall, registered shares	5.08
Zurich Insurance, registered shares	4.09
3. Banks (4)	**11.34%**
Credit Suisse, bearer shares	3.11
Union Bank of Switzerland, bearer shares	2.94
Swiss Bank Corporation, registered shares	2.82
Schweizerischer Volksbank	2.47
4. Other (3)	**12.54%**
Motor-Columbus	5.27
Electrowatt	4.09
Swissair, registered shares	3.18
Total: 25 companies	

Source: Credit Suisse.

Credit Suisse Index

The Credit Suisse Index[10] is a narrow-based index of only those 25 issues having the highest trading volume and capitalization out of over 2,500 that are listed on the Zurich Stock Exchange (Exhibit 7.46). It is considered by many to be the most prominent of all Swiss stock indexes. Maintained daily by Credit Suisse, one of Switzerland's "Big Three" banks,[11] the index is capitalization-weighted by the Paäsche formula and has a base level of 100 as of December 31, 1959. The index is divided into three major subindexes: Banking, Insurance, and Industrial. Unlike other Swiss stock indexes, bank stocks do not dominate the index.

---

[10] In German, the Credit Suisse Index is referred to as *Der Aktienindex der Schweizerischen Kreditanstalt*, or SKA Index.

[11] Switzerland's "Big Three" banks with their English and German equivalents are:
Credit Suisse (*Schweizerischer Kreditanstalt* [SKA])
Swiss Bank Corporation (SBC) (*Schweizerischer Bankverein* [SBV])
Union Bank of Switzerland (UBS) (*Schweizerischer Bankgesellschaft* [SBG])

FIGURE 7.30 Comparison of Credit Suisse Index with the DJIA

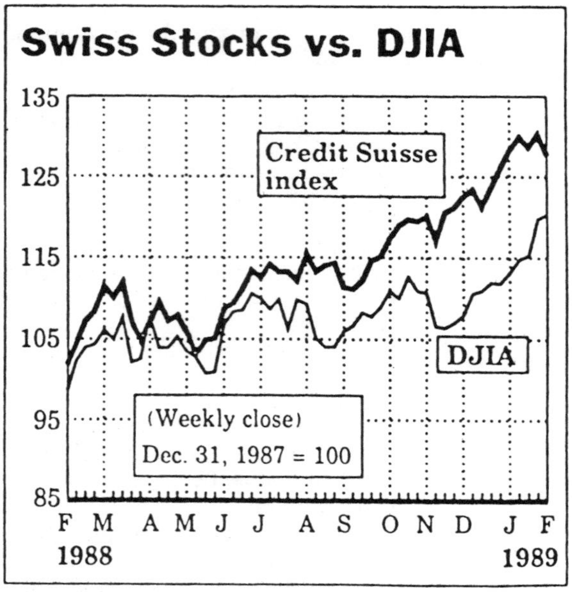
Swiss Stocks vs. DJIA
135
125
115
105
95
85
Credit Suisse index
DJIA
(Weekly close)
Dec. 31, 1987 = 100
F M A M J J A S O N D J F
1988
1989

Swiss Market Index

Started on June 30, 1988, the Swiss Market Index (SMI) is a narrow-based index of 24 stock issues representing 20 highly capitalized companies listed on the Zurich, Geneva, and Basel stock exchanges (Exhibit 7.47). The index was developed by the Association of Swiss Stock Exchanges and is presently calculated by Telekurs AG as a capitalization-weighted index according to the Laspeyres formula; its base level of 1,500 was assigned as of June 30, 1988.

As one might expect, Swiss bank stocks make up the largest share of the index by capitalization (39 percent), and two banks—Union Bank of Switzerland and Credit Suisse—make up approximately 25 percent. The SMI serves as the basis for European-style, cash-settled option contracts traded on the Swiss Options and Financial Futures Exchange (SOFFEX).

Swiss Performance Index

Prior to August 1988, the Swiss Performance Index (SPI) was called the *SwissIndex,* which was developed for the Association of Swiss Stock Exchanges by ECOFIN under contract to Telekurs AG. The SPI is a broad-based index of 364 stocks issued by 196 Swiss companies whose shares are traded on the Zurich, Geneva, and Basel stock exchanges, in addition to a few selected stock issues traded on "pre-bourse" markets *(Vorbörsen).* As shown in Exhibit 7.48, the SPI component stocks are classified in over 12 industry groups.

EXHIBIT 7.47 Swiss Market Index (SMI) Components

Industry Sector/Company/Class Share	Weight (%) (10/12/88)	
1. Banks (6 issues, 4 companies)	**39.00%**	
Union Bank of Switzerland, bearer shares		14.72%
Credit Suisse, bearer shares		10.39
Swiss Bank Corporation, bearer shares		6.85
Swiss Bank Corporation, participation certificates		3.31
Swiss Volksbank, bearer shares		2.34
Union Bank of Switzerland, participation certificates		1.39
2. Chemicals (4 issues, 3 companies)	**21.01%**	
Hoffman-La Roche, participation certificates		10.78
Sandoz, participation certificates		3.59
Ciba-Geigy, bearer shares		3.56
Ciba-Geigy, participation certificates		3.08
3. Foods (3 issues, 2 companies)	**18.09%**	
Nestlé, bearer shares		12.79
Jacobs Suchard, bearer shares		3.51
Nestlé, participation certificates		1.79
4. Industrial (4 issues, 4 companies)	**7.60%**	
Brown Boveri & Cie., bearer shares		3.06
Holderbank Financière Glarus, bearer shares		1.60
Oerlikon-Bührle, bearer shares		1.55
Société Internationale Perelli, bearer shares		1.39
5. Insurance (3 issues, 3 companies)	**7.26%**	
Zürich Insurance, bearer shares		2.91
Swiss Reinsurance, participation certificates		2.27
Winterthur Insurance, bearer shares		2.08
6. Other (4 issues, 4 companies)	**7.04%**	
Electrowatt, bearer shares		2.65
Pargesa Holding, bearer shares		2.27
Adia, bearer shares		1.29
Swissair, bearer shares		0.83
Totals: 24 issues, 20 companies		

Source: Swiss Options and Financial Futures Exchange.

EXHIBIT 7.48 Swiss Performance Index Components

Industry Sector	Capitalization Weight (%) (6/30/88)
1. Banks (55)	15.1%
2. Machinery (48)	13.2
3. Food and luxury goods (32)	8.8
4. Insurance (25)	6.9
5. Electrical engineering and electronics (24)	6.6
6. Retailers (23)	6.3
7. Building contractors and materials (21)	5.8
8. Chemicals and pharmaceuticals (20)	5.5
9. Utilities (16)	4.4
10. Transportation (13)	3.6
11. Metals (9)	2.4
12. Other (78)	21.4
Totals: 364 isssues/196 companies	

Source: Association of Swiss Stock Exchanges.

FIGURE 7.31   Swiss Market (SMI) and Swiss Performance (SPI) Indexes for 1988

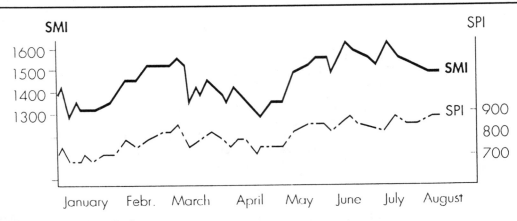

Source: Association of Swiss Stock Exchanges.

The index is calculated and published by Telekurs AG as a capitalization-weighted index according to the Laspeyres formula; its base level was set at 1,000 as of June 1, 1987. Unlike the SMI, the SPI does take into account the payment of dividends. Bank stocks make up the SPI's largest share, but they do not have as dominant a role as is the case with the SMI. Figure 7.31 graphs the movements of both the SMI and SPI for the first seven months of 1988.

Swiss Bank Corporation Indexes

Prior to April 1, 1988, the Swiss Bank Corporation (SBC) Index was based on 117 stocks; its base period was December 31, 1958. Now, it is a broad-based general index of 436 stocks issued by 246 Swiss companies whose shares are traded on the Zurich, Geneva, and Basel stock exchanges, as well as the pre-bourse markets (Exhibit 7.49). Besides the general index, there are 11 subindexes of two broad sectors—Industrials and Services—each of which is further subdivided. The 12 SBC indexes are summarized as follows:

1. SBC (General) Index
    2. Industrials Sector Index
        3. Food, Beverages, and Tobacco
        4. Chemical and Pharmaceutical
        5. Machinery, Metals, Electrical Engineering
        6. Miscellaneous Industrials
    7. Services Sector Index
        8. Banks
        9. Insurance
        10. Commerce
        11. Miscellaneous Services
12. SBC-100 Index

EXHIBIT 7.49 Swiss Bank Corporation Index Components

Company (All Share Classes)	Capitalization Weight (%) (7/29/88)
1. Nestlé	10.21%
2. Union Bank of Switzerland	7.96
3. Swiss Bank Corporation	6.19
4. Hoffman-La Roche	5.49
5. Ciba-Geigy	5.41
6. Sandoz	5.25
7. Credit Suisse	4.92
8. Zurich Insurance	3.92
9. Jacobs Suchard	2.71
10. Swiss Reinsurance	2.50
11. Wintherthur Insurance	2.50
12. Brown Boveri & Cie.	1.62
13. Michelin	1.36
14. Swiss Volksbank	1.28
15. Elektrowatt	1.24
16. Inspectorate	1.23
17. Surveillance	1.23
18. Holderbank Financière Glarus	1.18
19. Swissair	0.99
20. Bank Leu	0.91

Totals: 436 issues/246 companies

Source: Swiss Bank Corporation.

FIGURE 7.32 Swiss Bank Corporation Index (Second Quarter 1988)

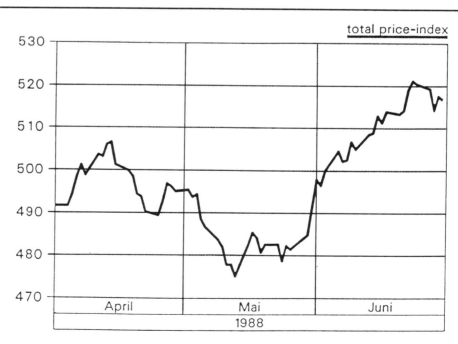

Source: Swiss Bank Corporation.

Since July 1987, the SBC has published the SBC-100 Index, which represents the top 100 highly traded stock issues that are part of the basic SBC Index.

Because any given company can issue several types of stock, each of the 12 SBC indexes is determined separately for three categories of stock issues:

- "Total" Index.   All categories of stock including bearer and registered shares, as well as participation and dividend-right certificates.
- "Bearer" Index.   Bearer shares, as well as participation and dividend-right certificates.
- "Registered" Index.   Registered shares only.

Consequently, there are, for example, three SBC Insurance Indexes calculated: one for all shares, one for bearer shares, and one for registered shares. As a result, there are 36 separate indexes.

Specifically, the SBC series of indexes was developed as (1) an aid in portfolio management and a benchmark in performance of Swiss stocks, similar to the S&P 500 Index used by U.S. money managers, and (2) an overview of the movements of the Swiss stock market. Consequently, each of the 12 indexes is calculated by two methods. In one method, a capitalization-weighted "price" index is calculated by using the Laspeyres formula, omitting dividends. The other method produces a total-return "performance" index, which includes reinvestment of all dividend payouts as well as rights offerings. Therefore, each of the 12 indexes is calculated for three stock category in terms of price and performance indexes. In total then, 72 indexes are calculated: 36 price indexes and 36 performance indexes. Although calculated daily by the SBC at the close of the markets, it is the Zurich, Geneva, and Basel stock exchanges, not the SBC, that determine which stocks are to be included in the general index.

All performance indexes have a base level of 1,000 as of April 1, 1987. On the other hand, a base level of 100 as of December 31, 1958, is used for all price indexes in those "new" SBC indexes that approximate the composition of the original 117-share SBC Index. For the Commerce, Miscellaneous Services, and Miscellaneous Industrials price indexes, which cannot be linked to the original index, a base level of 100 as of April 1, 1987, is used. For the SBC-100 Index, a base period of December 31, 1986, is used instead.

Swiss National Bank Index

The Swiss National Bank is Switzerland's central bank. It computes and publishes the broad-based Swiss National Bank Index of 131 stocks issued by 93 Swiss companies whose shares are traded on the Zurich, Geneva, and Basel stock exchanges in addition to pre-bourse markets (Exhibit 7.50). In addition, subindexes are calculated for 11 industry sectors. All 12 indexes are capitalization-weighted by the Laspeyres formula and have a base value of 100 as of 1966.

EXHIBIT 7.50 Swiss National Bank Index Components

Sector/Company

1. **Financial societies (29)**
   Allgemeine Finanzgesellschaft
   C. F. Bally
   Basler Handelsbank
   Eidgenössische Bank Finanzgesellschaft
   Elektrowatt
   Gutor Holding
   Hasler
   Holderbank Financière Glarus Interfood
   Intershop Holding
   Juvena Holding
   Laurens Holding
   Mikron Holding
   Motor-Columbus
   Naville Holding
   Pax Anlage
   Perrot, Duval & Cie.
   La Rente Immobilière
   SAEG
   Schweiz. Elektrizitäts und Verkehrsgesellschaft
   Schweiz. Gesellschaft für Kapitalanlagen
   Schweiz. Gesellschaft für Metallwerke
   Sociètè Financiere Italo-Suisse
   Sociètè Financiere Pirelli
   Südamerikanische Electrizitäts
   Sociètè Suisse de Ciment Portland
   Sociètè Generale pour l'Industrie
   Sopaftin
   Swiss-Argentine Society
2. **Machines and metals (17)**
   Adolf Saurer
   Appareillage Gardy
   Brown Boveri & Cie.
   Buss
   Cableries et Tréfileries de Cossonay
   Charmilles
   Ed. Dubied & Cie.
   Gebrüder Sulzer
   Georg Fischer
   Instruments de Physique
   Landis & Gyr
   LG International
   Monteforno Steel & Rolling Mill
   Paillard
   Sécheron
   Swiss Aluminum
   Von Roll
3. **Banks (15)**
   Aargauische Hypotheken- & Handelsbank
   Bank Leu & Co.
   Banque pour le Commerce Suisse-Iraélien
   Basellandschaftlische Hypothekenbank
   Crédit Founcier Vaudois
   Credit Suisse
   Handwerkerbank Basel
   Hypothekar- und Handelsbank Wintherthur
   Union Bank of Switzerland
   Swiss Bank Corporation
   Schweizerische Hypotheken- und Handelsbank

EXHIBIT 7.50 *(concluded)*

Sector/Company

Solothurner Handelsbank
Swiss National Bank
Schweizerische Bodenkredit-Anstalt
Waadtländer Kantonalbank

4. **Insurance (9)**
   Baloise-Holding
   Helvetia Swiss Fire and Accident Insurance
   La Genevoise Cie.
   Neuenberger
   Swiss National Insurance
   Swiss Reinsurance
   Swiss Accident Insurance, Winterthur
   Swiss General Insurance
   Zurich Insurance

5. **Power plants (8)**
   Aare-Tessin
   Aletsch, Mörel
   Centralscheizerische Kraftwerke
   EG Laufenberg
   Energie Electrique de Simplon
   Kraftwerk Bruslo
   Kraftwerk Laufenberg
   Sopracenerina

6. **Foods (5)**
   Brauerei Eichhof
   Hero Conserven Lenzburg
   Nestlé
   Roco Conserven Rorschach
   Ursina

7. **Transportation (4)**
   Brig-Visp-Zermatt Bahn
   Gornergratbahn
   Swissair
   Tramways

8. **Diverse enterprises (4)**
   Grand Passage
   Jelmoli
   Magazine zum Globus
   Publicitas

9. **Chemical and pharmaceutical (4)**
   Ciba-Geigy
   Lonza
   Sandoz
   Zyma

10. **Textile and leather (1)**
    AG für Seidenindustrie, Glarus

11. **Other (2)**
    Holzstoff
    Losinger
    Totals: 143 issues/98 companies

Source: Swiss National Bank.

Taiwan

The securities market in the Republic of China (Taiwan) stemmed from the 1953 "Land to the Tiller" land reform, whereby the government issued land bonds and shares of four large government-owned enterprises as compensation to those landowners who were required to redistribute their land. The Taiwan Stock Exchange, located in Taipei, was formed in 1961 to provide a basis for the development of a centralized,

EXHIBIT 7.51 Taiwan Stock Exchange Weighted Price Index Components as of December 31, 1988

Category A (93 Companies)

ADI
Ambassador Hotel
Asia Cement
Ban Yu Paper
Carnival
Cathay Construction
Cathay Life Insurance
Chang Hwa Bank
Charoen Pokthand Enterprises (Taiwan)
Cheng Hong Chemical
Cheng Loong
Cheng Shin Industries
Chia Hsin Cement
Chia Hsin Flour
Chien Tai Cement
China Chemical
China Development
China General Plastics Corporation
China Rebar
China Steel (preferred)
China Synthetic Rubber
China Wire & Cable
Chung Fu Textile
Chung Shing Textile
Chung Hwa Pulp
Dung Ho Textile
Eagle Food
Evergreen Marine
Far East Department
Far East Textile
First Bank
Formosa Chemical & Fibre
Formosa Plastic
Formosa Taffeta Company, Ltd.
Formosan Union Chemical
Fu I Industries
Great Wall Enterprise
Hua Engineering Wire & Cable
Hua Nan Bank
Hualon-Teijran
ICBC
International Bills Finance
Kolin
Kunnan Enterprise
Kuochan Development & Construction
Kwong Fong Industries
Lee Chang Yung Chemical Industries

Lien Hwa Industries
Liton Electronic
Long Chen Paper
The Medium Business Bank of Hsin Chu
The Medium Business Bank of Kaohsiung
The Medium Business Bank of Tainan
Mercuries & Associates
Microtek International
Namchow Chemical
Nan Ta Plastic
Nan-Yang Dyeing & Finishing
Oriental Union Chemical
Pacific Construction
Pacific Electric Wire
Picvue Electronics
President Enterprises
Rectron Ltd.
Reward Wool
Ruentext Industries
Sampo
San Fang Chemical
Shihlin Electric & Engineering
Shihlin Paper
Shinkong Synthetic Fiber
Southeast Soda
Taichung Business Bank
Tapei Business Bank
Taiwan Cement
Taiwan Fluorescent
Taiwan Glass
Taiwan Polypropylene
Taiwan Styrene Monomer
Taiwan Synthetic Rubber
Taroko Textile
Tatung
Teco Electric & Machinery
Tung Ho Steel
U-Lead Industries
United Micro Electronics
Universal Cement
USI Far East
Ve Wong
Walsin Lihwa Wire & Cable
Wei Chuan Food
Yue Loong Motor
Yuen Foong Yu Paper

EXHIBIT 7.51 *(concluded)*

Category B (34 Companies)

Asia Polymer	Right Way Industries
Chia Hsin Livestock	Shin Shin Supermarket
China Manmade Fibers	Shin Yen Industries
First Steamship	Sinkong Spinning
Garden Hotel	Sino-Japan Feed Industries
Grape King Industries	Tahchung Iron of Superior Quality
Hung Chou Chemical	Taita Chemical
Imperial Hotel	Taiwan Agriculture & Forestry
Kuoyang Construction	Taiwan Industry & Mining
Lucky Textile	Taiwan Paper
The Medium Business Bank of Taitung	Taiwan Pineapple
Min Hsing Cotton Mill	Tateh Agricultural Industries
Nan Kang Rubber Tire	Tay Feng Tire
Oceanic Beverage Company	Tong-Hwa Synthetic Fiber
Pao-Ku	Tung Kuan Enterprises
Pao Shiang Industries	Wan Hwa Enterprise
Pan Overseas Corporation	Yieh-Hsing
Total: 127 companies	

Source: Taiwan Stock Exchange Corporation.

regulated securities marketplace to replace a kind of over-the-counter market.

The sole measure of the stock activity on the Taiwan Stock Exchange is the broad-based composite Taiwan Stock Exchange Weighted Price Index of 127 issues (exclusive of banking and insurance issues) consisting of 94 Category A (1st Section) companies and 34 Category B (2nd Section) companies (Exhibit 7.51). The index is capitalization-weighted by the Paäsche formula and has a base level of 100 as of December 31, 1966.

To be listed as a Category A stock, a corporation must meet the following criteria:

• The amount of capital stock is not less than NT$200 million.
• The ratio of shareholder's equity to total assets for the latest year is not less than one third.
• The number of registered shareholders must be at least 2,000.
• The operating income and net income before taxes must meet one of the following conditions:
  1. The ratio of operating income and net income before taxes to the capital stock must not be less than 10 percent for each of the past two years.
  2. The amount of operating income and net income before taxes must be greater than NT$40 million, and the ratio defined in (1) must be greater than 5 percent for each of the past two years.
  3. Condition (1) must be met in one of the past two years and condition (2) in the other year.

To be listed as a Category B stock, a corporation must meet the following criteria:

• The amount of capital stock is not less than NT$100 million.

FIGURE 7.33 Taiwan Stock Exchange Weighted Price Index

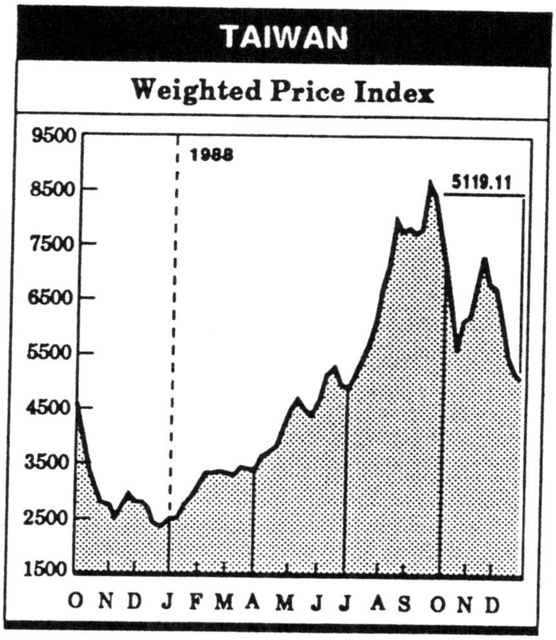

- The number of registered shareholders must be at least 1,000. A minimum of 10 million shares or 20 percent of the number of shares to be listed must be publicly held with not less than 500 shareholders each holding from 1,000 to 50,000 shares.
- The operating income and net income before taxes must meet one of the following conditions:
  1. The ratio of operating income and net income before taxes to the capital stock must not be less than 10 percent for the latest year.
  2. The average ratio of operating income and net income before taxes to the capital stock must be greater than 5 percent for each of the past two years, and the latest year must show better profitability than the previous year.

In addition to the broad Taiwan Stock Exchange Weighted Price Index, two subindexes comprising Category A and B stocks separately have been made available since January 5, 1981, as well as lesser-known indexes for the following eight industrial sectors:

Banking & Insurance

Cement

Construction

Electric & Machinery

Food

Plastics and Chemicals

Paper

Textiles

For each of these, the base levels equalled its capitalization on December 29, 1986.

Thailand

In 1962, a private group of investors organized the first stock exchange in Thailand, which was later incorporated as the Bangkok Stock Exchange Company. The present Securities Exchange of Thailand (SET), which opened on April 30, 1975, as a semi-official entity, is currently Thailand's sole stock exchange. Currently, there are two major indexes that reflect the price activity of the 100+ listed stocks on the SET: Securities Exchange of Thailand Index and the Book Club Index.

Securities Exchange of Thailand Index—SET

The Securities Exchange of Thailand Index, which is maintained by the SET, is a broad-based index composed of all the stocks listed on the SET. The index is capitalization-weighted by the Paäsche formula and has a base level of 100 as of April 30, 1975. On a day when there is no trading of a given stock, the stock's last closing price is used in calculation of the index.

FIGURE 7.34   Stock Exchange of Thailand (SET) Index

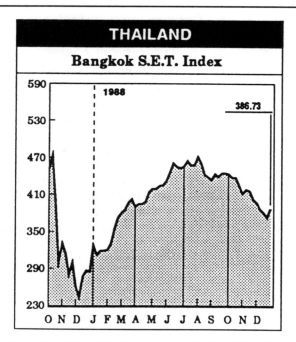

Book Club Index

The Book Club Index, which is maintained by the Book Club Finance and Securities Co., Ltd., is a broad-based index of all the stocks listed on the SET. Like the SET Index, the Book Club Index is capitalization-weighted by the Paäsche formula and has a base level of 100 as of April 30, 1975. However, on a day when there is no trading of a given stock, the average of the stock's last bid and offer prices is then used in calculation of the index. In addition, the formula for adjusting the index's base level is different from Equation 1.12, which is used for the SET Index. The formula used for adjusting the Book Club Index is:

$$\begin{array}{l} \text{New} \\ \text{base} \\ \text{value} \end{array} = \frac{\begin{array}{c} \text{Total capitalization} \\ \text{before adjustment} \end{array} + \begin{array}{c} \text{Adjusted} \\ \text{amount} \end{array}}{\begin{array}{c} \text{Total capitalization} \\ \text{after adjustment} \end{array}} \times \text{Old base value} \qquad (7.8)$$

West Germany

The first exchange list printed for the Frankfurt Stock Exchange (*Frankfurter Wertpapierbörse,* or FWB) dates from 1727; the first dividend-yielding shares were traded in 1820. There are now eight West German stock exchanges:

> Berlin Stock Exchange
>
> Bremen Stock Exchange
>
> Rhineland Westphalia Stock Exchange (Düsseldorf)
>
> Frankfurt Stock Exchange
>
> Hanseatic Stock Exchange (Hamburg)
>
> Lower Saxony Stock Exchange (Hannover)
>
> Bavarian Stock Exchange (Munich)
>
> Baden-Württemburg Stock Exchange (Stuttgart)

All of these belong to the Federation of the German Stock Exchanges. Of these eight exchanges, the Frankfurt Stock Exchange is the largest, listing over 700 shares and accounting for about 60 percent of the total turnover, while the Rhineland Westphalia Stock Exchange in Düsseldorf is Germany's second largest, with approximately 450 listed issues.

Currently, there are five indexes that reflect the price activity of the listed stocks on either the Frankfurt or Düsseldorf stock exchanges:

> Frankfurt Stock Exchange Composite Index
>
> Frankfurter Allgemeine Zeitung Index
>
> Commerzbank Index
>
> Börsen Zeitung Index
>
> The German Share Index

Frankfurt Stock Exchange Composite Index

The Frankfurt Stock Exchange Composite Index *(FWB-Gesamtindex)* is a broad-based index of the 233 most active stocks traded on the FWB (Exhibit 7.52). The index is capitalization-weighted according to the Laspeyres formula and has a base level of 100 as of December 31, 1968.

EXHIBIT 7.52   Frankfurt Stock Exchange (FWB) Composite Index Components as of June 30, 1988

Sector Subindex/Company

1.   Machinery (34)

Alderwerke	Kolbenschmidt
Allweiler	Krauss Maffei
Balcke-Dürr	Krones
Boge	KSB
CEAG	Linde
Deutsche Babcock & Wilcox	MAHO
FAG Kugelfischer	MAN Maschinenfabrik
Friedrich Deckel	MAN Roland Druckmaschinen
GESTRA	Moenus
GMN Georg Müller Nürnberg	Pittler Maschinenfabrik
G. M. Pfaff	Rheinmetall
Hertel	SABO Maschinenfabrik
Industrie-Werke Karlsruhe-Ausburg	Schiess
J. Vögele	Schubert & Salzer
Klöckner-Humboldt-Deutz	Seitzenzinger Noll
Kochs Adler	Traub
Koenig & Bauer	VDO Adolph Schindling

2.   Chemicals and pharmaceuticals (25)

Altana	Hoechst
BASF	Kali-Chemie
Bayer	Kali und Salz
Biotest	Phoenix
Cassella	Pirelli
Continental Gummiwerke AG	Riedel de Haen
Degussa	Rütgerswerke
Deutsche Texaco	Schering
Enka	C. Schlenk
Fresenius	Schwäbische Zellstoff
Fuschs Petrolub	Wella
Thyssen Goldschmidt	Zanders Feinpapier
Henkel KGaA	

3.   Breweries (17)

Bayerische Brauerei Schuck-Jaenisch	Löwenbräu
Binding-Brauerei	Mainzer Aktien-Bierbrauerei
Die Blauen Quellen	Parkbrauerei
Dortmunder Ritterbrauerei	Reichelbräu
Dortmunder Union Schultheiss	Sinalco
Eichbaum-Brauerei	Sinner
Heidelberger Schlossquellbrauerei	Stuttgarter Hofbräu
Henniger-Bräu	Tucher Bräu
Kupferberg & Company	

4.   Utilities (17)

Badenwerk	Neckarwerke Electrizitätsversorgungs
Berlin Power and Light	Rheinelecktra
CONTIGAS	RWE
Gelsenwasser	Thüga

EXHIBIT 7.52 *(continued)*

Sector Subindex/Company

Kraftwerk Rheinfelden
Kraftwerk Altwürttemberg
Lahmeyer
Lech-Elektrizitätswerke
Main-Kraftwerke

Überlanwerke Unterfranken
VEBA
VEW
Württemburigsche Electrizitäts

5. Electronics (15)

AEG
Brown Boveri & Cie.
Braun
Brilliantleuchten
Deutsch-Atlantische Telegraphen
Felten & Guilleaume
Hagen Batterie
Hartmann & Braun

Kabel und Metallwerke
Nixdorf Computers, preferred
Philips Kommunikations-Industrie
Schneider Rundfunkwerke
SEL
Siemens
Varta

6. Lending banks (14)

Allgemeine Deutsche Credit-Anstalt Bank
Baden-Württembergische Bank
Bayerische Hypotheken- und Weschselbank
Bayerische Vereinsbank
Berliner Bank
Berliner Handels- und Frankfurter Bank
Commerzbank

Deutsche Bank
Deutsche Verkehrs-Kredit Bank
Dresdner Bank
Frankfurter Bankgesellschaft
Industriekreditbank
Trinkhaus & Burkhardt
Vereins- und Westbank

7. Insurance (14)

Aachen and Munich Beteilung
Aachen and Munich Insurance
Aachen Reinsurance
Albingia
Allianz
Allianz Life Insurance
Colonia

Deutscher Continental Reinsurance
Frankona
Magdeburg Fire
Mannheimer Insurance
Munich Reinsurance
Thuringia Insurance
Würtemberg & Bad Insurance

8. Construction (13)

Bilfinger + Berger
Didier-Werke
DLW
Dyckerhoff & Widmann
Dyckerhoff Cement
Flachglas
Grünzweig + Hartmann and Glasfaser

Heidelberg Cement
Hochtief
Pegulan-Werke
Philipp Holzmann
Strabag-Bau
VGT

9. Iron and steel (12)

Buderus
Edelstahlwerk Witten
Hindrichs-Auffermann
Hoesch
Klockner-Werke
Krupp Stahl

Mannesmann
Stahlwerke Peine-Salzgitter
Thyssen AG
Thyssen Industrie
Vereinigte Deutsche Metallwerke
Württembergische Metallwarenfabrik

10. Department stores (11)

Andreae-Noris Zahn
ASKO Deutscher Kaufhaus
CO OP
Deutscher Eisenhandel
GEHE
Hornbach

Horten
Massa
Karstadt Group AG
Kaufhof
Stumpf

11. Mortgage banks (7)

Braunschweig-Hannoversche Hypotheken Bank
Deutsche Centralbodenkredit-AG
Deutsche Hypothekenbank Frankfurt-Bremen
Deutsche Hypothekenbank Hannover und Berlin
Frankfurter Hypothekenbank
Pfälzische Hypothekenbank
Rheinische Hypothekenbank

EXHIBIT 7.52 *(concluded)*

Sector Subindex/Company

12. **Textiles and leather (7)**
   Bremer Wollkämmerei   Puma
   Dierig Holding   Salamander
   ESCADA   VERSIDAG
   Hugo Boss
13. **Automobiles (6)**
   Audi   Mercedes-Automobil-Holding
   Bayerische Motoren-Werke   Porsche
   Daimler-Benz   Volkswagen
14. **Commerce (3)**
   Eisenbahn-Verkehrsmittel-AG für Transport und Lagerung
   Lufthansa
   Hamburger Hochbahn AG
15. **Miscellaneous (38)**
   Aesculap-Werke   Mauser Waldeck
   AGAB   Metalgesellschaft
   AG für Industrie und Verkerswessen   Monachia
   Bremer Vulkan   Oberland Glas
   Concordia   Otavi Mining
   DEWB   Preussag
   DSK   PWA Papierwerke Waldhof
   Feldmühle Nobel   Rosenthal
   Hamborner Bergbau   Schmalbach-Lubeca
   Hannover Papierfabrik   Axel Springer
   Harpener   Stolberger Zinc
   Herlitz   Stollwerk
   Hussel Holding   Süddeutsche Zucker
   Hutschenreuther   Vereinigte Kunstmühlen
   Industrieverwaltungs Gesellschaft   VIAG
   Leifheit   Wanderer Werke
   Linotype   Wickrather
   Markt & Technik   Ymos
   Maschinenfabrik Esslingen   Zeiss Ikon

   Total: 233 companies

Source: Frankfurt Stock Exchange.

**EXHIBIT 7.53   Frankfurt Stock Exchange (FWB) Most
Active Shares Index Components as of June 30, 1988**

Most Active Shares Index

AEG   Dresdner Bank
Allianz Life Insurance   Hoechst
BASF   Mannesmann
Bayer   RWE
Bayerische Hypotheken- und Weschselbank   Schering
Commerzbank   Siemens
Daimler-Benz   Volkswagen
Deutsch Bank

Total: 15 companies

Source: Frankfurt Stock Exchange.

EXHIBIT 7.54   Frankfurt Stock Exchange (FWB) Industrial Index Components as of June 30, 1988

Composite Index Sectors	Companies
1. Machinery	34
2. Chemicals and pharmaceuticals	25
3. Electronics	15
4. Construction	13
5. Iron and steel	12
6. Textile and leather	7
7. Automobiles	6
Total: 112 companies	

Source: Frankfurt Stock Exchange.

The FWB Index is broken down into 14 sector indexes plus 38 shares that are not assigned to any specific industry sector. In addition, there is the FWB Index of Most Active Shares *(Publikumswerte)*, which is a narrow-based index of the stocks of the 15 companies listed in Exhibit 7.53, as well as the FWB Industrial Index, which is a composite index of all the 112 stocks from the following seven sectors (listed in Exhibit 7.54) of the FWB Composite Index: Machinery, Chemicals and Pharmaceuticals, Electronics, Construction, Iron and Steel, Textiles and Leather, and Automobiles. Both the Most Active Shares and Industrial indexes are also capitalization-weighted according to the Laspeyres formula, and each has a base level of 100 as of December 31, 1968.

Frankfurter Allgemeine Zeitung Index—FAZ

The *Frankfurter Allgemeine Zeitung* is one of Germany's major daily newspapers. Since 1961, its Frankfurter Allgemeine Zeitung (FAZ) Index has been considered the major stock index in Germany. The FAZ is a narrow-based index of the 100 most highly capitalized stocks traded on the FWB (Exhibit 7.55). The index is capitalization-weighted according to the Laspeyres formula and has a base level of 100 as of December 31, 1958. It is used as a short-term gauge by those who watch the market and for long-term calculations by financial analysts.

The FAZ Index is broken down into 12 sector indexes, of which the Chemical and Rubber sector accounts for approximately 25 percent of the index's weight. The original index of 1958 remained unchanged until July 20, 1970, after which it was revised to take into account changes in the stock exchange list.

Commerzbank Index

The Commerzbank is one of Germany's "Big Three" banks. Its index, the Commerzbank Index, is Germany's oldest indicator and is a narrow-based index of 60 leading blue-chip stocks that are traded on the stock exchange in Düsseldorf. The index is capitalization-weighted according

EXHIBIT 7.55   Frankfurter Allgemeine Zeitung (FAZ) Index Components

Sector/Company	Capitalization Weight (%) (6/30/88)
1. Chemicals and rubber (11)	**25.02%**
Bayer	7.64%
Hoechst	6.72
BASF	6.67
Continental Gummiwerke AG	0.93
Degussa	0.88
Schering	0.68
Chemie-Verwaltungs	0.43
Altana	0.32
Rütgerswerke	0.29
Thyssen Goldschmidt	0.15
Pirelli	0.12
2. Auto and machine tool manufacturers (16)	**16.82%**
Mercedes-Automobil-Holding	0.64
Bayerische Motoren-Werke (BMW)	1.80
Daimler-Benz	5.09
Volkswagen	3.60
Mannesman-Demag	0.66
Deutsche Babcock & Wilcox	0.69
Industrie-Werke Karlsruhe-Ausburg	0.20
MAN	1.16
KHD	0.76
Gutehoffnungshütte	0.00*
Thyssen-Industrie	1.13
Schubert & Salzer	0.06
Linde	0.57
KSB	0.09
Rheinmetall	0.22
G. M. Pfaff	0.14
3. Banks and insurance (13)	**16.63%**
Deutsche Bank	4.26
Dresdner Bank	3.15
Commerzbank	2.50
Allianz Insurance	1.80
Bayerische Hypotheken- und Weschselbank	1.64
Bayerische Vereinsbank	1.19
Berliner Handels- und Frankfurter Bank	0.53
Aachen and Munich Insurance	0.42
Allianz Life Insurance	0.40
Colonia Insurance	0.31
Frankfurter Hypothekenbank	0.19
Deutsche Centralbodenkredit	0.17
Deutsche Hypothekenbank Hannover	0.07
4. Utilities (7)	**11.76%**
VEBA	4.78
RWE	3.52
VEW	1.65
Bewag	0.91
CONTIGAS	0.38
Thüinger	0.36
Badenwerk	0.18
5. Electronics (9)	**8.77%**
Siemens	5.72
AEG	1.64
Brown Boveri & Cie.	0.38
Philips Kommunikations-Industrie	0.36
Varta	0.24
Rheinelektra	0.22
SEL	0.13
Ceag	0.07
Hartmann & Braun	0.02

EXHIBIT 7.55 *(concluded)*

Sector/Company	Capitalization Weight (%) (6/30/88)
6. Iron works (4)	**8.28%**
Thyssen	3.76%
Mannesmann	3.06
Hoesch	0.86
Klöckner-Werke	0.60
7. Commerce (3)	**3.12%**
Lufthansa	2.62
Hapag-Lloyd	0.28
Agiv	0.22
8. Trade (6)	**3.06%**
Kaufhof	0.94
Karstadt	0.87
Horten	0.60
Neckermann	0.33
Hussel	0.25
Andreae-Noris-Zahn	0.07
9. Raw materials (7)	**3.01%**
Preussag	0.97
Metallgesellschaft	0.67
PWA Papierwerke Waldhof	0.48
Kali Chemie	0.34
Kali + Salz	0.30
Didler	0.22
Otavi Minen	0.03
10. Construction (9)	**1.76%**
Hochtief	0.48
Heidelberg Cement	0.30
Philipp Holzmann	0.22
Bilfinger + Berger	0.17
Dywidag	0.14
DLW	0.14
Dyckerhoff Cement	0.12
Flachglas	0.10
Pegulan-Werke	0.09
11. Consumer goods (13)	**1.37%**
Dortmunder Union Schultheiss-Brauerei	0.36
Süddeutsche Zucker	0.21
Salamander	0.18
Henniger-Bräu	0.11
WMF	0.10
Stollwerck	0.10
Binding	0.09
Dierig Holding	0.07
Rosenthal	0.07
Wicküler	0.04
Stuttgarter Hofbräu	0.03
Löwenbräu München	0.02
Parkbrauerei	0.01
12. Mining (2)	**0.40%**
Harpner	0.31
Hamborner Bergbau	0.09
Total: 100 companies	

* Less than 0.01%.
Source: *Frankfurter Allgemeine Zeitung.*

FIGURE 7.35   Frankfurter Allgemeine Zeitung (FAZ) Index

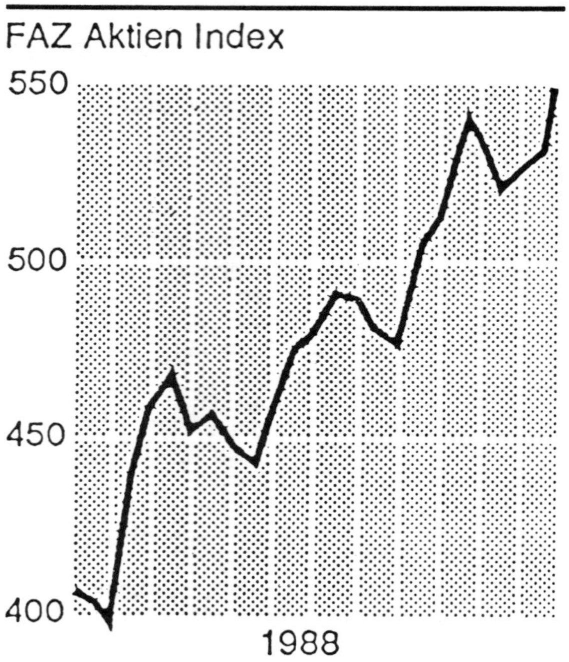

FAZ Aktien Index

Reprinted by permission of *Financial Times.*

to the Laspeyres formula and has a base level of 100 as of December 1953. It comprises approximately 75 percent of the aggregate market value of all the officially quoted shares on the exchange. Like the FAZ Index, the Commerzbank Index is calculated once daily from official midday share prices.

Börsen Zeitung Index

The Börsen Zeitung Index is a narrow-based index of 30 stocks traded on the Frankfurt Stock Exchange. Maintained and published since 1959 by the *Börsen Zeitung* (Bourse Journal), a specialized financial newspaper, the index is capitalization-weighted. Since the introduction of the German Share Index, the Börsen Zeitung Index has declined in popularity and since February 1, 1988, has listed the same stock issues as the DAX.

The German Share Index—DAX

The German Share Index (*Deutscher Aktienindex,* or DAX) is the newest of the German stock indexes, introduced on July 1, 1988. The DAX is a narrow-based index of 30 of the most heavily traded stocks listed on the FWB, representing over 75 percent of the total turnover in German equities (Exhibit 7.56). Unlike the older FAZ and Commerzbank indexes, which are calculated once daily on the basis of official midday share prices, the DAX is a "real-time" index similar to the Dow Jones

EXHIBIT 7.56   German Share Index (DAX) Components

Company	Capitalization Weight (%) (7/1/89)
1. Daimler-Benz	11.87%
2. Bayer	8.47
3. Allianz Insurance	8.37
4. Siemens	8.33
5. BASF	6.92
6. Hoechst	6.82
7. Deutsche Bank	6.71
8. VEBA	5.03
9. RWE	4.52
10. Volkswagen	3.29
11. Bayerische Motoren-Werke (BMW)	3.27
12. Dresdner Bank	2.97
13. Bayerische Hypotheken und Wechselbank	2.44
14. Commerzbank	2.17
15. Thyssen	1.60
16. Kaufhof	1.59
17. Lufthansa	1.59
18. Bayerische Vereinsbank	1.52
19. Nixdorf Computer, preferred	1.52
20. Karstadt Group	1.50
21. Mannesmann	1.26
22. Linde	1.21
23. Degussa	1.13
24. VIAG	1.01
25. Schering	0.98
26. MAN (GHH)	0.92
27. Feldmühle Nobel	0.83
28. Henkel KGaA	0.83
29. Continental Gummiwerke	0.81
30. Deutsche Babcock & Wilcox	0.52

Source: Frankfurt Stock Exchange.

Industrial Average and is continuously updated at one-minute intervals throughout the trading day.

The DAX is capitalization-weighted according to the Laspeyres formula and has a base level of 1,000 as of December 31, 1987. It replaced the older Börsen Zeitung Index on December 31, 1987, at an index level of 100. In terms of capitalization, Daimler-Benz and Bayer currently account for approximately 20 percent of the index's weight.

World Stock Market Indexes

As the result of the economic rise of many foreign countries, many money managers and private investors have invested in overseas funds, ADRs, or the foreign stocks themselves. As a gauge of the performance of their portfolios against those of the world, two major sources are frequently used: the Morgan Stanley Indexes and the AMEX International Market Index.

Morgan Stanley Indexes

Morgan Stanley Capital International (MSCI), a unit of Morgan Stanley & Co., maintains and publishes two broad-based international indexes: the MSCI World Index and the MSCI Europe, Australia, and Far East (EAFE) Index.

The MSCI World Index is based on over 1,400 securities listed on 19 of the world's stock exchanges in the United States, Europe, Canada, Australia, South Africa, and the Far East (Exhibit 7.57). It aims to account for approximately 60 percent of the capitalization of each nation's market, and nearly 99 percent of the component stocks are easily purchasable by U.S. investors. The notable exceptions are the restricted shares issued in Sweden and Switzerland.

Besides the World Index, MSCI also maintains regional indexes for Europe and for the combination of Europe, Australia, and the Far East. The latter is commonly referred to as the EAFE Index, which includes over 900 stocks and is the benchmark against which money managers measure the performance of their international portfolios. All indexes are capitalization-weighted according to the Laspeyres formula, and have a base level of 100 as of January 1, 1970. Both the World and EAFE indexes are computed as arithmetic averages of the individual indexes of the component countries.

EXHIBIT 7.57   Morgan Stanley Capital International World Index Component Countries

Regional Index/Country	Approximate Weight (%) (November 1987)	
Europe	**22.5%**	
Austria		0.1%
Belgium		0.6
Denmark		0.2
France		2.7
Germany		3.5
Italy		2.1
Netherlands		1.5
Norway		0.2
Spain		0.6
Sweden		0.8
Switzerland		1.9
United Kingdom		8.3
Europe, Australia, and Far East (EAFE)	**59.0%**	
Europe (as above)		22.5
Australia		1.5
Hong Kong		0.8
Japan		33.7
Singapore/Malaysia		0.5
World	**100%**	
EAFE (as above)		59.0
Canada		2.9
South African Gold Mines		0.4
USA		37.7

Source: Morgan Stanley Capital International.

FIGURE 7.36   Morgan Stanley Capital International EAFE and S&P Indexes

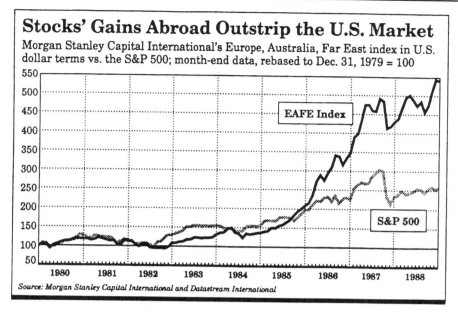

Stocks' Gains Abroad Outstrip the U.S. Market

Morgan Stanley Capital International's Europe, Australia, Far East index in U.S. dollar terms vs. the S&P 500; month-end data, rebased to Dec. 31, 1979 = 100

Source: Morgan Stanley Capital International and Datastream International

The EAFE aims to account for approximately 60 percent of the capitalization of each nation's market, and nearly 99 percent of the component stocks are easily purchasable by U.S. investors. The notable exceptions are the restricted shares of Swedish and Swiss firms.

AMEX International Market Index

The AMEX International Market Index is a narrow-based index developed jointly by the American Stock Exchange and the Coffee, Sugar & Cocoa Exchange (New York). It is based on the share prices of 50 major blue-chip foreign companies from Europe, Australia, and Japan (Exhibit 7.58). The underlying stocks of these companies are registered either as ADRs or New York Shares[12] in the United States and are actively traded in dollars on the NYSE, AMEX, or through NASDAQ's OTC and National Market systems.

To be included in the index, component stocks must be either registered under Section 12 of the Securities Exchange Act of 1934, or eligible for exemption from Section 12 by complying with the provisions of SEC Rule 12g3–2. Furthermore, (1) monthly volume of at least 75 percent of the underlying stocks must average 50,000 shares and none can trade less than 20,000, (2) minimum capitalization must be $100 million, and (3) there must be at least eight market makers for each NASDAQ-traded issue. Unlike other international stock indexes, such

---

[12] A New York Share is similar to an ADR in that it trades in the United States and is fully redeemable for a company's underlying ordinary shares. However, it differs from an ADR in that a New York Share is shown on the company's balance sheet as a separate class of stock, whereas ADRs are not treated as such.

EXHIBIT 7.58   AMEX International Market Index Components

	Company	Country	Exchange	ADR Ticker Symbol	Capitalization Weight (%) (7/29/88)
1.	Toyota Motor Corp.	Japan	OTC	TOYOY	12.04%
2.	Hitachi Ltd.	Japan	NYSE	HIT	8.43
3.	Matsushita Electric Co.	Japan	NYSE	MC	8.12
4.	Royal Dutch Petroleum Co.	Netherlands	NYSE	RD	6.25
5.	British Petroleum Co. Ltd.	UK	NYSE	BP	5.04
6.	NEC Corp.	Japan	OTC/NMS	NIPNY	5.04
7.	Nissan Motor Corp. Ltd.	Japan	OTC	NSANY	4.17
8.	Honda Motor Co. Ltd.	Japan	NYSE	HMC	3.33
9.	Japan Airlines Co. Ltd.	Japan	OTC	JAPNY	3.01
10.	Glaxo Holdings PLC	UK	NYSE	GLX	2.54
11.	Sony Corp.	Japan	NYSE	SNE	2.46
12.	Imperial Chemical Ind.	UK	NYSE	ICI	2.41
13.	Ito-Yokado Co. Ltd.	Japan	OTC/NMS	IYCOY	2.35
14.	BAT Industries	UK	AMEX	BTI	2.30
15.	Fuji Photo & Film Co.	Japan	OTC	FUJIY	2.27
16.	Broken Hill Proprietary	Australia	NYSE	BHP	2.11
17.	Sanyo Electric Co.	Japan	OTC	SANYY	1.92
18.	Unilever NV	Netherlands	NYSE	UN	1.84
19.	Hanson Trust PLC	UK	NYSE	HAN	1.80
20.	Mitsui & Co.	Japan	OTC	MITSY	1.63
21.	National Westminster PLC	UK	NYSE	NW	1.51
22.	Kyocera Corp.	Japan	NYSE	KYO	1.44
23.	Compania de Telef Nacnls	Spain	NYSE	TEF	1.38
24.	Canon, Inc.	Japan	OTC/NMS	CANNY	1.35
25.	Barclays PLC	UK	NYSE	BCS	1.07
26.	TDK Corp.	Japan	NYSE	TDK	0.96
27.	Tokio Marine & Fire	Japan	OTC/NMS	TKIOY	0.90
28.	Pioneer Electric Corp.	Japan	NYSE	PIO	0.88
29.	Novo Industries AS	Denmark	NYSE	NVO	0.88
30.	Volvo AB	Sweden	OTC/NMS	VOLVY	0.84
31.	Cadbury Schweppes PLC	UK	OTC/NMS	CADBY	0.78
32.	Philips NV	Netherlands	NYSE	PHG	0.78
33.	Banco Central SA	Spain	NYSE	BCM	0.75
34.	Reuters Holdings PLC	UK	OTC/NMS	RTRSY	0.74
35.	ASEA AB	Sweden	OTC	ASEAY	0.65
36.	Beecham Group PLC	UK	OTC/NMS	BECHY	0.64
37.	Norsk Hydroelectric	Norway	NYSE	NHY	0.58
38.	Montedison SPA	Italy	NYSE	MNT	0.55
39.	Electrolux	Sweden	OTC/NMS	ELUXY	0.54
40.	Rank Organisation PLC	UK	OTC	RANKY	0.53
41.	News Corporation	Australia	NYSE	NWS	0.47
42.	Fisons PLC	UK	OTC	FISYD	0.43
43.	Pacific Dunlop Ltd.	Australia	OTC/NMS	PDLPY	0.34
44.	Burmah Oil PLC	UK	OTC	BURMY	0.33
45.	Ericsson Telephone Co.	Sweden	OTC/NMS	ERICY	0.32
46.	Pharmacia AB	Sweden	OTC/NMS	PHABY	0.26
47.	KLM Royal Dutch Airlines	Netherlands	NYSE	KLM	0.20
48.	Saatchi & Saatchi Co.	UK	NYSE	SAA	0.20
49.	Jaguar PLC	UK	OTC/NMS	JAGRY	0.18
50.	Norsk Data AS	Norway	OTC	NORKZ	0.05

Source: American Stock Exchange.

as Morgan Stanley's EAFE Index, any of the component shares can be held by U.S. investors.

The index is capitalization-based and is computed from the last sale price of each stock. It has a base level of 200 as of January 2, 1987. Based on market capitalization, the 50 stocks represent nine

EXHIBIT 7.59   AMEX International Market Index Components by Country

Country	Companies	Percent of Index (7/29/88)
Japan	17	60.32%
United Kingdom	15	20.91
Netherlands	4	9.07
Australia	3	2.92
Sweden	5	2.60
Spain	2	2.13
Denmark	1	0.88
Norway	2	0.62
Italy	1	0.55

Source: American Stock Exchange.

different countries, with the 17 Japanese component companies accounting for approximately 60 percent of the index (Exhibit 7.59). Notable omissions are stocks from France, Germany, Hong Kong, and Switzerland because their ADRs do not qualify.

The International Market Index serves as the basis for European-style, cash-settled index option contracts that traded on the AMEX under the ticker symbol ADR as well as cash-settled index futures contracts traded on the Coffee, Sugar & Cocoa Exchange using the commodity code DR.

FIGURE 7.37   AMEX International Market Index (IMI) and EAFE Index

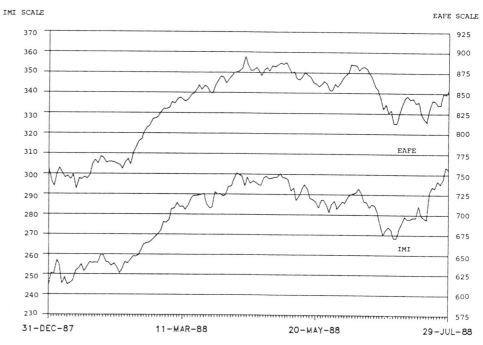

IMI vs. EAFE

Daily Levels, 1988

Source: American Stock Exchange.

Chapter

8

Miscellaneous Financial Indexes, Averages, and Indicators

Introduction

This chapter is primarily concerned with technical indicators which are used by both fundamental and technical analysts to guide their financial decisions. For some, the calculation is easier than the interpretation of the result.

Advance-Decline Measures

There are several popular measures based on the number of advancing and declining issues of NYSE-listed stocks, and all are indicators of the breadth of the stock market.

Absolute Breadth Index

The Absolute Breadth Index is simply the absolute difference between the number of advancing and declining issues. In calculating the absolute difference, the algebraic sign (+ or −) is ignored, and only the number's magnitude is important. In theory, a market bottom is near when the index is high, since a selling spree often occurs near a market bottom.

Advance-Decline Line

The Advance-Decline Line is intended to be an accumulative measure of stock market breadth, and its trend is compared to some other stock average or index, such as the Dow Jones Industrial average. It is computed by starting with a base value, such as 10,000, and the net of the advances and declines is added or subtracted from this base value. Each day's net is added to or subtracted from the previous day's total. Figure 8.1 illustrates the movement of the Advance-Decline Line against the price movements of the DJIA.

FIGURE 8.1 DJIA Advance-Decline Line

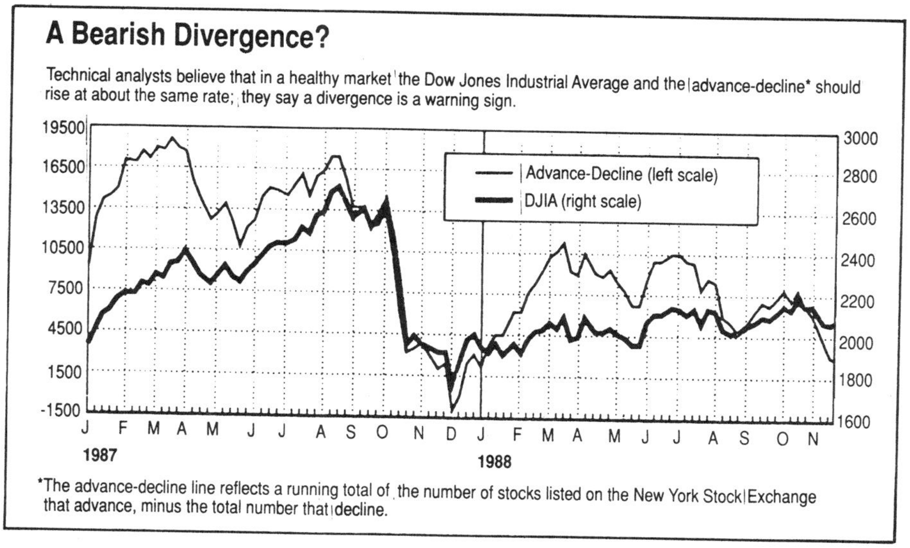
A Bearish Divergence?
Technical analysts believe that in a healthy market the Dow Jones Industrial Average and the advance-decline* should rise at about the same rate; they say a divergence is a warning sign.
19500
16500
13500
10500
7500
4500
1500
-1500
3000
2800
2600
2400
2200
2000
1800
1600
Advance-Decline (left scale)
DJIA (right scale)
J F M A M J J A S O N D J F M A M J J A S O N
1987
1988
*The advance-decline line reflects a running total of the number of stocks listed on the New York Stock Exchange that advance, minus the total number that decline.

In the following table, the following characteristics of the advance-decline line are compared with another market indicator:

A-D Line	Market Indicator	Signal
Rising	Rising	Bullish
Below corresponding market indicator peak	Near or at previous top	Bearish
Above corresponding market indicator peak	Near or at previous top	Bullish
Above previous bottom	Near or at previous bottom	Bullish
Below previous bottom	Near or at previous bottom	Bearish
Rising	Falling	Bullish

Example 8.1

The following illustrates the calculation of the Advance-Decline Line:

Day	A-D Line Value	Advances	Declines	Difference	A-D Line Final Value
1	10,000 (initial)	1,000	500	+500	10,500
2	10,500	200	900	−700	9,800
3	9,800	300	1,200	−900	8,900
4	8,900	600	400	+200	9,100

Advance-Decline Nonaccumulative Indicator

The Advance-Decline Nonaccumulative Indicator is also referred to as the Hughes Breadth Index. It is calculated by using the following formula:

$$\text{Hughes Breadth Index} = \frac{\left(\begin{array}{c}\text{Number of}\\ \text{advancing issues}\end{array}\right) - \left(\begin{array}{c}\text{Number of}\\ \text{declining issues}\end{array}\right)}{\text{Total number of issues traded}} \qquad (8.1)$$

Advance/Decline Ratio

The Advance/Decline Ratio is frequently used as an overbought/oversold indicator. Based on either daily or weekly data, it is simply the ratio of the number of NYSE-listed advancing issues to the number of NYSE-listed declining issues. When a 10-day moving average is used to smooth out day-to-day fluctuations, an advance/decline ratio above 1.25 is taken as a bearish (overbought) sign, while a ratio below 0.75 is considered bullish (oversold).

Breadth Advance/Decline Indicator

The Breadth Advance/Decline Indicator was developed by Martin Zweig, who publishes the *Zweig Forecast,* for NYSE-listed stocks. It is similar to the standard advance/decline ratio except that it uses the 10-day moving average of the number of advancing issues divided by the 10-day average of the number of declining issues.

Insider Buy/Sell Ratio

As its name implies, the Insider Buy/Sell Ratio is the ratio of insider sell to buy transactions. An *insider* is a corporate officer or director who has access to sensitive information not publicly available to the average investor, and can (and usually does) profit by buying and selling stock in his or her company at advantageous times.

Regulations do limit this advantage, however. First, insiders are required to report to the Securities and Exchange Commission any changes in their company ownership by the tenth day of the month following the transaction. Also, insiders are not allowed to realize profits from any transaction until at least six months has passed; otherwise shareholders can challenge the transaction and the insider is required to return all profits to the company.

A high ratio of sellers to buyers indicates an overbought condition and that their stocks are overvalued. A low ratio of sellers to buyers indicates an oversold condition and that their stocks are undervalued. The ratio is computed weekly by Vickers Stock Research Corporation. They use the following criteria to evaluate the ratio:

- Buy when the buy/sell ratio is less than 1.5.
- Sell when the buy/sell ratio is more than 2.0 *and* either when the stock market has dropped 5 percent from the buy level or 5 percent from a subsequent high.

The importance of this type of indicator is such that it is one of the 10 components of the Wall Street Week Technical Market Index.

Moving Averages

Moving averages provide information about basic trends by removing short-term variations. Comparing the average against the actual day-to-day movements, in theory, is supposed to help the investor. Three basic moving averages are used by investors—simple, weighted, and exponential smoothing—any of which can be calculated for any interval (as little as several days to as long as 200 days, for example); these choices are left to the individual. In all cases, moving averages smooth out variations within the time interval of the average, and they emphasize variations for time intervals greater than the average. As a general rule, short intervals are used for short-term trading; longer intervals for long-term trading.

Simple Moving Average

The basic N-day moving average is determined by taking the average of the closing prices of the previous N trading days. The process is then repeated for each following day, adding the latest closing price and dropping the earliest one from the average. Results are usually plotted on the same scale as the daily levels. As with most arithmetic averages, all prices in the interval are given equal weight.

The correct method includes "centered" plotting, so that the moving average lags behind the price level by half its length. Most traders who use moving averages, however, plot their moving average on the same date as the last closing price. As an example, Figure 8.2 illustrates the smoothing effect of a 200-day moving average on the weekly values of the DJIA over a two-year period.

FIGURE 8.2 Dow Jones Industrial Average with Its 200-Day Moving Average

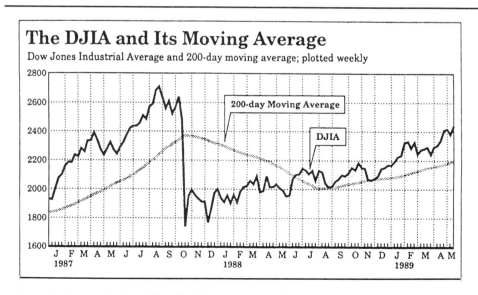

The most common trading strategy focuses on crossings of the two lines. The basic trading rules for simple moving averages are as follows:

- *Buy* when the daily price crosses *above* the moving average line.
- *Sell* when the daily price crosses *below* the moving average line.

This is the opposite of the old axiom: Buy low, sell high.

Example 8.2

The values of the DJIA for the 10-day period from May 9 to May 23, 1989, and those of the five-day moving average are as follows:

Date	DJIA Close	Five-Day Moving Average	Trading Strategy
May 9	2371.33		
10	2374.45		
11	2382.88		
12	2439.70		
15	2463.89	2406.45	Buy
16	2453.45	2422.87	
17	2462.43	2440.47	
18	2470.12	2457.92	
19	2501.10	2470.20	
22	2502.02	2477.82	
23	2478.01	2482.74	Sell

The five-day moving average for the first five-day period (from May 9 to May 15) is:

$$\text{5-Day MA} = \frac{2371.33 + 2374.45 + 2382.88 + 2439.70 + 2463.89}{5}$$

$$= \mathbf{2406.45}$$

For the next five-day period, May 10–16, the moving average is:

$$\text{5-Day MA} = \frac{2374.45 + 2382.88 + 2439.70 + 2463.89 + 2453.45}{5}$$

$$= \mathbf{2422.87}$$

and so on.

Weighted Moving Average

The weighted moving average provides for some flexibility in determining the relative contributions of each of the prices within the interval. For example, heavier weights may be assigned to the more recent prices.

Exponential Moving Average

Of the three moving averages, the exponential moving average is the most sophisticated and is more responsive than a simple moving average. Mathematically, it is determined as follows:

$$MA = \beta P_i + (1 - \beta)X_{i-1} \tag{8.2}$$

where

P_i = Current day's or period's price
X_{i-1} = Previous day's or period's exponential moving average
β = Exponential smoothing constant.

The smoothing constant (β) is a weight between zero and 1, which adjusts the difference between the previous day's or period's moving average value and the actual price. In most applications, its value is best calculated as follows:

$$\beta = \frac{2}{T+1} \qquad (8.3)$$

where T is the time interval for the moving average. If a four-day exponential moving average is required, then $\beta = 2/(4 + 1)$, or 0.4. For the first day or period only, the exponential moving average has the same value as that day's (or period's) closing price (MA = P_i).

Example 8.3

The values of the DJIA for the same 10-day period as Example 8.2 (May 9 to May 23, 1989) and those of a 4-day exponential moving average are as follows:

Date	DJIA Close	4-Day Exponential Moving Average
May 9	2371.33	2371.33
10	2374.45	2372.58
11	2382.88	2376.70
12	2439.70	2401.90
15	2463.89	2426.70
16	2453.45	2437.40
17	2462.43	2447.41
18	2470.12	2456.49
19	2501.10	2474.34
22	2502.02	2485.41
23	2478.01	2482.45

The smoothing constant is $\beta = 2/(4 + 1)$, or 0.4. The 4-day exponential moving average for the first day (May 9) is the same as that day's closing price,

MA = **2371.33**

For May 10, the exponential moving average is determined from Equation 8.2 as follows:

MA = (0.4)(2374.45) + (1 − 0.4)(2371.33)
= **2372.58**

For May 11,

MA = (0.4)(2382.88) + (1 − 0.4)(2372.58)
= **2376.70**

and so on.

Overbought/Oversold Indicators

A variety of technical indicators are used to signal that the market is either overbought or oversold, a condition that precedes the inevitable correction. The precise point at which the market becomes overbought or oversold is about as difficult to define as the measure used to define the market itself.

Measures considered in this chapter as overbought/oversold indicators include the Advance/Decline Ratio, Insider Buy/Sell Ratio, Relative Strength Index, and the TRIN. Another measure is the so-called +30%/−10% rule as applied to the S&P 500 Index. When the 12-month change of the S&P 500 is greater than +30 percent, the market is overbought and one should sell, either long or short. On the other hand, when the 12-month change is less than −10 percent, the market is oversold and one should buy.

Another overbought/oversold indicator is based on data for the last 10 trading days, as follows:

$$\text{O/O Indicator} = \frac{(\text{Current price}) - (\text{10-day low price})}{(\text{10-day high price}) - (\text{10-day low price})} \times 100\% \quad \textbf{(8.4)}$$

Example 8.4

As an example, the values of the DJIA for the 10-day period from May 16 to May 30, 1989, are as follows:

| | | DJIA | |
Date	High	Low	Close
May 16	2469.76	2439.88	2453.45
17	2478.74	**2439.70**	2462.43
18	2482.77	2448.86	2470.12
19	2509.35	2468.29	2501.10
22	**2521.63**	2481.30	2502.02
23	2501.83	2467.19	2478.01
24	2494.68	2458.03	2483.87
25	2498.72	2467.56	2482.59
26	2501.83	2473.06	2493.77
30	2510.66	2459.74	2475.55

The 10-day high (May 22) and low (May 17) levels are shown in boldface. If on May 31, the current level of the DJIA is 2496.87, the calculation is:

$$\text{O/O Indicator} = \frac{(2496.87) - (2439.70)}{(2521.63) - (2439.70)} \times 100\%$$
$$= \textbf{69.8\%}$$

which is neutral.

The market is overbought when this indicator is greater than 90 and is oversold when it is less than 10.

Put/Call Options Premium Ratio

The Put/Call Options Premium Ratio is considered a short-term contrary technical indicator. It is calculated by taking the ratio of the average premium on all listed put options to the average premium on all listed call options. A *put option* is an option, but not the obligation, to sell a given number of shares of a stock at a given price before a given expiration date. On the other hand, a *call option* is an option, but not the obligation, to buy a given number of shares of a stock at a given price before a given expiration date. In effect, a call option is a bet that the price of the stock will go up, while a put option places the opposite bet. The price paid to acquire either type option is called the *premium*.

As a contrary indicator, put premiums are generally high when investors are pessimistic, and as a result, the put/call ratio will be high. In contrary terms, this high ratio is considered bullish for the stock market. When investors are optimistic, on the other hand, call premiums are generally high, and the put/call ratio is low and is considered bearish for the market.

Relative Strength Index

The Relative Strength Index (RSI) is a technical analysis tool often used by chartists. Developed by J. Welles Wilder in 1978, the RSI for a particular stock, bond, commodity, or index is based on the closing prices of the last 14 trading days. Mathematically, it is calculated as follows:

$$RSI = 100 - \frac{100}{1 + RS} \qquad (8.5)$$

where

$$RS = \frac{14 \text{ day average of UP closes}}{14\text{-day average of DOWN closes}}$$

In the absence of other factors, high RSI values are considered as indicating that the market is overbought; low ratios are judged to indicate an oversold condition.

Example 8.5

As an example, the values of the DJIA for the 14-day period from May 9 to May 30, 1989, were as follows:

Date	DJIA Close	Close Up	Close Down
May 9	2371.33		
10	2374.45	3.12	
11	2382.88	8.43	
12	2439.70	56.82	
15	2463.89	24.19	
16	2453.45		10.44
17	2462.43	8.98	
18	2470.12	7.69	
19	2501.10	30.98	
22	2502.02	0.92	
23	2478.01		24.01
24	2483.87	5.86	
25	2482.59		1.28
26	2493.77	11.18	
30	2475.55		18.22
Totals		155.05	53.95
Average		**11.08**	**3.85**

The average in each case is obtained by dividing the total by 14, even though there may not be 14 values. The value for RS is then:

$$RS = \frac{11.08}{3.85}$$
$$= 2.88$$

From Equation 8.5,

$$RSI = 100 - \frac{100}{1 + 2.88}$$
$$= \mathbf{74.23}$$

Short Ratios

A "short sale" occurs when an investor sells a borrowed security with the hope of buying it back later at a lower price to realize a profit. There are a number of technical indicators used to gauge the short selling activity in the marketplace. These in general are essentially the same, and differ primarily by the type of investor they measure. Short sale data are published weekly by the NYSE for both members and nonmembers.

Member Short Ratio

The Member Short Ratio is calculated by dividing the number of short sales of NYSE members by the total number of short sales:

$$\text{Member Short Ratio} = \frac{\text{Short sales of NYSE members}}{\text{Total short sales}} \tag{8.6}$$

Its use is based on the assumption that professional investors are generally correct about the direction of the market. In the absence of other factors, high ratios are considered bearish; low ratios are bullish.

Odd Lot Short Ratio

An odd lot is any order of fewer than 100 shares of stock; such orders are typically placed by small individual investors. The Odd Lot Short Ratio is determined by dividing the total odd-lot short sales by the average of odd-lot purchases and sales:

$$\text{Odd Lot Short Ratio} = \frac{\text{Total odd-lot short sales}}{\text{Average of odd-lot purchases and sales}} \quad \textbf{(8.7)}$$

As a contrary technical indicator, its use is based on the assumption that the small, individual investor belongs to the "wrong way" crowd—he is wrong about the direction of the market more times than he is right. Consequently, in the absence of other factors, high ratios are considered bullish; low ratios are bearish.

Public Short Ratio

The Public Short Ratio is calculated by dividing the number of short sales by non-NYSE members by the total number of short sales:

$$\text{Public Short Ratio} = \frac{\text{Short sales by non-NYSE members}}{\text{Total short sales}} \quad \textbf{(8.8)}$$

Like the Odd Lot Short Ratio, the Public Short Ratio is a contrary technical indicator. In the absence of other factors, high ratios are considered bullish; low ratios are bearish.

Public/Specialist Short Ratio

A *specialist* works on the exchange floor and is responsible for maintaining an orderly market for the stock(s) he specializes in by balancing incoming buy and sell orders. Specialists are in the center of the market and must often risk their own funds in order to maintain an orderly market. Like member firms, they are generally right about market trends more often than the average investor.

The Public/Specialist Short Ratio is calculated by dividing the total number of public (nonmember) short sales by the total number of short sales by specialists:

$$\frac{\text{Public/Specialist}}{\text{Short Ratio}} = \frac{\text{Total public short sales}}{\text{Total specialist short sales}} \quad \textbf{(8.9)}$$

In the absence of other factors, high ratios are considered bearish; low ratios are seen as bullish.

Short Interest Ratio

The Short Interest Ratio is calculated by dividing the total monthly NYSE short interest by the average daily trading volume:

$$\text{Short Interest Ratio} = \frac{\text{Total monthly NYSE short interest}}{\text{Total short sales}} \qquad \textbf{(8.10)}$$

It is a contrary technical indicator: when high, the indicator is considered bullish because the total number of short sales is low and the short sellers will have to cover their positions by buying back stocks, tending to increase market prices.

Specialist Short Ratio

The Specialist Short Ratio is calculated by dividing the total specialist short sales by the total number of short sales from all sources:

$$\text{Specialist Short Ratio} = \frac{\text{Total specialist short sales}}{\text{Total short sales}} \qquad \textbf{(8.11)}$$

In the absence of other factors, high ratios are considered bearish; low ratios are seen as bullish.

Total Short Ratio

The Total Short Ratio is calculated by dividing the total specialist short sales by the total volume, usually on a monthly basis:

$$\text{Total Short Ratio} = \frac{\text{Total specialist short sales}}{\text{Total trading volume}} \qquad \textbf{(8.12)}$$

It is considered to be a contrary indicator. In the absence of other factors, high ratios are considered bullish; low ratios are seen as bearish.

TICK and TRIN

TICK and TRIN both are short-term technical indicators that are designed to measure the strength of the stock market. TICK is the difference between the number of all NYSE stocks whose last sale occurred on an up-tick and the number of all NYSE stocks whose last sale was on a down-tick:

$$\text{TICK} = \left(\begin{array}{c} \text{Number of NYSE stocks} \\ \text{whose last sale} \\ \text{occurred on an up-tick} \end{array} \right) - \left(\begin{array}{c} \text{Number of NYSE stocks} \\ \text{whose last sale} \\ \text{occurred on a down-tick} \end{array} \right) \qquad \textbf{(8.13)}$$

The TICK value can be either positive or negative. A high positive reading would be considered by some as a short-term bullish signal, while a large negative value would be considered bearish. However, there are analysts who interpret TICK readings as a contrary indicator. A high positive TICK value can then be regarded as a short-term overbought signal, while a large negative value signals an oversold situation.

The TICK is displayed for the NYSE stocks throughout the trading day on quote machines; it is identified by the symbol TICK. In addition, *Barron's* publishes the closing TICK values separately for NYSE, AMEX, and DJIA stocks, as illustrated in Figure 8.3.

FIGURE 8.3   Closing TICK for NYSE, AMEX, and DJIA Stocks

Closing Tick				
Daily	Mar. 20	Mar. 21	Mar. 22	Mar. 23 Mar. 24
NYSE	−90	− 99	− 58	− 155
Amex	−144	− 51	− 10	+ 41
DJIA	+16	− 20	+ 18	− 10

The tick shows the number of stocks whose last change in price was an increase, less the number whose last change was a downtick. It is computed for the NYSE, the American Stock Exchange and for the stocks in the Dow Jones Industrial Average. High positive figures indicate a strong market near the close, while negative ones indicate a weak one.

The TRIN is an index that measures the strength of the volume of advancing stocks with respect to that of declining stocks. It is called TRIN because of the symbol used to identify it on quote machines; it is also known as the Arms Short-Term Trading Index, after its developer, Richard W. Arms. It is calculated by taking the advance/decline ratio (a measure of the market's breadth) and dividing it by the ratio of up volume to down volume:

$$\text{TRIN} = \frac{\text{Number of advances/Number of declines}}{\text{Up volume/Down volume}} \qquad (8.14)$$

On days when the stock market rises considerably, the TRIN often drops to low levels (0.5 or less) since the up/down volume ratio is usually much larger than the advance/decline ratio. On down market days, the TRIN is usually greater than 1.0 because of the heavy down volume.

As is shown in Figure 8.4, *Barron's* publishes the closing TRIN (Arms Index) values separately for NYSE, AMEX, and NASDAQ OTC

FIGURE 8.4   Arms Index (TRIN) for NYSE, AMEX, and NASDAQ Stocks

Arms Index				
Daily	Mar. 20	21	22	23	24
NYSE	1.22	.74	1.24	1.34	....
AMEX	1.00	.61	1.09	1.27	....
NASDAQ	1.12	.50	1.02	.53	....

The Arms index, also known as the short term trading index, is the average volume of declining issues divided by the average volume of advancing issues. It is computed separately for the NYSE, the American Stock Exchange and Nasdaq. A figure of less than 1.0 indicates more action in rising stocks.

stock issues. The TRIN is one of the 10 technical market indicators used to compute the Wall Street Week Technical Market Index.

Wall Street Week Technical Market Index

The Wall Street Week Technical Market Index is a consensus barometer of 10 individual technical market indicators (Exhibit 8.1). It was developed by Robert J. Nurock, who publishes *Investor's Analysis* and is a regular panel member of the weekly PBS television show *Wall Street Week,* which gives the index its name. Its objective is to either confirm the continuation of an existing intermediate (3- to 6-month) trend or signal an impending reversal of the trend.

EXHIBIT 8.1   Wall Street Week Technical Market Index Components

Technical Indicator	Bottom Indication (Positive Reading)	Top Indication (Negative Reading)
1. Short-Term Trading Index (TRIN) 10-day moving average	Above +1.2. Readings between −0.8 and +1.2 are neutral.	Lower than −0.8
2. Dow Jones Industrial Average Momentum Ratio	DJIA is more than 3% below its 10-day moving average.	DJIA is more than 3% above its 10-day moving average.
3. Low-Price Activity Ratio	Less than 2.82%	Above 7.59%
4. Market Breadth Indicator	When the indicator goes from below +1000 to the point where it peaks and then drops 1000 points from this peak. Readings between −1000 and +1000 are neutral.	When the indicator goes from above −1000 to the point where it bottoms and then rises 1000 points from this bottom.
5. Prices of NYSE Stocks selling above their 10-week and 30-week moving averages	10-week below 30% *and* 30-week below 40%	10-week above 70% *and* 30-week above 60%
6. NYSE High-Low Indicator	10-day moving average from less than 10 until it exceeds the average number of new lows.	10-day moving average from less than 10 until it exceeds the average number of new highs.
7. Put/Call Options Premiums Ratio	Above 95.5%	Below 42%
8. Corporate Insider Buy/Sell Ratio	Below 1.42	Above 3.61
9. Federal Reserve Monetary Policy	Below 103%	Above 125%
10. Investment Advisors Bearish Sentiment Index	Above 51.5%	Below 35.3%

Source: *Futures* magazine.

The index reflects the influence on stock prices of a wide variety of factors such as market action, speculation, investor psychology, and monetary conditions. In effect, it virtually ignores fundamental figures related to corporate earnings, dividends, or the economy. In fact, it is not an index at all, but an indicator, which assigns a +1 for a bullish trend, a 0 for neutral, or a −1 rating for a bearish trend for each of the 10 market measures that make up the index. The index is the algebraic sum of the 10 ratings.

The 10 market indicators used to construct the Wall Street Week Technical Market Index are as follows:

1. Arms Short-Term Trading Index (TRIN). This indicator, discussed elsewhere in this chapter, is the advance/decline ratio of NYSE stocks, divided by the ratio of up volume to down volume. Exhibit 8.1 summarizes the guidelines used for positive (+1), neutral (0), and negative (−1) ratings.

2. Dow Jones Industrial Average Momentum Ratio. This indicator measures the percent difference between the Dow Jones Industrial Average and the average of its prices for the last 30 days. The current DJIA closing price is divided by the average of the DJIA's average of the last 30 days' prices.

3. Low-Price Activity Ratio. This indicator, which is reported weekly in *Barron's,* measures the activity of low-priced speculative stocks in comparison to that of the DJIA blue-chip issues. The market often peaks when low-price stock volume increases relative to blue-chip volume.

4. Market Breadth Indicator. This is a 10-day moving average of the difference between advances and declines.

5. Prices of NYSE Stocks selling above their 10-week and 30-week moving averages. This indicator measures the percentage of NYSE stocks that are priced above both their 10-week and 30-week moving averages.

6. NYSE High-Low Index. This indicator contrasts the number of NYSE-listed stock reaching new highs and lows on a daily basis over the last 10 trading days. Very few stocks achieve new high prices at market bottoms, while very few stocks achieve new low prices at market tops.

7. Put/Call Options Premiums Ratio. This indicator, discussed earlier in this chapter, is the ratio of the average premium on all listed put options to the average premium on all listed call options.

8. Corporate Insider Buy/Sell Ratio. This indicator, which is discussed earlier in this chapter, is the ratio of insider sell to buy transactions, computed on a weekly basis by Vickers Stock Research Corporation.

9. Federal Reserve Monetary Policy. This indicator tries to sense the direction of Federal Reserve Board policy. It is computed daily by taking the ratio of the closing bid price on Fed funds to the discount rate. The Fed funds rate is the rate charged for overnight borrowing between member banks of the Federal Reserve System; the discount rate is the rate charged member banks by the Fed.

A four-day moving average is computed from the ratios for Friday, Monday, Tuesday, and Thursday, while Wednesday values are ignored as they have been considered as being unusually volatile. When the Fed funds rate equals or falls below the discount rate, the Fed has eased up on monetary policy.

10. Investment Advisors Bearish Sentiment Index. This indicator summarizes the forecasts of approximately 100 stock market newsletters. It was developed by A. W. Cohen of Chartcraft, Inc., and is computed by *Investor's Intelligence*.

In theory, the Wall Street Week Technical Market Index can range from -10 to $+10$. A reading of $+5$ or higher is taken as an immediate buy signal, whereas a -5 or lower is an intermediate sell signal. Readings between these levels are assigned the following meanings:

$+5$ and above	Extremely bullish; buy now
$+4$	Strongly bullish; get ready to buy
$+3$	Bullish
$+2$	Mildly bullish
-1 to $+1$	Neutral
-2	Mildly bearish
-3	Bearish
-4	Strongly bearish; get ready to sell
-5	Extremely bearish; sell now

West Coast Index

The West Coast Index, also referred to as the Monthly Cost of Funds Index, has been published for the Eleventh District[1] of the Federal Home Loan Bank (FHLB), which has its headquarters in San Francisco, since August 1981. The index is a monthly weighted average of the cost of funds—the interest that is being paid by savings institutions on their various sources of mortgage money. It has been proved popular, and many banks outside the district use it to index their adjustable rate mortgages (ARMs).

The greatest source of funds for home loans in the FHLB's Eleventh District is money deposited in savings accounts; lesser amounts arise from loans through FHLB credit programs (called "Advances") and money borrowed from commercial banks and other sources. Because the major component of the Cost of Funds Index is the interest paid on savings accounts, the index does not change as rapidly as other market rates. Consequently, a lag might occur because many accounts are medium- and long-term time deposits.

The funds used as the basis for computing the index are (1) money on deposit, (2) money borrowed from an FHLB bank (Advances), and (3) all other borrowed money, such as reverse repurchase agreements

---

[1] There are 12 district Federal Home Loan Banks, which are part of the Federal Home Loan Bank System created by Congress in 1932. Currently, more than 200 savings and loan associations and banks are part of the Eleventh FHLB District, which includes the three states of Arizona, California, and Nevada.

EXHIBIT 8.2 Cost of Funds Index Adjustment Factors

Days in Month	Adjustment Factor
28	1.086
29*	1.052
30	1.014
30*	1.017
31	0.981
31*	0.984

* Leap-year months.

and mortgage-backed bonds. All of these are the main liabilities of District savings institutions. The formula used for the index is:

$$\begin{matrix}\text{Weighted} \\ \text{average} \\ \text{cost of} \\ \text{funds}\end{matrix} = \frac{\begin{matrix}\text{Interest paid on savings,} \\ \text{advances, and other} \\ \text{borrowings}\end{matrix}}{\begin{matrix}\text{2-month average of total} \\ \text{outstanding of the total} \\ \text{of savings, capital, FHLB} \\ \text{advances, and other} \\ \text{money}\end{matrix}} \times \begin{matrix}\text{Adjustment} \\ \text{factor}\end{matrix} \times 12 \times 100\%$$

(8.15)

The adjustment factor takes into account the differing number of days in a month. It is found by dividing the average month of 30.417 days (based on a 12-month, 365-day year) by the actual number of days in any month. For a 28-day month, this adjustment factor would be equal to 30.417/28, or 1.086. For leap years, the average month has 30.500 days. Exhibit 8.2 summarizes the adjustment factors for common and leap years.

Example 8.6

Suppose that the data for Eleventh District savings institutions are as follows for the month of March in 1989 (31 days):

Cost of interest on savings, advances, and other borrowings	$ 2,000,000,000
2-month average funds	
Savings	$200,000,000,000
Advances	30,000,000,000
Other borrowings	40,000,000,000
Total	$270,000,000,000

From Equation 8.15, with an adjustment factor of 0.981 for a 31-day month in a common year,

$$\begin{aligned}\text{Cost of funds index} &= \frac{\$2,000,000,000}{\$270,000,000,000} \times 0.981 \times 12 \times 100\% \\ &= \textbf{8.72\%}\end{aligned}$$

---

9 On the Lighter Side

This final chapter concerns itself with several financial benchmarks that, while they may not be universally known, accepted, or discussed at trading desks or cocktail parties, nevertheless poke a little fun at what lengths financial analysts will go to try to relate or predict the price movements of virtually anything carrying a price tag.

The Big Mac Index

From its humble beginnings in the early 1950s, McDonald's Corporation has grown to be a corporate giant, has gained a spot on the Dow Jones Industrial Average, and its Big Mac hamburger sandwich is widely recognized as an unofficial synonym for "hamburger." Several years ago, McDonald's Corporation aptly described the Big Mac in an advertising jingle as "Two all-beef patties, special sauce, lettuce, cheese, pickles, onions, on a sesame-seed bun."

The popularity of this double-decker hamburger sandwich has spawned a variety of look-alikes over the years. In fact, McDonald's won a court suit against a Tel Aviv, Israel, restaurant to stop it from making and selling a *Mac David* hamburger sandwich that was a non-kosher imitation.

The Big Mac Index, whose origin, in 1984, is attributed to Georg Grimm, an advisor to West German Chancellor Helmut Kohl, is a novel way of explaining global foreign exchange rates that ignores the effects of trade deficits and intervention of foreign central banks. Although simplistic, it nevertheless is a concept that is easily understood without having to attend MacDonald's Hamburger U.

The index simply looks at worldwide prices of the Big Mac sandwich at today's exchange rates (Exhibit 9.1). By comparing the cost of the Big Mac in New York City to its cost elsewhere, the index quickly shows which foreign currencies are relatively strong or weak, and by how much. For example, the *Biggu Maku* in Tokyo costs the equivalent of $2.78 compared to $2.19 in New York City. In my hometown of Wilmington, Delaware, where we don't have a sales tax and life is not in the fast lane, the Big Mac costs even less at $1.60.

EXHIBIT 9.1 The Big Mac Index Components

Country	Local Price*	U.S. Equivalents*	Over/Under New York Value
Norway	28 kronen	$4.21	+92%
Finland	16.6 markka	3.84	+75
Switzerland	4.50 francs	2.99	+37
France	17.2 francs	2.81	+28
Japan	370 yen	2.78	+27
Italy	3500 lire	2.60	+19
Spain	280 pesetas	2.30	+ 5
West Germany	4.05 marks	2.23	+ 2
New York City	**2.19 dollars**	**2.19**	—
England	1.04 pounds	1.78	−19
Wilmington, DE	1.60 dollars	1.60	−27
Australia	2.00 dollars	1.59	−27
Yugoslavia	2300 dinars	1.47	−33
Singapore	2.80 dollars	1.37	−37
Hong Kong	7.60 dollars	0.97	−56
Turkey	1300 liras	0.95	−57
Hungary	43 forints	0.74	−66

* Local prices and exchange rates as of 9/23/88.
Source: *The Wall Street Journal.*

The Japanese yen is therefore overvalued, as is also the case with most West European currencies. In the words of George Anders of *The Wall Street Journal,* the price of the Big Mac in Norway, $4.21, might be said to be a "whopper." By contrast, a Big Mac bought in Budapest, Hungary, is a real bargain at 74¢. If you can't swallow the concept of an index using a hamburger sandwich to relate the purchasing power of different foreign currencies, then swallow a Big Mac instead for lunch; it's easier.

Moët Luxury Index

Unlike the market basket of basic staples measured by the Consumer Price Index, the producers of Moët & Chandon champagnes annually describe a cost of living indicator applicable to certain luxury goods. The Moët Luxury Index follows the prices of a dozen luxuries in New York City, selected to typify what it costs to live in the style of *La Dolce Vita,* or "the good life."

Annually since 1982, the index has surveyed a market basket of those goods and services the well-to-do should not be without. In its survey, the average annual percent change is compared with the domestic CPI cost-of-living index for the same year. Exhibit 9.2 lists the 12 staples, which in 1988 ranged from a one-pound box of imported Swiss chocolate truffles at $36.00 (not including the New York City 8.5% sales tax) to the Rolls-Royce Corniche convertible at $205,500 (which does not include dealer preparation, freight, license fees, and taxes).

The annual index is determined by taking the arithmetic average of the annual percent changes of all 12 items. Unlike traditional indexes,

EXHIBIT 9.2 Moët Luxury Index Components (New York City Prices)

Item	1988 Price	Percent Change from 1987
1. Petrossian Beluga caviar, 30 grams	$47.00	41.4%
2. Rolls-Royce Corniche convertible	205,500.00	12.0
3. Rolex Oyster perpetual day-date watch with President bracelet	11,700.00	12.0
4. Round trip airplane ticket, New York-Paris on Air France Concorde	4,876.00	10.2
5. Dom Perignon Champange, 750 ml	69.97	8.5
6. Hennessy X.O. Cognac, 750 ml	78.95	7.0
7. Broadway theater ticket, Orchestra seat for "CATS"	50.00	5.3
8. Wash, cut, & blow dry at Bumble & Bumble hair salon	70.00	4.5
9. Mink coat, woman's full-length	17,000.00	3.0
10. Maid service, 1 day, from Maids Unlimited	80.00	0
11. Limousine rental, 1 hour, from Dav El	40.00	0
12. Teucher's imported (Swiss) chocolate truffles, 1 pound	36.00	0
Average change		+8.7%

Sources: Wilmington News Journal; Schieffelin & Sommerset Co.

it has no base-period figure for comparison other than its change from the previous year.

The Misery Index

Developed by the late Arthur Okun, the so-called "Misery Index" came to prominence during the term of President Jimmy Carter (1977–81) who was plagued by the record double-digit inflation rates of the late 1970s. As graphed in Figure 9.1, the Misery Index is determined simply by adding together the current inflation rate and the unemployment rate:

$$\text{Misery Index} = \text{Inflation rate} + \text{unemployment rate}$$

Because of the stock market's sensitivity to inflation and general downturns in the economy, the Misery Index generally varies inversely to the current state of the stock market, but it has virtually no value as a barometer in predicting future market trends.

An alternate method of calculating the Misery Index, given by Colby and Meyers,[1] includes the prime rate at which banks lend money to their most creditworthy customers:

$$\text{Misery Index} = \text{Inflation rate} + \text{Unemployment rate} + \text{Prime rate}$$

---

[1] Colby, Robert W., and Thomas A. Meyers, *The Encyclopedia of Technical Market Indicators* (Homewood, Ill.: Dow Jones-Irwin, 1988), p. 278.

FIGURE 9.1   The Misery Index

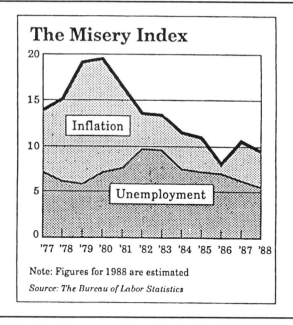

Note: Figures for 1988 are estimated

Source: *The Bureau of Labor Statistics*

Super Bowl Indicators

Every January, the champions of the National Football League's National and American Conferences square off for football immortality in the Super Bowl. By far this country's most watched and heaviest wagered (legal and illegal) event, it touches virtually everyone. Interest in the Super Bowl is now worldwide, although not quite as extensive as soccer's World Cup, which is contested every four years. "Football widows" eagerly await "Super Bowl Sunday," for it (finally!) marks the end of the long football season. For others, who follow the stock market, the winner of the Super Bowl serves as an almost uncanny leading indicator of the direction of the stock market for the coming year.

If an original National Football League (NFL) team wins the Super Bowl, the Dow Jones Industrial Average will be higher at year's end; if an original American Football League (AFL) team wins, the stock market will drop. In the first 23 years of the Super Bowl, this method has correctly picked the Dow's direction 20 times. Exhibit 9.3 lists the original NFL and AFL teams before they were merged into the present day NFL in 1970.

On the other hand, if the Super Bowl can call the direction of the stock market, why can't stocks predict the Super Bowl? According to some, including *The New York Times,* this is not too far from reality. If the Dow is "down" from November to January's Super Bowl Sunday, the team whose name is closest to the beginning of the alphabet will

EXHIBIT 9.3   Super Bowl Indicator

Original NFL Teams (16)

Atlanta Falcons	Minnesota Vikings
Chicago Bears	New Orleans Saints
Cleveland Browns	New York Giants
Dallas Cowboys	Philadelphia Eagles
Detroit Lions	Phoenix Cardinals[2]
Green Bay Packers	Pittsburgh Steelers
Indianapolis Colts[1]	San Francisco Forty-Niners
Los Angeles Rams	Washington Redskins

Original AFL Teams (10)

Buffalo Bills	Kansas City Chiefs
Cincinnati Bengals	Miami Dolphins
Denver Broncos	New England Patriots[4]
Houston Oilers	New York Jets
Los Angeles Raiders[3]	San Diego Chargers[5]

[1] Formerly the Baltimore Colts.
[2] Formerly the St. Louis Cardinals.
[3] Formerly the Oakland Raiders.
[4] Formerly the Boston Patriots.
[5] Formerly the Los Angeles Chargers.

win. On the other hand, a rising market during this period gives the winning nod to the team whose name is closest to Z. Including 1989's Super Bowl, this barometer has worked 13 of the last 15 times. The name of the teams' city, rather than its nickname, is used as the basis.

For the 1989 Super Bowl, the San Francisco Forty-Niners, an original NFL team, played the Cincinnati Bengals, an original AFL team. From November 1987 to January 1988, the Dow Jones Industrial Average was up and the name of the team closest to the end of the alphabet was San Francisco. Guess who won? Right! Now only time will tell if this original NFL team's Super Bowl victory has had a bullish effect on the Dow at the end of 1989.

Nikkei Golf Membership Index

In Japan, where land is at a premium and can cost several thousand dollars per square inch, golf is a very popular game among the salarymen. There are brokers who act as the middlemen, matching eager golfers with available memberships at area golf courses. The worth of such memberships, which can give the holder a decided advantage in the world of Japanese business and politics, if not enormous prestige, is tracked periodically by the *Nihon Keizai Shimbun* (Japan Economic Journal) in the form of the Nikkei Golf Membership Index (Figure 9.2).

Each week, the index tracks the average price of memberships of the 400 leading golf clubs in Japan. Its base level was set at 100 on December 31, 1981. Up to 1985, the index was a lagging indicator of stock prices on the Tokyo Stock Exchange. Immediately following the October 1987 world-wide stock market crash, many memberships were

FIGURE 9.2   The Nikkei Golf Membership Index

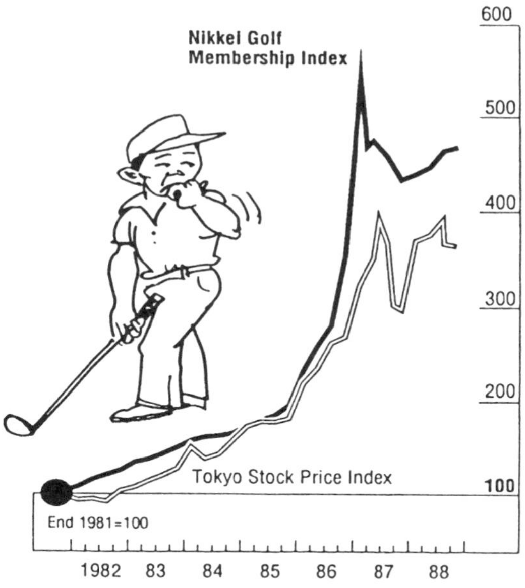

Source: Reprinted by permission from *The Economist*.

sold to cover stockmarket losses and margin calls. For virtually all the clubs, prices of membership also collapsed. Membership at the prestigious Koganei Club in Tokyo held firm around ¥304 million (about $2.4 million), while memberships at more spartan clubs sold for less than ¥5 million ($40,000).

The evaluation of the underlying asset value of a Japanese golf club membership is complicated by the fact that a member is also co-owner of the land on which the golf course is located. Since land is very valuable and expensive, so are memberships.

The Sotheby Index

The Sotheby Index, which was formerly called the Sotheby Art Index, tracks the price trends of certain *objets d'art* and antiques prized by the investor and collector. Exhibit 9.4 summarizes the 12 categories that make up the index, which is designed to reflect representative niches in a broad spectrum of art-market sectors. It is prepared by Sotheby's Holdings Inc., which runs well-known auction houses in New York and London.

The index is constructed in a manner similar to the Consumer Price Index. While the CPI uses actual prices for its market basket, however, the Sotheby Index is based on a fixed basket of 25 to 65 representative types of art in each of 12 categories. Rather than confining itself to specific items—say a ceramic vase from China's Ming dynasty, which may be extremely rare or may come up for sale only once in a generation—the index actually tracks given categories. Al-

EXHIBIT 9.4   The Sotheby Index Components

Category	Percent Weight (7/15/85)
1. Impressionist and Postimpressionist paintings	18%
2. Old-master paintings	17
3. 19th-century European paintings	12
4. Modern paintings (1900–50)	10
5. Chinese ceramics	10
6. English furniture	7
7. French and continental furniture	7
8. Continental silver	5
9. English silver	5
10. American furniture	3
11. American paintings (1800–WW II)	3
12. Continental ceramics	3

Source: *Barron's;* Sotheby's.

though the divisions are not shown in Exhibit 9.4, some of the categories are divided further. For example, paintings drawn by the old masters are subdivided by Sotheby into Italian, German, French, Spanish, and Dutch/Flemish. Other categories, such as Chinese ceramics, are not divided, so that disagreements arise as to what is meant by "Chinese ceramics." 17th century? 19th century?

Each month, Sotheby has two to four experts in each of the 12 categories reappraise the marketbasket in light of recent auctions, private sales, exhibitions, and the winds of prevailing market conditions. Each of the index's categories is then weighted by its dollar volume to show its importance in relation to the total market. The aggregate average is determined by first multiplying the value for each category by its percent weighting, and then adding up the results. The index was started in 1975 with a base price of 100.

Although the index is designed to track the world market, it nevertheless succumbs to certain biases and realities of the marketplace. American furniture, for example, although primarily collected by Americans, is included in the index to reflect the importance of the American auction market. Since antiques are one-of-a-kind items and often do not come on the market for decades or generations, the prices set are often based on subjective judgment.

Critics claim that artworks, unlike stocks, are not indexable because each is unique in its own way. Others claim that the index is not adjusted for inflation, that it focuses on auction prices and downplays the importance of sales through dealers. Worst of all, it probably contains an upward bias as it never tracks the losers because those items that have fallen in value are not generally put up for sale. Despite these shortcomings and the fact that the Sotheby Index is not as precise a mathematical index as some would like, it nevertheless attracts a wide following as the only such game in town.

The Delaware Ten Index

The Delaware Ten Index is included here for purely symbolic and sentimental reasons. The little state where I was born and still live in has only one member in the House of Representatives and was the first state to ratify the U.S. Constitution (on December 7, 1787). Despite its small size, Delaware nevertheless enjoys its role as king of the

FIGURE 9.3   The Delaware Ten Stock Index, 1988

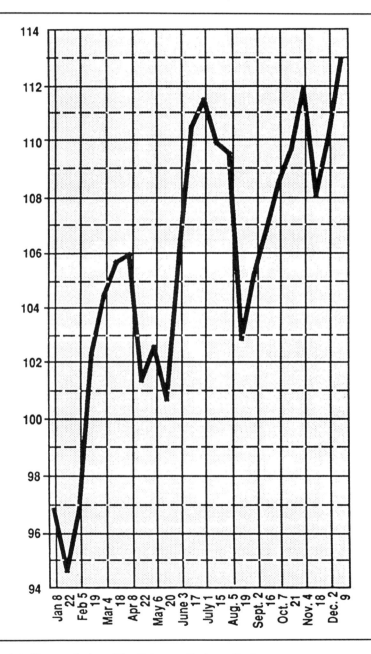

Source: Reprinted by permission of the *Delaware Business Review.*

mountain in being the corporate home to almost half of the companies listed on the New York Stock Exchange as well as over half of the Fortune 500 companies. It also lays claim to the birthplace and headquarters of the Du Pont Company, which is one of the nation's highest capitalized companies and a long-time component of the Dow Jones Industrial Average. Furthermore, other nationally known giants such as Hercules, General Motors, American International Group, Chase Manhattan Bank, and Avon Products have major offices and plants here.

The components of the Delaware Ten Index are summarized in Exhibit 9.5; the index is published weekly in the *Delaware Business Review*. Like most stock indexes, it is capitalization-weighted, with a base price of 100, set at the close of trading on December 31, 1987.

EXHIBIT 9.5   Delaware Ten Index Components

Company	Ticker Symbol	Capitalization Weight (%) (12/30/88)
1. General Motors	GM	38.47
2. E.I. Du Pont de Nemours	DD	30.68
3. American International Group	AIG	15.79
4. Hercules	HPC	3.42
5. Chase Manhattan Bank	CMB	3.40
6. Great Atlantic & Pacific Tea Co.	GAP	2.63
7. Columbia Gas System	CG	2.18
8. Avon Products	AVP	2.03
9. Delmarva Power & Light	DEW	1.15
10. Bank of Delaware	BDEL	0.25

Source: *Delaware Business Review*.

Selected Bibliography and References

Arms, R. W. *The Arms Index (TRIN): An Introduction to the Volume Analysis of Stock and Bond Markets.* Homewood, Ill.: Dow Jones-Irwin, 1988.

Berlin, H. M. *The Dow Jones-Irwin Guide to Buying and Selling Treasury Securities* (2nd ed.). Homewood, Ill.: Dow Jones-Irwin, 1988.

Colby, R. W., and T. A. Meyers. *The Encyclopedia of Technical Market Indicators.* Homewood, Ill.: Dow Jones-Irwin, 1988.

Fabozzi, F. J., and I. M. Pollack, eds. *Handbook of Fixed Income Securities* (2nd ed.). Homewood, Ill.: Dow Jones-Irwin, 1987.

Fabozzi, F. J., and H. I. Greenfield, eds. *The Handbook of Economic and Financial Measures.* Homewood, Ill.: Dow Jones-Irwin, 1984.

Luskin, D. L. *Index Options & Futures: The Complete Guide.* New York: John Wiley & Sons, 1987.

Mesler, D. T. *Stock Index Options.* Chicago: Probus Publishing, 1985.

Nix, W., and S. Nix. *The Dow Jones-Irwin Guide to Stock Index Futures and Options.* Homewood, Ill.: Dow Jones-Irwin, 1984.

Nix, W., and S. Nix. *The Dow Jones-Irwin Guide to International Securities, Futures, and Options Markets.* Homewood, Ill.: Dow Jones-Irwin, 1988.

Rowley, A. *Asian Stockmarkets: The Inside Story.* Homewood, Ill.: Dow Jones-Irwin, 1987.

Stillman, R. J. *Dow Jones Industrial Average.* Homewood, Ill.: Dow Jones-Irwin, 1986.

Viner, A. *Inside Japanese Financial Markets.* Homewood, Ill.: Dow Jones-Irwin, 1988.

The Spicer & Oppenheim Guide to Securities Markets Around the World. New York: John Wiley & Sons, 1988.

Appendix

Useful Addresses

The following is a list of names and addresses of the world's major securities and commodities exchanges, as well as those miscellaneous banks and financial newspapers that maintain major market indexes. The list is arranged alphabetically by country for each category.

1. Stock Exchanges

Argentina:
Buenos Aires Stock Exchange
(Bolsa de Comercio de Buenos Aires)
Sarmiento 299
Buenos Aires

Australia:
Stock Exchange of Adelaide
55 Exchange Place
Adelaide, 5001 South Australia

Brisbane Stock Exchange
Network House
344 Queen Street
Brisbane, 4001 Queensland

Stock Exchange of Melbourne
351 Collins Street
Melbourne, 3001 Victoria

Stock Exchange of Perth
68 St. George's Terrace
Perth, 6001 Western Australia

Sydney Stock Exchange
20 Bond Street
Sydney, 2000 New South Wales

Austria:
Vienna Stock Exchange
(Wiener Börsenkammer)
Wipplingerstrasse 34
A-1011 Vienna

Belgium:
Brussels Stock Exchange
(Bourse de Bruxelles)
Palais de la Bourse
1000 Bruxelles

Brazil:	Rio de Janiero Stock Exchange *(Bolsa de Valores de Rio de Janiero)* Praca XV de November 20 Rio de Janiero RJ
Canada:	Alberta Stock Exchange 300 5th Avenue, S.W. Calgary, Alberta T2P 3C4
	The Montréal Exchange *Tour de la Bourse* 800 Square Victoria Montréal, Quebec H4Z 1A9
	The Toronto Stock Exchange The Exchange Tower 2 First Canadian Place Toronto, Ontario M5X 1J2
	Vancouver Stock Exchange Stock Exchange Tower 609 Granville St. Vancouver, British Columbia V7Y 1H1
Chile:	Santiago Stock Exchange *(Bolsa de Comercio de Santiago)* Casilla 123-D Santiago
Colombia:	Bogotá Stock Exchange *(Bolsa de Bogotá)* Carrere 8, 13–82 Piso 8 Bogotá
Denmark:	Copenhagen Stock Exchange *(Københavns Fondsbørs)* Nikolaj Plads 6 Post Box 1040 DK-1007 København K
Ecuador:	Quito Stock Exchange *(Bolsa Valores de Quito)* Avenue Rio Amazonas 540 y Jeronimo Carrion, Piso 8 Apartado Postal 3772 Quito
Egypt:	Cairo Stock Exchange 4-A Cherifein Street Cairo
Finland:	Helsinki Stock Exchange *(Helsingin Arpvopaperipörssi)* Fabianinkatu 14, PL 429 SF-00100 Helsinki
France:	Bordeaux Stock Exchange *(Bourse de la Bordeaux)* Palais de la Bourse 13-Bordeaux

Lille Stock Exchange
(Bourse de la Lille)
Palais de la Bourse
59-Lille

Lyon Stock Exchange
(Bourse de la Lyon)
Palais du Commerce
Palais de la Bourse
69289 Lyon

Marseille Stock Exchange
(Bourse de la Marseille)
Palais de la Bourse
Marseille

Nancy Stock Exchange
(Bourse de la Nancy)
40 Rue Henri Poincare
54000 Nancy

Nantes Stock Exchange
(Bourse de la Nantes)
Palais de la Bourse
Place du Commerce
44-Nantes

Paris Stock Exchange
(Bourse de Paris)
4, Place de la Bourse
75080 Paris Cedex 02

Great Britain:	London Stock Exchange Old Broad Street London EC2N 1HP
Greece:	Athens Stock Exchange 10 Sophocleous Street Athens 121
Hong Kong:	The Stock Exchange of Hong Kong 1st Floor, Exchange Square GPO Box 8888
India:	Bombay Stock Exchange Dalal Street Fort, Bombay 400001
	Calcutta Stock Exchange Association 7 Lyons Range Calcutta 700001
	Delhi Stock Exchange Association 3 & 4/4B Asaf Ali Road New Delhi 110002
	Madras Stock Exchange Stock Exchange Building 11 Second Line Beach Madras 600001

Indonesia: Stock Exchange of Indonesia
Perserikatan Perdagangan
Uang dan Efek-Efek
P.O. Box 1224/Dak
Jakarta-Kota

Israel: Tel Aviv Stock Exchange
54 Ahad Ha'am Street
Tel Aviv 65543

Italy: Bologna Stock Exchange
(Borsa Valori di Bologna)
Piazza della Constuzione, 8
Pallazzo degli Affari
40100 Bologna

Florence Stock Exchange
(Borsa Valori di Firenze)
Piazza Mentana, 2
50122 Florence

Genoa Stock Exchange
(Borsa Valori di Genova)
Via G. Boccardo, 1
16121 Genoa

Milan Stock Exchange
(Borsa Valori di Milano)
Comitato Direttivo
degli Agenti di Cambio
Piazza Degli Afferi, 6
20123 Milan

Naples Stock Exchange
(Borsa Valori di Napoli)
Via S. Aspreno, 2
80133 Naples

Palermo Stock Exchange
(Borsa Valori di Palermo)
Via E. Amari, 11
90139 Palermo

Rome Stock Exchange
(Borsa Valori di Roma)
Via del Burro, 147
00186 Rome

Turin Stock Exchange
(Borsa Valori di Torino)
Via S. Francesco da Paola, 28
10123 Turin

Trieste Stock Exchange
(Borsa Valori di Trieste)
Via Cassa di Risparmio, 2,
34100 Trieste

Japan:	Fukuoka Stock Exchange 2–14–2 Tenjin, Chuo-ku Fukuokashi
	Hiroshima Stock Exchange 14–18 Ginzancho Hiroshimashi
	Kyoto Stock Exchange 66 Tateuri Nishimachi Tohdohin Higashihairu Shijohdohri, Shimokyoku Kyoto
	Nagoya Stock Exchange 3–3–17 Sakae, Naka-ku Nagoyashi
	Niigata Securities Exchange 1245 Hachibancho Kamiohkawamaedhri Niigatashi
	Osaka Securities Exchange Kitahama 2-Chome Higashi-ku Osaka 541
	Sapporo Stock Exchange 5–14–1 Nishi Minami Ichijoh, Chuo-ku Sapporoshi
	Tokyo Stock Exchange 1–1 Nihombashi-Kayaba-cho 2-chome, Chuo-ku Tokyo 103
Kenya:	Nairobi Stock Exchange Stanbank House Moi Avenue P.O. Box 43633 Nairobi
Korea:	Korea Stock Exchange 33 Yoido-Dong Youngdeungpo-ku Seoul 150–010
New Zealand:	New Zealand Stock Exchange PO Box 2959 Caltex Tower 286–292 Lambton Quay Wellington
Nigeria:	Nigerian Stock Exchange NIDB House, 15th Floor 63/71, Broad Street P.O. Box 2457 Lagos
Norway:	Oslo Stock Exchange (Oslo Børs)

	Tollbugt. 2, Box 460, Sentrum 0105 Oslo 1
Pakistan:	Karachi Stock Exchange Stock Exchange Road Karachi 2
	Lahore Stock Exchange 17 Bank Square Lahore
Philippines:	The Makati Stock Exchange MSC Building, Ayala Avenue Corner Makati Avenue Makati Metro Manila
	The Manila Stock Exchange MSE Building Prensa Street Corner Muella de la Industria Binondo Manila
Portugal:	Lisbon Stock Exchange *(Bolsa de Valores de Lisboa)* Praca do Comercio Torreao Oriental Lisbon
Singapore:	Singapore Stock Exchange 1 Raffles Place #24/25–00 Oub Centre Singapore 0104
South Africa:	Johannesburg Stock Exchange Diagonal Street, PO Box 1174 Johannesburg 2000
Spain:	Barcelona Stock Exchange *(Bolsa de Barcelona)* Paseo Isabel II, Consuldo 2 Barcelona
	The Madrid Stock Exchange *(Illustre Colegio de Agentes de Cambio y Bolsa)* 1, Plaza de la Lealtad Madrid 28014
Sri Lanka:	Colombo Brokers' Association P.O. Box 101 59 Janadlipathi Mawatha Colombo 1
Sweden:	Stockholm Stock Exchange *(Stockholms Fondbörs)* Box 1256 S-111 82 Stockholm

Switzerland:	Basel Stock Exchange *(Börsenkammer des Kantons Basel-Stadt)* Freie Strasse 3 CH-4001 Basel
	Bern Stock Exchange *(Berner Börsenverein)* Aabergergasse 30 CH-3011 Bern
	Geneva Stock Exchange *(Chambre de la Bourse de Genève)* 10, Rue Peitot Casa Postale 228 CH-1211 Geneva
	Lausanne Stock Exchange *(Bourse de Lausanne)* Societé de Banque Suisse 16, Place St-François CH-1003 Lausanne
	Neuchâtel Stock Exchange *(Bourse de Neuchâtel)* Coq d'Inde 24 2000 Neuchâtel
	Zurich Stock Exchange *(Effektenbörsenverein Zürich)* Bleicherwege 5 CH-8021 Zurich
Taiwan:	Taiwan Stock Exchange Corporation 10th Floor, City Building 85 Yen-Pin South Road Taipei
Thailand:	Securities Exchange of Thailand Siam Center, 4th Floor 965 Rama 1 Road Bangkok, Metropolis 5
United States:	American Stock Exchange (AMEX) 86 Trinity Place New York, NY 10006
	Boston Stock Exchange One Boston Place Boston, MA 02108
	Cincinnati Stock Exchange 205 Dixie Terminal Building Cincinnati, OH 45202
	Intermountain Stock Exchange 373 South Main Street Salt Lake City, UT 84111
	Midwest Stock Exchange 440 South LaSalle Street Chicago, IL 60606

New York Stock Exchange (NYSE)
11 Wall Street
New York, NY 10005

Pacific Stock Exchange (PSE)
301 Pine Street
San Francisco, CA 94014

Philadelphia Stock Exchange (PHLX)
1900 Market Street
Philadelphia, PA 19103

Spokane Stock Exchange
225 Peyton Building
Spokane, WA 99201

West Germany: Berlin Stock Exchange
(Berliner Wertpapierbörse)
Hardenbergstrasse 16–18
1000 Berlin 12

Rhineland Westphalia Stock Exchange
(Düsseldorf)
(Rheinisch Westfälische Börse zu Düsseldorf)
Ernst-Schneider-Platz 1
4000 Düsseldorf

Frankfurt Stock Exchange
(Frankfurter Wertpapierbörse)
6 Frankfurt am Main
Postfach 2913

Hanseatic Stock Exchange (Hamburg)
(Hanseatische Wertpapierbörse Hamburg)
Adolph, Börse, Zimmer 151
2000 Hamburg 11

Bavarian Stock Exchange (Munich)
(Bayerische Börse im München)
Lenbachplatz 2 a
8000 Munich 2

2. Commodity Futures and Options Exchanges

Australia: Sydney Futures Exchange
13–15 O'Connell Street
Sydney, New South Wales 2000

Brazil: Brazilian Futures Exchange
(Bolsa Brasileira de Futuros)
Rua Do Mercado
7–2 Andar E. Sobreloja
Rio de Janeiro, 20010

Canada: The Toronto Futures Exchange
2 First Canadian Place
Toronto, Ontario M5X 1J2

The Winnipeg Commodity Exchange
500 Commodity Exchange Tower

	360 Main Street
	Winnipeg, Manitoba R3C 3Z4
France:	*Marché à Terme International de France* (MATIF)
	108 Rue de Richelieu
	Paris 75002
Great Britain:	Baltic International Freight Futures Exchange, Ltd. (BIFFEX)
	The Baltic Exchange
	24/28 St. Mary Axe
	London EC3A 8EP
	London International Financial Futures Exchange, Ltd. (LIFFE)
	The Royal Exchange
	London EC3V 3PJ
Hong Kong:	Hong Kong Futures Exchange, Ltd.
	Hutchinson House, 2nd Floor
	Harcourt Road
The Netherlands:	European Options Exchange (EOE)
	Rokin 65, P.O. Box 19164
	1000 GD Amsterdam
	Fianciele Termijnmarkt Amsterstam N.V.
	Nes 49, Amsterdam 1012 KD
New Zealand:	New Zealand Futures Exchange
	Stock Exchange Centre
	191 Queen Street
	Auckland, AK1
Singapore:	The Singapore International Monetary Exchange, Ltd. (SIMEX)
	1 Maritime Square, No. 09–39
	World Trade Centre
	Singapore 0409
Sweden:	Stockholm Options Market
	(Stockholms Optionsmarknad OM Fondkomission AB)
	Brunkebergstog 2
	Box 16305
	10326 Stockholm
	Sweden's Options and Futures Exchange (SOFE)
	P.O. Box 7267
	10389 Stockholm
Switzerland:	Swiss Options and Financial Futures Exchange (SOFFEX)
	Neumattstrasse 7
	CH-8953 Dietikon
United States:	Chicago Board of Trade (CBOT)
	141 W. Jackson Blvd.
	Chicago, IL 60604

Chicago Board Options Exchange (CBOE)
400 S. LaSalle Street
Chicago, IL 60605

Chicago Mercantile Exchange (CME)
International Monetary Market (IMM)
Index and Options Market (IOM)
30 S. Wacker Drive
Chicago, IL 60606

Coffee, Sugar & Cocoa Exchange (CSCE)
4 World Trade Center
New York, NY 10048

Commodity Exchange (COMEX)
4 World Trade Center
New York, NY 10048

Kansas City Board of Trade
4800 Main Street, Suite 303
Kansas City, MO 64112

MidAmerica Commodity Exchange
141 W. Jackson Blvd.
Chicago, IL 60604

Minneapolis Grain Exchange
150 Grain Exchange Building
Minneapolis, MN 55415

New York Cotton Exchange (NYCE)
Financial Instrument Exchange (FINEX)
4 World Trade Center
New York, NY 10048

New York Futures Exchange (NYFE)
20 Broad Street
New York, NY 1005

New York Mercantile Exchange (NYMEX)
4 World Trade Center
New York, NY 10048

Philadelphia Board of Trade (PBT)
1900 Market Street
Philadelphia, PA 19103

3. Banks

Austria:	Creditanstalt-Bankverein Schottengasse 6–8 A-1010 Vienna
Italy:	Banca Commerciale Italiana Direzione Centrale Piazza Della Scala, 6 PO Box 926 20121 Milan
New Zealand:	Barclay's Bank New Zealand, Ltd. PO Box 754 Wellington

West Germany: Commerzbank
                       PO Box 100505
                       Neue Mainzer Strasse 32–36
                       6000 Frankfurt am Main 1

4. Financial Newspapers & Magazines

England: *Financial Times*
                       Number One Southwark Bridge
                       London SE1 9HL

                            or

                       14 East 60th Street
                       New York, NY 10022

                       The Economist
                       25 St. James Street
                       London SW1A 1HG

Japan: Nihon Keizai Shimbun, Inc.
                       9–5 Ohtemachi, 1-chome, Chiyoda-ku
                       Tokyo 100–66

                       The Japan Economic Journal
                       1221 Avenue of the Americas, Suite 1802
                       New York, NY 10020

Singapore: *Straits Times*
                       Straits Times Press (1975) Ltd.
                       Times House, 390 Kim Seng Road
                       Singapore 0923

Sweden: *Affärsvärlden*
                       Box 1234
                       11182 Stockholm

United States: Dow Jones & Company, Inc.
                           *(Barron's, The Wall Street Journal, Wall
                           Street Journal Europe, Asian Wall
                           Street Journal)*
                       200 Liberty Street
                       New York, NY 10281

                       Investor's Daily
                       1941 Armacost Avenue
                       Los Angeles, CA 90025

West Germany: *Allgemeine Zeitung für Deutschland*
                       Hellerhofstrasse 2–4
                       Postfach 10 08 08
                       6000 Frankfurt am Main 1

5. Associations

France: International Federation of Stock Exchanges
                       *(Federation Internationale des Bourses de
                           Valeurs)*
                       22, Bld. de Courcelles
                       75017 Paris

United States:

National Association of Securities
  Dealers, Inc.
1735 K Street, N.W.
Washington, DC 20006

Index